1991

# The English Alliterative Tradition

University of Pennsylvania Press
MIDDLE AGES SERIES
*Edited by Edward Peters*
Henry Charles Lea Professor
of Medieval History
University of Pennsylvania


A complete listing of the books in this series
appears at the back of this volume

# The English
# Alliterative Tradition

*Thomas Cable*

**uʃʃ**

University of Pennsylvania Press

*Philadelphia*

The following publishers have generously given permission to use quotations from copyrighted works: From T. S. Eliot, *Collected Poems 1909–1962*. Copyright © 1936 by Harcourt Brace Jovanovich, Inc.; copyright © 1943, 1963, 1964 by T. S. Eliot; copyright © 1971 by Esme Valerie Eliot. Used by permission of Harcourt Brace Jovanovich, Inc. and Faber and Faber, Ltd. From F. Klaeber (Editor). *Beowulf and the Fight at Finnsburg*. Third Edition. Copyright © 1950 by D. C. Heath and Company. Used by permission. From Larry D. Benson (Editor). *The Riverside Chaucer*. Third Edition. Copyright © 1987 by Houghton Mifflin Company. Used by permission. From J. J. Anderson (Editor). *Cleanness*. Copyright © 1977 by Manchester University Press. Used by permission. From G. L. Brook and R. G. Leslie (Editors). *Laȝamon: Brut*. Copyright © 1963 by the Early English Text Society. Used by permission of the Council of the Early English Text Society.

Library of Congress Cataloging-in-Publication Data

Cable, Thomas, 1942–
   The English alliterative tradition / Thomas Cable.
      p.      cm. — (Middle Ages series)
   Includes bibliographical references and index.
   ISBN 0-8122-3063-9
   1. English poetry—Middle English, 1100–1500—History and
criticism.   2. Alliteration in literature.   I. Title.   II. Series.
PR317.A55C33   1991
821'.109—dc20                                            91-9184
                                                          CIP

To Carole

# Contents

# Acknowledgments

Long enough ago so that it is embarrassing to say, the American Council of Learned Societies supported the beginnings of this work in a project of the same name. Support has also come from the University of Texas at Austin through the University Research Institute, which funds Faculty Research Assignments, and through Project Quest, which in cooperation with IBM has provided the computer hardware that made parts of the research possible. For this institutional help I wish to thank Deans William S. Livingston, Eugene H. Wissler, and Robert D. King, and at IBM, John Tiede. Where institutional support has its sources in the personal, it is a pleasure to thank Jane and Roland Blumberg, who have been generous over the years in their service to the University of Texas and in their establishment of professorships in several of its colleges.

For reading and commenting in detail on the whole manuscript and prompting substantial revisions, I am indebted to Mary Blockley, to Geoffrey Russom, and to Ann Matonis, who has generously shown me drafts of her own book on Middle English. Constance Hieatt and R. D. Fulk have given insightful readings to several successive versions of the parts on Old English meter; indeed, the final version of Chapter Six depends heavily on Fulk's own work in progress. In helping me work through the overlapping claims of linguistic theory and English philology, C. B. McCully has been especially helpful (and here I must name again both Mary Blockley and Geoffrey Russom).

Parts of this book have been presented in lectures at Rice, Cornell, Harvard, and UCLA, and at various MLA and Kalamazoo conferences. For arranging these programs, I am grateful to Jane Chance, Robert Farrell, Larry Benson, Donka Minkova, Robert Stockwell, Daniel Calder, Richard Osberg, Gilbert Youmans, and Thomas Seiler. A version of Chapter Three appeared in *Standardizing English: Essays in the History of Language Change in Honor of John Hurt Fisher*, edited by Joseph B. Trahern, Jr., whose tactful guidance has long meant much to me. I wish to thank the University of Tennessee Press for permission to reprint that essay of 1989, and also John Alford and M. Teresa Tavormina, editors of Colleagues Press, for permission to reprint a few paragraphs that appeared in an essay in Volume 2 (1988) of *The Yearbook of Langland Studies*. Some of the ideas in the book have appeared or will appear in essays under the editorship of Helen Damico, Patrick J. Gallacher, T. V. F. Brogan, Alfred Bammesberger, and Teresa Kirschner, all of whom have a knack for helping prose attain clarity in a small space.

Because the book has been through several versions and different formats, some of the following people may not see the connection between what they once read and what is here published. But they have all been helpful in quite specific ways: Angus McIntosh, Marie Borroff, Hoyt Duggan, Daniel Donoghue, Tess Tavormina, Jane Roberts, Donka Minkova, Robert Stockwell, F. H. Whitman, Ruth Lehmann, James Wimsatt, Rebecca Baltzer, Jacqueline Henkel, C. L. Baker, W. O. S. Sutherland, Thomas Shippey, Mary Richards, A. N. Doane, Edwin Duncan, John Schmit, Burns Cooper, Steven Brehe, John Ruffin, and Karl Hagen.

As always it is a pleasure to thank Carole Cable for more than I can say—but not least for the cartoons in the *Chronicle of Higher Education* that have helped keep it all in perspective.

# Introduction

This study began several years ago with both empirical and theoretical aims, separate at first, but eventually intertwined. The empirical aim might be formulated as, "Revise Oakden"—the theoretical as something like, "Explore the implications of the Old English metrical paradigm." The Old English metrical paradigm was mainly the classic formulation by Eduard Sievers, with some minor refinements introduced in my *Meter and Melody of* Beowulf in 1974.[1]

The resulting project has covered much of J. P. Oakden's ground anew, at least parts of the metrical survey, but it has hardly touched the topics under his dialect survey.[2] Thus, I have revised selected aspects of Oakden's large topic and have gone on to deal with other topics, both earlier and later in the history of English poetry, that were beyond his purview. The parts that I have reexamined, I have done with instruments of analysis which were not available fifty years ago and which reveal features that never showed up in Oakden's study. These newly noted features lead to strikingly different conclusions about the tradition, including its beginnings in Old English.

The new techniques of analysis in themselves would probably not have led to the new conclusions had they not been set within a certain theoretical context, which shaped the whole investigation. Influenced most directly by developments in linguistics during the past quarter century, this theoretical context might be called "Cartesian" in the Chomskyan sense, or "rationalist," or "cognitive."[3] It finds parallels between the transmission and development of language and the transmission and development of literary tradition. In the study of these subjects, the implications of Peircean *abduction* can be a significant key to the understanding of linguistic and literary continuity and change.[4] The present work was not written under the banner of the New Philology, which had not yet flown, and indeed the emphasis on individual cognition in the following chapters departs from some of the stated assumptions of this newly emerging set of theories and attitudes.[5] But if Oakden is a fine exemplar of the Old Philology—a positivistic tradition that is still manifested in most studies of Old and Middle English phonology and meter—then the present work can fairly separate itself by claiming part of the scholarly landscape of the New Philology.

The first chapter is a reconsideration of standard features in traditional metrical theories of Old English, including my own. The problem that is posed concerns the hierarchy of statements in a descriptive theory. One theory might start with certain features as basic and derive other features from them. Another theory might reverse the ordering of features. Virtually all serious theories of Old English meter include, at some point in the description, a limit on the number of syllables that occur in certain places in the verse. The view presented in Chapter One takes a count of syllables as the statement of most importance in the hierarchy and shows that other familiar statements can either be derived directly from the statement of syllable count or can be shown to be supplementary and subsidiary.

This priority of syllable count in the structure of the half-line is surprising. Because Old English meter obviously allows lines of varying length, it has always been considered the antithesis of syllabic meter. However, the key to the meter is in understanding that the expansion which causes the varying line length can occur in only one place in each half-line. In locating that place, we must deal again with technical matters such as resolution, but also with more philosophical matters such as the level of representation of a theory and the meaning of derivativeness. Geoffrey Russom's recent study of Old English meter is an excellent model of this more theoretically oriented discussion.[6]

Chapter Two finds that in the century after the Norman Conquest a basic change has occurred in the metrical grammar. Middle English alliterative poetry from the twelfth century to the beginning of the fourteenth century returns to a form that is familiar from standard handbook descriptions of the "strong-stress" tradition. In contrast with Old English poetry (the flexibility of which is only apparent because of strict rules regulating syllable count, stress, and syllabic length), Early Middle English poetry has a truly flexible line. For poems such as Lawman's *Brut* (c. 1200), a fairly adequate description simply posits two stresses to the half-line and a varying number of metrically unstressed syllables. Syllable count figures only in the minimum length of the line—at least five syllables to the half-line. Such a system is profoundly different from the principles of the Old English meter which preceded (and also, as we shall see, from the principles of the Alliterative Revival which followed). Thus, one argument of Chapter Two is that Middle English poetry does not show the continuity of tradition that standard authorities such as Oakden assert. With the Norman Conquest came a clear break, and what followed was a drastic misreading of what had preceded.

A second argument of Chapter Two is that this rupture of the poetic tradition can also be seen as a continuation of the rhythmical prose tradition. The most frequent patterns in Ælfric's late tenth-century saints' lives, which we now call rhythmical prose, are also the most frequent patterns in Lawman's *Brut*. We are led to the conclusion that the modern, clear distinction between poetry and prose would have been seen differently in late Old English and early Middle English times, and that in fact there was a continuum of overlapping modes.

Chapter Three addresses the problem of final -*e* in fourteenth-century texts. Most familiar in the context of Chaucer's poetry, the solution there has been aided by the relative firmness of the iambic pentameter. Although dissenters persist, over the past century a majority opinion and a standard reading have developed. With the alliterative tradition, however, we seem to be faced with a meter that has only flexibility as its essence (except for patterns of alliteration) and therefore no firm peg to which to tie the vexing -*e*. In fact, as this chapter and the next show, the firm patterns are there once the phonology and metrics of final -*e* are understood.

The two halves of the long line in fourteenth-century poetry have strikingly different patterns that have not been perceived in previous studies. Beginning with the hypothesis of a feminine ending for the second half-line and either a masculine or a feminine ending for the first half-line, one can put together a picture of the predictable rules of final -*e* as it occurs variously in native words and in Old French and Old Norse loans—in nouns, adjectives, verbs, and the other parts of speech. The conclusion of Chapter Three is that the phonology of the West Midlands alliterative poems was more conservative than standard Middle English grammars have recognized, and that a regular meter depends on restoring inflectional and etymological endings that prevailing scholarly opinion would assume to have been lost.

Chapter Four explains how an investigation of the phonology of final -*e* can proceed simultaneously with an investigation of the abstract metrical form without being viciously circular. Toward this end it presents some remarkable facts of distribution. To say that regular metrical patterns emerge from a certain treatment of final -*e* could indeed be tautological if

-*e* were optional and its occurrence or absence depended on the pattern aimed for. Something of that difficulty has always discomfited the treatment of Chaucerian -*e*, although the standard view of variable -*e* in the iambic pentameter appears to be essentially correct. By the proposed theory of the present study, however, the final -*e* of the alliterative texts is not variable. For each etymological and grammatical category it either occurs or does not occur, according to the rules established in Chapter Three, and thus there is no question in a given line of choosing an option that would bias the distribution.

In this sense, Middle English alliterative meter is even more highly controlled than the Chaucerian meter. Certain patterns of stressed and unstressed syllables turn out to be appropriate only for the first half-line and other patterns only for the second half-line. This distribution is the main evidence for a new paradigm of Middle English alliterative meter. The mutual exclusivity of the various patterns for the two halves of the line, by my present understanding, is something over 90 percent; in *Cleanness,* for example, 93 percent of the hemistichs occur in the half of the line that is appropriate for its type. Whether we should speak of rules with exceptions or of strong tendencies is a matter of metatheoretical orientation. What is important is that nothing in previous discussions gives an indication of any degree of mutual exclusivity that differentiates the two halves of the long line except for an occasional remark that the first half-line is often longer than the second.

The length of the half-line is indeed one of the determining features, but it is not the central feature. Chapter Five examines the internal rhythmical structure of the patterns of the two halves of the line with the aim of accounting at a higher level of adequacy for the descriptive paradigm of Chapter Four. This investigation leads to a comparison of the meters of Middle English and Modern English, and to the central theoretical issues in English prosody of the past century.

In brief, the model presented in Chapter Five identifies five simple elements (strong stress, syllabism, quantity, the foot, and alternating stress) and four compound modes of English meter. By this classification, the meter of Chaucer and, a century and a half later, of Gascoigne (based on alternating stress and syllabism) is significantly different from the English iambic pentameter from Sidney to Yeats (based on the foot and syllabism). The difference shows up in the kinds of substitutions that are typical of these two compound meters. Old English meter and Middle English alliterative meter fit into the typology according to the principles established in earlier chapters: the *Beowulf* meter is a compound of syllabism, strong stress, and quantity while the meter of the Alliterative Revival is a compound of strong stress and foot meter. The rhythmical principles of strong stress are essentially those of the rhythmical grid as described in Mark Liberman and Alan Prince's seminal article of 1977 and in Liberman's 1975 dissertation; and the principles of alternating stress are essentially those of another major prosodic rule in English, which Elisabeth Selkirk follows Henry Sweet in calling the Principle of Rhythmic Alternation.[7]

Hovering around all these problems, but especially around the problems of rhythm, time, and linguistic gaps in Chapter Five, are certain enduring philosophical questions about the locus of existence of the literary text and about tradition. The final chapter investigates these matters on two levels. The middle two sections (6.3 and 6.4) present technical analyses of specific temporal structures—first in the iambic pentameter and then in Old English meter. The return to Old English meter and the sketch of a tentative rhythmical analysis of the long line depend upon much of the intervening discussion since Chapter One. Some of the rules of the first chapter might now be seen, from the perspective of the last chapter, as surface phenomena resulting from deeper principles. If these deeper principles are indeed valid, they can probably best be understood through the kind of historical survey and typology of general prosody that Chapters Two through Five offer.

The first two and the last two sections of Chapter Six relate these quite specific metrical patterns in medieval and modern texts to current issues in criticism. Central to this discussion is a distinction between grammars and texts, which has been a theme of both linguistics and literary criticism during the past quarter century. Focusing on the grammar makes us realize that multiple texts were possible at the time that our particular extant text was set down. If we see as our goal an understanding of the grammar that produced the text, then we aspire to nothing less than access to a part of the mind of the poet. The written text that was selected from the set of comparable, variant texts is thus an epiphenomenon, but in great poetry that selection attains the illusion of inevitability.

# 1. Old English Meter

## 1.1 Misreadings of Old English Meter

Metrists studying English alliterative poetry have tended to emphasize the continuity of the tradition from the seventh century to the fifteenth. This continuity is said to be characterized, from Cædmon to Langland, by "strong-stress meter." One of the results of the chapters that follow will be to call into question the most familiar meanings of "the English alliterative tradition."

W. K. Wimsatt, Jr. and Monroe C. Beardsley present an account that is often cited because of its succinctness and clarity: "the clutter of weaker syllables in a strong-stress meter is against an accurate syllable-stress reading, most often prevents it entirely. A few lines of *Piers Plowman* or of *Everyman* ought to suffice to show what is what."[1] The authors contrast the meter of *Piers Plowman* with the syllable-stress meter of the English iambic pentameter (Chaucer, Shakespeare, Milton, Pope, Wordsworth) and suggest that Langland's meter is "older in English poetry and may be more natural to the English tongue, though again it may not be. Here only the major stresses of the major words count in the scanning. The gabble of weaker syllables, now more, now fewer, between the major stresses obscures all the minor stresses and relieves them of any structural duty. . . . Thus we have *Beowulf, Piers Plowman, Everyman*, Spenser's *February Eclogue*, Coleridge's *Christabel*, the poetry of G. M. Hopkins (who talks about 'sprung rhythm' and 'outrides'), . . . the poetry of T. S. Eliot, and many another in our day" (p. 592).

One of the main arguments of my *Meter and Melody of* Beowulf was that *Beowulf* and the rest of Old English poetry did not belong in this group.[2] A main argument of the present study is that *Piers Plowman* and other poems of the fourteenth-century Alliterative Revival do not belong either—or rather that to use the rubric "strong-stress meter" to group *Piers Plowman* and *Christabel* is to misrepresent the fourteenth-century meter in an essential way. The *Piers* meter is obviously strong stress but, I shall argue, not essentially so (as the phrase is usually understood), just as it is alliterative, but not essentially so.

Middle English meter has always been more problematic than Old English meter. The past two centuries of metrical scholarship have not revealed a system with the regularity that Eduard Sievers discovered in the Five Types of the Old English half-line.[3] The argument of Chapters Three and Four is that there is a comparable system in late Middle English meter and that the principles which regulate that system are not as exotic as one might imagine. The principles operate in present-day varieties of English meter, and an understanding of them will help to explain some of the enduring rifts in the study of the prosody of Modern English (as we shall see in Chapter Five).

While Middle English alliterative meter is generally recognized as an intractable conundrum, theories of Old English meter, for all their divergence, give the sense of a core of agreement in the solidity of Sievers' Five Types. My 1974 refinement of Sievers' system provided what I considered a base for tracing the development of the alliterative tradition into Middle English. However, the actual process of working through the later meters made clear that the refinement of Sievers' system had not gone far enough. The extraordinary variety of metrical patterns that occur in Middle English reminds one of what is missing in Old English. This is knowledge that any reader of Old and Middle English has at a certain level of consciousness; yet the significance of it may not be felt until one scans and parses thousands of verses that are at once so similar and so different from the verses of Old English. The absence of scores of patterns in Old English meter must be attributed to the paradigm of meter. Yet of the many modern descriptions of Old English meter—including Sievers' system, my own refinements of that system, and the long lists of occurring patterns in A. J. Bliss's and John C. Pope's studies—none lays out in a descriptively adequate way the principles that regulate the paradigm.

Sievers' Five Types have been the traditional starting point both for teaching Old English meter and for theoretical inquiry. For reference it will be useful to list them in their standard form:[4]

| A  | / x  \|  / x | gomban gyldan |
| B  | x /  \|  x / | on sīdne sǣ |
| C  | x /  \|  \ x | mid scipherge |
| D1 | /  \|  / \ x | wīs wēlþungen |
| D4 | /  \|  / x \ | bād bolgenmōd |
| E  | / \ x  \|  / | flōdȳþum feor |

Word stress is the main determinant of the meter, but syllabic quantity, which functioned phonemically in Old English, is also important. Generally, metrical stress occurred on a long syllable (containing a long vowel or else a short vowel followed by two consonants) or its resolved equivalent; however, there were certain clear contexts in which "suspension of resolution" was allowed and in which metrical stress thus fell on a short syllable. (See section 1.4, below.) One feature of Sievers' original formulation that was generally overlooked in subsequent summaries and adaptations of it was the specification of four *Glieder,* or members, in the great majority of verses. Thus, *gomban gyldan* has not only two stresses (on the first syllables of *gomban* and *gyldan*) and two feet (indicated by the vertical line), but also four members (two stresses and two dips). A verse such as *wēox under wolcnum* has an extra syllable in the first dip, but it still has only four members because the two unstressed syllables of *under* form a single dip—a single member:

$$\overset{\prime}{\text{w}}\bar{\text{e}}\text{ox} \overset{\text{x}}{\text{un}}\overset{\text{x}}{\text{der}} \overset{\prime}{\text{wol}}\overset{\text{x}}{\text{cnum}} \quad (8a)$$

This particular example, with a difference in degree of linguistic stress on the two syllables of *under,* reminds us that metrical stress does not track linguistic stress in a one-to-one fashion but forms a separate abstraction. The main exception to the four-member pattern, as presented by Sievers, was the five-member pattern of "expanded D," or D*—in verses such as *Beowulf* 223a, with a dip in the first foot:

$$\overset{\prime}{\text{s}}\bar{\text{i}}\text{de} \overset{\text{x}}{\text{}} \overset{\_}{\text{sæ}}\overset{\backslash}{\text{næ}}\overset{\text{x}}{\text{ssas}}$$

Finally there were precise rules for alliteration, some of which are only now being understood in the full complexity of the interaction between alliterating syllables and patterns of stress. The most familiar generalization is that alliteration occurs only on the first stressed syllable of the second half-line, but on either one or two stressed syllables of the first half-line.

With so many specifications operating on such a small domain of poetic language (the verse, or half-line), it is not surprising that subsequent interpretations of Sievers' system took one specification or another as basic and attempted to show how the other patterns of features could be derived from it. This, in fact, has been the main story of Old English metrics during the past one hundred years. My own refinement of Sievers' system focused on the four-member specification. The abstractness of the concept, however, has never been completely satisfactory: its aesthetic and psychological reality as a means of composing verse is not immediately clear. Studies by later investigators—some of them from unrelated theoretical perspectives—have revealed how frequently the *Glied,* or member, is realized as a single syllable or a syllable equivalent. Thus, if the abstract concept of *member* can be tied more directly to the concrete entity of the *syllable,* we may gain a better insight into the structure of Old English meter.

## 1.2 Syllable Count

Indeed, the general principle of Old English meter that forms the basis of a more adequate theory is the not very obvious requirement of a regular count of syllables. A strong and simple description of Old English meter can begin with the specification of four syllables, or syllable equivalents, to the half-line:

1   2  3   4
gomban gyldan  (11a)

The phrase "syllable equivalents" refers to the familiar processes of resolution of a short syllable with the following syllable:

1   2     3    4
/\         ̄
monegum mægþum  (5a)

Here we should note that there is not a one-to-one mapping of the linguistic abstraction (the syllable) onto the metrical abstraction (the syllable-equivalent) and that this is a perfectly normal state of affairs. In every meter in every language there are points at which the ordinary linguistic units and the metrical units do not coincide. This is simply a truism, for otherwise there would be no separate, definable domain of meter. The determination of specific points of coincidence or divergence between the two systems is, of course, an empirical question.

Traditional accounts of Old English meter extend the lack of a one-to-one mapping beyond resolution to stretches of unstressed syllables, as in the three syllables *-ne ofer* of *Beowulf* 46a:

1    2  3  4

ǣnne ofer ȳðe

The three unstressed syllables are seen as filling a single metrical unit, a dip, just as the first syllable of *ǣnne* fills a single unit, a stress. There is nothing logically wrong with the concept. Empirically, however, there are certain problems. Three unstressed syllables can occur in the first or the second of the four numbered positions in an Old English verse, but they do not occur in the third or fourth. In the *Gawain* meter, by contrast, any number of consecutive unstressed syllables can occur anywhere in the first half-line; for example:

For to telle of þis teuelyng     of þis trwe kny3tez  (1514)

Most theories of Old English meter, if they recognize this constraint at all, handle it by an ad hoc statement: three unstressed syllables cannot occur in the third or fourth positions of a verse (or in the appropriate "foot," "breath-group," or "measure," depending on the terms of the theory). The problem with such a statement is that it does not hook up with any principles of general prosody, and the reason for such a constraint is obscure. It may be observationally adequate, but it has no psychological reality.

The accordion-like flexibility of the dip in "strong-stress meter" seems to be such an essential element that it usually gets mentioned immediately after the element of strong stress itself—or in the same breath, since "strong stress" depends for its full meaning on the "gabble of weaker syllables" that can occur before, between, and after the strong stresses. But the "gabble of weaker syllables," whatever it might do in the *Gawain* meter, does not occur freely in Old English meter, as we have noted. Suppose that instead of beginning a description of Old English meter with the idea of a gabble of weaker syllables and then disallowing it in half of the half-line, we turned the problem on its head. Suppose that the most basic situation is a one-to-one matching of a single syllable or its resolved equivalent and a single metrical unit. A perfectly normal variation of this pattern could then be specified as a stretch of two or more unstressed syllables. It is not surprising that such a variation would be more acceptable near the beginning of the verse than near the end (as is the case with some of the most important variations of metrical patterns in various European languages).

What does it mean to speak of a basically syllabic pattern and a variation that adds unstressed syllables near the beginning of the verse? One way of conceiving the structure would be to say that in certain specific contexts the syllabic principle is overridden by a "strong-stress" principle that allows two or more consecutive unstressed syllables in place of one syllable (just as in the iambic pentameter an anapest can sometimes substitute for an iamb). The problem with this formulation is that the strong-stress principle appears to be just as basic as the syllabic principle. Old English meter is founded on two equal principles, which pull in opposite directions: syllabism gives a regular count of syllables; strong stress gives a varying count of syllables between stresses and provides the basis for alliteration. About half of the verses in *Beowulf* have four syllables or the resolved equivalent and about half are longer than four syllables because of the occurrence of two or more unstressed syllables between stresses.

Let us call such a sequence of unstressed syllables a "strong dip." Although previous scholarship makes no distinction between one-syllable dips and multisyllable dips, we shall see that the strong dip is a key to the meter. Setting aside verses with anacrusis, 3,037, or 47.7 percent of the verses in *Beowulf* have four syllables or the resolved equivalent. By exempting verbal prefixes from the count, along lines established elsewhere,[5] more than half of the verses have four syllables or the resolved equivalent—that is, they do not have a strong dip. From the syntactic structure of the verses and from the distributions of the metrical patterns, it is difficult to say that either the minimum length of verse or a slightly longer length is the ideal norm. Recognition of syllable count obviates the need for certain ad hoc constraints and for long lists of attested patterns that are familiar in traditional studies. Continued recognition of strong stress is also necessary for two of the most obvious features of Old English meter—the variable length of the verses and the assignment of alliteration.

There is actually a third principle of Old English meter, syllabic length, as we shall see when we consider resolution in section 1.4 and again in Chapter Six. Indeed, nearly all traditional accounts recognize the importance of syllabic quantity, and the present description has slipped in a recognition of the feature in the phrase "a single syllable or its resolved equivalent." Syllabic quantity is intrinsically bound up with the assignment of stress. Were the meter purely syllabic without the strong-stress principle, there would probably be no need for the determination of syllabic quantity. Such a close relationship of metrical stress and syllabic quantity suggests that the two principles might be reduced to one. Although the exact form of this relationship is still not clear, R. D. Fulk has recently taken the problem in a promising direction by assigning priority to quantity at the tertiary level of stress (see note 15 below).

The strong-stress pattern with its strong dip turns out to be much more highly constrained than one might gather from descriptions of Old English prosody in the handbooks, where the typical focus is on a supposedly indeterminate number of unstressed syllables. If there is a common theme in current studies of Old and Middle English meter, it is the attention to constraints on unstressed syllables, which until recently have generally been considered unregulated.[6] The strong dip can normally occur only once in a verse, if it occurs at all, and then only in the first two positions of the verse. If we consider a verse to have four positions, this restriction, if it is correct, has the effect of limiting the strong dip to the first dip of types A, B, and C (where x x can be further extended to as many as four syllables in type A and as many as five syllables in types B and C):

A    / x x / x
B    x x / x /
C    x x / / x

Types D and E have primary and secondary stresses in the first two positions. Thus, of the twenty possible positions among the five types of four positions, only three positions would account for most of the wide variation in length that we think of as typical of the Old English line.[7]

Is the restriction correct? Let us consider the hypothesis that a strong dip can occur only in the first half of a half-line in Old English. A survey of *Beowulf* shows that of the 6,342 half-lines that are not hypermetric, 171, or 2.7 percent, have a strong dip in the second half of the half-line, contrary to the restriction; for example:

$$\overset{x}{\text{ond}} \overset{x}{\text{him}} \overset{\prime}{\text{fæs}}\overset{x}{\text{te}} \overset{x}{\text{wi}}\overset{\prime}{\text{ðfeng}} \quad (760a)$$

What does it mean to say that a hypothesized restriction holds 97.3 percent of the time? It means nothing in isolation. Statements of frequencies, tendencies, and rules have significance only within a full theoretical context. Because much of the analysis in the chapters that follow involves frequencies, tendencies, and rules, it will be useful to sort out some of the issues at the beginning. These issues concern principles of scientific explanation and—related but not identical—principles of explanation in the humanities. The hypothesis before us concerning the number and placing of strong dips in Old English poetry can serve as a specific example.

## 1.3 Tendency Statements as Constraints on Dips

In linguistic theory it is generally understood that speakers of a language do not apply their internalized "rules" with the same consistency and predictability that physical matter shows in following the "laws" of science. Two of the main approaches to linguistic theory during the past quarter century consider it obvious that substantive linguistic rules do not apply with 100 percent regularity: generative grammar frames the problem in terms of a distinction between "competence" and "performance"; sociolinguistic theory invokes "variable rules," in which statistical superscripts showing probability of occurrence are sometimes incorporated into the rules themselves. In studies of literary meter, however, "exceptions to the rules" cause considerable controversy and confusion.

One reason for the special difficulty in literary studies is the question of emendation *metri causa*—a question naturally more prominent in editing medieval and Renaissance texts than in editing later poetry. The often implicit assumption that all authorial lines are metrical cannot, of course, be sustained as a general principle because in the medieval period it cannot be demonstrated, and in the modern period it can be shown to be wrong. One could simply say that Homer sometimes nods, except that this way of thinking about the problem biases the conception. So too does the use of the idea of "competence" from generative grammar, especially if its technical meaning is misunderstood and the metrist considers a poet who breaks a rule to be somehow incompetent or less competent than otherwise. Finally, the familiar examples of conscious breaking of rules for a specific effect—the sort of thing that Alexander Pope does well—are interesting special cases but should not be taken as the norm, lest one seek to justify every metrical deviation in terms of these textbook examples.

Perhaps the most useful and most cautious attitude to take to the meter of these medieval texts is the combination of certainty and agnosticism that is natural in reading Eliot—as discussed in section 5.2, below. One can be certain that there is a regular metrical form about which generalizations can be made, and which in many poems by Eliot can be called "iambic pentameter." One can also be certain that there are lines within those poems that do not fit that form. If the generalization were changed to accommodate those lines, the usefulness and power of the generalization would be lost. It is better to call the unruly lines "exceptions," and remain uncertain as to why Eliot wrote them. In the case of texts transmitted by medieval scribes, the reasons for agnosticism are more numerous, including the uncertainties of scribal emendation and the variant forms of a changing language. If we let the most adequate generalizations stand as temporary heuristics, we will often find that additional facts do indeed rationalize the apparent exceptions.

In some instances this rationalization by additional facts will result from the discovery of a presently unknown and unspecified property.[8] Even without the unspecified property we have a useful generalization that in *Beowulf* is 97.3 percent accurate. Furthermore, the hypothesis of the existence of an unspecified property points directions for further inquiry. The unspecified property serves the function that exceptions did for the Neogrammarians ("For every exception there must be a rule.") If our hypothesis has any merit, then the specification of the unknown property becomes the goal of our research program. What reasons are there for supposing that the restriction on the extended second dip has any merit? After all, the prohibited pattern occurs 171 times in *Beowulf*. Here is where a scansion of Middle English alliterative poetry can change the perception of Old English meter. As we shall see in Chapters Two and Four, verses with two strong dips are very common in Middle English alliterative poetry, setting the standard pattern for the first half-line. Therefore, the simple difference in frequency of occurrence of the structure in the two periods should claim our attention in itself. Furthermore, as we shall see, not only frequency is important but also the distribution: verses with two strong dips were carefully avoided in the second half of the line in the poems of the Alliterative Revival. Thus, of the infinite number of statistical facts that one might extract from the text of *Beowulf*, this one has some relevance to future developments of alliterative poetry in English.

Now we can begin to make sense of the data through a property that was recently discovered by Edwin W. Duncan: the majority of Old English verses that appear to contain a strong dip in the second half of the half-line get the extra length from a verbal prefix: *ge-*, *wið-*, *be-*, *on-*, *ā-*, etc.[9] This is the case in 135 of the 171 possible verses with a strong second dip, or 78.9 percent. To put it another way, there are only 36 verses with a strong second dip that does not contain a verbal prefix. These amount to 0.6 percent of the nonhypermetric verses in *Beowulf*. Again, this statistic might or might not be significant, depending on the shape of the total theory. The extreme difference between the frequencies of this structure in Old English meter and those that we shall see in fourteenth-century English meter are compelling.

However, there is a further observation, which can be made at this point and without reference to Middle English. Identifying the unknown property as the capacity optionally to include a verbal prefix that is not counted in the metrical scheme hooks up with other relevant facts about Old English meter. Perhaps the most useful contribution that came out of my earlier studies of Old English meter was the suggestion that this structure is relevant in determining constraints on anacrusis in type A. In two-thirds of the type A verses that appear to have anacrusis, the extrametrical syllables are prefixes. Daniel Donoghue has extended the idea to what looks like an extra position between the clashing stresses of type C.[10] If these syllables are regarded as invisible to the metrical template, the number of type A verses with other, inexplicable kinds of anacrusis amount to only one half of one percent of the lines of *Beowulf*—about the same as the number of verses with two strong dips when the prefixes are regarded as extrametrical and invisible.[11]

There is a further connection between the results of this approach and other surprising facts of Old English meter—facts which the approach both reveals and rationalizes. The statement of the percentages above followed the usual practice of exempting the twenty-two hypermetric verses from the count. However, with the new principles in mind, we can see that even these longer verses, where one would expect more than one "gabble of weaker syllables," follow the restriction that limits strong dips to the first dip. (I scan the second syllable of *Scyldinga* in 1166a and 1168b with some degree of metrical stress; see Chapter Six, section 6.4.) In the five verses that appear to have a second strong dip the extra syllable is *ge-* (in two nouns, a pronoun, and two verbs):

sǽton suhtergefǽderan  (1164a)

ǽrfæst æt ecga gelácum  (1168a)

ðín ofer þéoda gehwylce  (1705a)

Ic þé sceal míne gelæstan  (1706b)

syðða[n] híe ðá mærða geslógon  (2996b)

Hypermetric verses in other Old English poems follow this tendency as well. Chapters Four and Five will argue that the strong dip is a significant feature of Middle English alliterative meter and of the Modern English iambic pentameter, as well as of Old English meter.

Let us summarize our paradigm for the meter of Old English poetry at this point:

*Old English Meter*
Old English meter is alliterative-syllabic, each verse containing four positions. These positions are realized as single syllables (or resolved equivalents) except for one optional expansion of unstressed syllables in either of the first two positions of the verse.

A corollary to this statement would address the metrical status of verbal prefixes such as *ge-*. A further corollary would address the status of the important group of D* verses. One possibility would be to consider D* verses, following Sievers, as a second basic type of the normal half-line—a five-member type. Another possibility, which will be presented in Chapter Six, is to find a base of equivalences in the overall rhythmic structure of the verse and the long line. Any solution depends on a fuller consideration of the meaning of "resolution" than is usually given in Old English metrics, a topic to which we now turn.

## 1.4  Resolution, Kuhn's Laws, and the Antepenultimate Syllable

In this section we shall consider two problems that contribute to making the study of Old English meter as complex as it is: the contexts for resolution of short syllables and the contexts for stressing syllables of ambiguous status. The proliferation of rules regulating these patterns seems at times to put a full understanding of Old English meter out of the reach of any one person—Anglo-Saxon poet or modern metrist. The argument of this section is that the underlying simplicity is to be found in the metrical pattern itself.

Resolution, although rooted in Old English phonology, is an artifice of meter. Metrical stress is determined mainly by grammatical category (noun, adjective, etc.), but the assignment of stress must also pay attention to the quantitative structure of the stressed syllable within the particular word. Normally metrical stress falls on a "long" syllable (one that has a long vowel or diphthong or is closed by a consonant). If the syllable is "short," then it must be "resolved" for metrical purposes by being scanned with the following syllable as a single unit. However, resolution is not always required. If the preceding syllable is stressed and long, resolution is often "suspended"—but often not. Preferable terms would be "heavy" and "light," but the following discussion retains the traditional terms "long" and "short" for easy comparison with earlier studies of Old English meter.[12]

Resolution occurs in all of the Five Types and in various places in each; for example, on the first metrical stress of type A, the second metrical stress of type B, and the first metrical stress of type D:

sceaþena þrēatum (4b)

siþðan grimne gripe (1148a)

sele Hröðgāres (826b)

These are only a few of the contexts in which resolution occurs.

A glance at any catalogue of metrical patterns in Old English will reveal a seemingly arbitrary use of resolution—or suspension of it where it does not seem to be needed. For example, in the following verses the conventional assignment of the second metrical stress occurs on a short syllable:

on bēorsele (492a, 1094a)

in nīdgripe (976a)

Such patterns raise the question of whether resolution is simply used or not used as needed to make the meter come out right.

A. J. Bliss looked carefully at the contexts for resolution and suspension of resolution and found a rough correlation between the prehistoric phonology of certain grammatical categories and the patterning of those categories in meter.[13] For example, the unstressed syllable that resolves with the preceding short, stressed syllable is itself normally short. When "suspension of resolution" occurs, the unstressed syllable is often long. According to Bliss, these tendencies are even clearer if one considers the prehistoric quantities of the vowels. In compounds in the type A pattern, $/ \setminus x$ / x, the third syllable was usually short historically, but in compounds in the type D pattern, $/ / \setminus x$, the relevant syllable, the last, was usually long in prehistoric Old English:

frēowine folca (430a)   Type A

lēof landfruma (31a)   Type D

The main problem with Bliss's analysis, as he acknowledges, is that many categories do not pattern as neatly as compounds do—for example, weak verbs of the second class, which occur in both the A and D contexts.

Indeed, any attempt to extend Bliss's idea beyond the small set of compounds that he analysed encounters contrary evidence immediately. Even Bliss's cautious summary may be an overstatement: "It seems very likely that we can observe in *Beowulf* the decay of a poetic tradition" (p. 35). The decay of what he calls the "primitive equivalences" ("a short syllable followed by a short vocalic ending was equivalent to a single long syllable, but a short syllable followed by a consonantal or a long vocalic ending could only be equivalent to a long syllable followed by a similar ending " [p. 35]) has progressed so far that it may be more accurate to say that a few isolated structures still show reflexes of the older phonology.

Is there anything in the existing verse itself that clearly establishes the need for resolution or its suspension in a given instance? In the great majority of instances the stressed, short, unresolved syllable is the penultimate syllable of the verse; and in the great majority of these instances the preceding antepenultimate syllable is stressed and long. Because previous theories of Old English meter have not had a component of syllable count, this way of looking at the verse has not arisen in the normal course of analysis. It is impossible to give an exact count of verses that are involved until we have an understanding of what is meant by "stressed syllable," a subject to which we shall return in Chapter Six. At this point it is sufficient to say that there are in *Beowulf* between 800 and 900 instances of what is generally understood to be suspension of resolution. Of these, there are very few exceptions to either of the contexts just named, and nearly all of these verses are familiar for being problematic in other theories of Old English meter; for example, there are three verses ending in *fæder* without an immediately preceding long, stressed syllable:

Wæs mīn fæder  (262a)

þone þīn fæder  (2048a)

Geslōh þīn fæder  (459a)

There are also about 17 verses in which suspension of resolution does not occur on the penultimate syllable; for example:

þēodcyninga  (2a)

eorðcyninges  (1155b)

Let us set aside as problematic and possibly exceptional the verses with *fæder* (for which *fædder* has been suggested by several scholars) and the handful of similar verses. For verses like *þēodcyninga,* Chapter Six will propose a solution based on a specific definition of secondary stress.

Our focus is on the large number of verses in which a penultimate syllable with unresolved stress is preceded by a syllable that is stressed and long. For example:

grim andswaru  (2860b)

The key syllable here is the antepenultimate syllable of the verse, regardless of what precedes it:

$$\cdots \sigma\ \sigma\ \sigma$$
$$\uparrow$$

Let us formulate the following rule:

*Antepenultimate Syllable Rule for Resolution*
If the antepenultimate syllable of a verse is long and stressed, the last two syllables are unresolved, regardless of their stress. All other short syllables bearing rhythmic stress must be resolved.[14]

If we recall the simplified schemes of the Five Types, we see that the context just stated applies regularly to all of the types except A. (By "stressed syllable" we include syllables with secondary stress.)

| | | | | |
|---|---|---|---|---|
| A | ´ | x | ´ | x |
| B | x | ´ | x | ´ |
| C | x | ´ | ´ | x |
| D | ´ | ´ | ` | x |
| E | ´ | ` | x | ´ |

Among type A verses, those with secondary stress in the first dip are also included:

´ [`] ´͜ x
wonsceaft wera (120a)

We now have clear metrical contexts for resolution and suspension of resolution. When the antepenultimate syllable is long and stressed, syllables to the right of it do not undergo resolution. All other short syllables bearing rhythmic stress must be resolved.[15]

Various patterns on first thought may appear to be exceptions. For example, types B and E with a long stressed second syllable have resolution at the end:

x ´ x ´͜x
þurh sīdne sefan (1726a)

´ ` x ´͜x
Folcwaldan sunu (1089b)

These follow the pattern. It is the antepenultimate *syllable,* not metrical *position,* that must be long and stressed. The antepenultimate syllable in 1726a is *-ne,* in 1089b *-an.* Thus, resolution must occur wherever in the verse short syllables bear metrical ictus.

How do we know which syllables bear metrical ictus? This question leads us to the second topic of the present section, Kuhn's Laws. The subject of Hans Kuhn's influential 1933 study was the syntactic placement of certain grammatical categories in the older Germanic languages and their concomitantly variable stress.[16] Some categories, like nouns, nearly always receive metrical stress; other categories, like prepositions, seldom do; and still other categories, including finite verbs and adverbs, vary in stress according to their context. Kuhn saw the context as primarily syntactic, but an argument can be made that the meter itself establishes the context that is the major determinant of stress. Because a full critique of Kuhn's Laws is beyond the scope of the present study, we shall move directly to the metrical considerations that arguably can replace the most interesting phenomena described by Kuhn's Laws. Here again the antepenultimate syllable of the verse is the key.

First it is necessary to recognize the idea of a grammatical hierarchy of stress that goes back to Sievers' studies of the older Germanic languages. Different investigators have found different levels of categorial stress. Kuhn rejected the binary distinction between stressed words and unstressed words, by which a *Satzteil*, or sentence constituent, such as "the boy," can consist of an unstressed proclitic, or *Satzteilpartikel* ("the") and a stressed element ("boy"). He proposed that between these two possibilities for stress assignment lay a third categorially defined group of words for which he had to coin the name of *Satzspartikel*, usually translated as "particle," although quite different from the present-day linguistic definition. These are words whose stress, according to Kuhn, derives from their position in the clause. When they occur together early in the clause, either before the first stressed word or immediately after it, Kuhn noted that the meter shows that they are unstressed. But words that belong to the *Satzpartikel* group may occur later in the clause, and when they do, the meter shows that the word has stress. Kuhn proposed that the meter simply exploited the archaic syntax and revealed what the prose concealed about the tripartite division of words into categories eligible for sentential stress.

The present analysis follows the arguments given at length elsewhere for rejecting Kuhn's tripartite division.[17] Instead, the main division is between stressed, lexical categories, which bear metrical ictus, and all other categories, which do not bear ictus unless they occur in certain positions:

*Hierarchy of Stress*
I.  Ictus-bearing categories
    Adjectives, Nouns, Infinitives, Participles, Lexical Adverbs, Finite Lexical Verbs
II. Nonictus-bearing categories
    Pronouns, Auxiliaries, Conjunctions, Prepositions, Articles

Sometimes finite lexical verbs and lexical adverbs do not bear metrical stress, as in:

$$\overset{x}{d}\overset{x}{r}uncon\ \overset{/}{w}\bar{\imath}n\ \overset{/}{w}\overset{x}{e}ras\ (1233a)$$

$$\overset{x}{þ}\overset{x}{e}nden\ w\overset{/}{o}r\overset{x}{d}um\ w\overset{/}{e}old\ (30a)$$

Thus, the hierarchy can be refined as follows:

*Hierarchy of Stress*
I.  Ictus-bearing categories
    A.  Always stressed: Adjectives, Nouns, Infinitives, Participles
    B.  Demotable: Lexical Adverbs, Finite Lexical Verbs
II. Nonictus-bearing categories (but promotable)
    Pronouns, Auxiliaries, Conjunctions, Prepositions, Articles

This revision admittedly returns us to a tripartite division, but one quite different from Kuhn's. The determinants of what is demotable and what is promotable turn out to be mainly metrical rather than mainly syntactic, and the resulting taxonomy distributes Kuhn's particles through all three of the new categories.

The adjectives, nouns, infinitives, and participles give fixed points from which to begin. They will never occur in dips. A good diagnostic for identifying items in the ictus-bearing category (I) is the first position of a type D, which can be occupied by a noun or adjective:

þegn Hróðgáres  (235a)

wís wélþungen  (1927a)

and also by a finite lexical verb or a lexical adverb, provided it alliterates:

bát bánlocan  (742a)

eft eardlufan  (692a)

But the first position of a type D cannot be occupied by words of the non-ictus-bearing category (II), because the verse then becomes a type C:

ofer hronráde  (10a)

þonne hé Hróðgáres  (1580a)

What is interesting about these verses is that the last three positions are filled by a single noun or adjective, and the antepenultimate syllable of that verse is the one that receives metrical stress. As in the establishment of resolution and suspension of resolution, the antepenultimate syllable of the verse is the key for establishing the pattern—in this case, the overall stress pattern. Kuhn's Laws, in focusing on the first dip, have it backwards. The substitute for Kuhn's two laws assigns stress from the right edge of the verse rather than the left:

*Antepenultimate Syllable Rule for Stress*
If the antepenultimate syllable (or resolved equivalent) of the half-line is the stressed syllable of a noun or adjective, then it is assigned metrical ictus and anything preceding it which is not the stressed syllable of a noun or adjective (or the stressed, *alliterating* syllable of a verb or adverb) is metrically unstressed.

The metrical patterns that are especially relevant to the operation of this rule (and of Kuhn's Laws) are types B and C, which generally have a stressed antepenultimate syllable or resolved equivalent. (Thus, this rule applies after the Antepenultimate Syllable Rule for Resolution has determined syllable-equivalents.) Types D and E also have stressed antepenultimate syllables (secondary stress in type E), but they do not have sequences of metrically unstressed syllables. Type A, which with types B and C provides contexts for Kuhn's Laws, does not fit the antepenultimate context. It can be handled in a straightforward way, but it will not be dealt with here. Words which in other contexts might receive metrical stress are thus metrically unstressed in 2401a and 250b:

$$\overset{x}{G}\overset{x}{e}\overset{x}{w}\overset{/}{a}t \ \overset{x}{þ}\overset{/}{a} \ twelfa \ sum \quad (2401a)$$

$$\overset{x}{n}\overset{x}{æ}\overset{x}{f}ne \ \overset{x}{h}im \ \overset{/\_x}{h}is \ \overset{/}{w}hite \ \overset{x}{l}eoge \quad (250b)$$

One might reasonably ask *why* the antepenultimate rules should work as they do. What is the meaning of assigning resolution and stress by working *backwards* in a verse? Doesn't this approach assume that the verses and lines come already divided and set off by white spaces as we have them in modern editions? Indeed, it does assume that potential verses and lines must be taken as wholes before a determination of the metrical pattern is possible.

From this point of view, the insistence by Robert P. Creed that an essential part of the prosody of *Beowulf* should deal with the extraction of verses and lines from the manuscript seems odd.[18] Creed takes as one of his goals a computer program to replicate the methods used by the early editor John Mitchell Kemble, whose lineation has been accepted by subsequent editors. But even if we could gain access to Kemble's methods of lineation, this information is not necessarily relevant to determining the meter of the poem. The paradigm of meter has no logical connection to the manuscript representation of the possible verses that it tests, or to any procedure for lineating that representation. The meter simply tests the possible verses, from whatever source, filtering out unmetrical sequences from metrical ones (if it is the correct meter). This traditional way of viewing the problem presumably puts us closer to the mental structures of the poet than would a focus upon the derivative object of the manuscript. (The edited text, of course, would not be possible without an extant manuscript, but the edited text stands as a hypothesis of a less derivative level of linguistic representation, just as a modern grammar of Old English does.) One application of a rigorously explicit meter might indeed be to lineate the manuscript, or we might choose not to make that application.

It is helpful to think in a very practical way about the nuts and bolts of meter. If a certain meter allows flexibility at the beginning of a verse but screws down the constraints tightly at the end, then clearly it is necessary to know the end of the verse in order to know what kinds of adjustments to make at the beginning. Among the elements that introduce flexibility and allow these adjustments are the semi-rigid categories of the Hierarchy of Stress: adverbs and finite verbs are basically ictus-bearing but demotable; function words are basically nonictus-bearing but promotable.

The implications of assigning metrical stress from the right edge of the verse connect with a host of ideas from current work in metrics, although the way toward reconciling these ideas is not immediately clear. For example, the English Stress Rule of the present day works from the right edge of the word in accordance with well-known Latinate influences.[19] C. B. McCully and R. M. Hogg argue persuasively that the Old English Stress Rule works in "mirror-image fashion" from the left edge of the word.[20] If so, then the directions of word-stress assignment and of metrical-stress assignment appear to be mirror images within Old English. To these theories one can add Russom's theory that metrical stress in Old English essentially reflects word stress. There appears to be a set of principles toward which these sometimes contradictory (or apparently contradictory) ideas are converging.

If the issues seem to belong too much to the rarefied world of medieval literary metrics, it is helpful to remember that some of the most practical and apparently commonsensical statements in the historical grammars depend upon such metrical theories. If the theory can be shown to be inadequate and superseded, then it is time to revise the grammars. In a discussion of "half-stress" that involves these patterns and others like them, Alistair Campbell states that the second elements of compounds that "did not retain their original semantic force fully" have no intrinsic half-stress but rather acquire it or lose it depending on the syllables that precede or follow.[21] The relevance of the immediate context in determining patterns of stress is not in itself controversial. Much recent work in metrical phonology has dealt with stress shift when stresses "clash." Thus:

$$\text{thirt\`een m\'en} \rightarrow \text{th\`irteen m\'en}$$

As a result of the shift, the clash is alleviated and a more "eurhythmic" spacing is achieved.

The problem in the discussions of both resolution and half-stress is that the context for assigning stress is just the opposite of that in recent phonological theory, and it also runs counter to expectations that would be derived from the facts of historical development. What is the rationale for saying, as Campbell does, that half-stresses on heavy derivative suffixes, "require to be preceded by a long syllable or its equivalent" (p. 35): thus, *síngènde* but *wésende*? It is as though the middle syllable gained some of its weight from the length of the preceding syllable. Yet this would not be a normal relationship between two consecutive syllables. To the contrary, extra length and stress on one syllable could be expected to contribute to the reduction of the following syllable, as in examples of stress clash and stress shift from many languages and in historical developments that are well attested in English. This is what happened, for example, in Old English nouns of all three genders. In the familiar examples of neuter nouns, the long-stem plural *word* loses the *-u* that follows, but short-stem plural *scipu* retains it.

The problem with Campbell's analysis is that he took a structure of the literary meter to be a structure of the ordinary, nonmetered phonology. There is nothing in the ordinary phonology of Old English to correspond to the context "antepenultimate syllable of the verse." Yet this metrical context is what accounts for the difference in distribution between *singende*, which begins with a long syllable, and *wesende*, which begins with a short syllable that must be resolved under conditions of metrical ictus.

Perhaps a cautionary note should be sounded for the phrasing of The Antepenultimate Syllable Rule for Resolution. Because penultimate and antepenultimate syllables figure prominently in purely phonological processes such as the well-known Romance Stress Rule (and consequently, as mentioned above, the English Stress Rule), it may be easy to make the slip that Campbell did from meter to presumed phonology. The significance of a long, stressed antepenultimate syllable is simply that at this point in the highly constrained meter of Old English verse, one can look both to the left and to the right and say succinctly which metrical patterns are possible—succinctly enough to state as the two antepenultimate rules. It is at this point that any optional extended dip has come to an end, and the verse must return to the basic syllable-counting pattern.

R. D. Fulk's terms *onset* and *coda* have much to recommend them, because they are clearly metrical and not phonological (see note 15). The onset of a verse is from the beginning to the last full stress; the coda is the rest of the verse. For all of the relevant structures at the end of the verse, there is an overlap between the domains specified by the Antepenultimate Syllable Rule for Resolution and those specified by Fulk's Rule of the Coda. Because the present theory takes the antepenultimate syllable as pivotal not only for indicating suspension of resolution at the end of the verse but also for indicating certain patterns of stress at the beginning (those associated with Kuhn's Laws), I shall continue to use the more narrow terminology. Future inquiry may reveal ways of stating Old English metrical theory in Fulk's felicitous terms of *onset* and *coda* so as to include the phenomena of Kuhn's Laws as well as those of resolution and its suspension.

Chapter Six will sketch some principles of general prosody that may underlie both of these rules. If the principles can be established, then the "rules" as they appear here may turn out to be derivative surface phenomena. The deeper principles, however, depend for their explanation on the exposition of the intervening chapters, including an analysis of temporal elements. In the English language of all periods, temporal elements cannot be separated from the topics of alternating rhythm and clashing stress.

## 1.5 Alternating Rhythm and Clashing Stress

In light of the discussion of resolution, let us restate our description of Old English meter and consider how its interacting principles account for the many types and subtypes of verse:

*Old English Meter*
Old English meter is alliterative-syllabic, containing four positions. These positions are realized as single syllables (or resolved equivalents) except for

one optional expansion of unstressed syllables in either of the first two positions of the verse.

As we unpack these terms we can see that they state or imply principles that sometimes reinforce each other and sometimes conflict. This is why the familiar catalogues of Old English verse types contain many patterns that are clearly and easily metrical and other patterns that are more difficult. The continuum shades from the obviously metrical to the complex, the ambiguous, and finally the downright unmetrical.

One of the key terms, about which little thus far has been said (beyond its appearance in the title of this book), is "alliterative." As any handbook of versification will tell us, alliteration—like rhyme—normally occurs on stressed syllables. Now if the concept of "stressed syllable" is a basic element of the meter, it may well conflict with another basic element, syllable count—as discussed in section 1.2 and as used in the descriptive statement above, where "syllabic" is hyphenated with "alliterative." Indeed many metrists have seen stress and syllable count as existing in an unbalanced relationship that in a stress-timed language such as English always defeats pure syllable count. Paul Fussell, with reference to the syllabic experiments of Robert Bridges, W. H. Auden, Marianne Moore, and others, writes:

> But despite sporadic successes, even these poets would probably agree that syllabism is not a natural measuring system in a language so Germanic and thus so accentual as English.
>
> Indeed, when syllabic meter does produce engaging effects, they will often be found the result of a lurking system of stresses which the poet has not been able to wish away.[22]

There are, of course, many verses in Old English that exemplify both the principle of a four-syllable count and stress-based alliteration. When the stressed and unstressed syllables alternate evenly, the "lurking system of stresses" presents no more difficulty than do the patterns of the iambic pentameter in Modern English. We can start with these alternating patterns and work toward the harder cases:

/    x  / x  Type A
beorhtre bōte (158a)

x    / x    /    Type B
ond hālig God (1553b)

There are quite a few verses as regular as these: exactly four syllables with an alternating pattern of stress, the stresses falling on long syllables that do not require resolution. Of the 6,342 verses in *Beowulf,* 1,302 (or 20.5 percent) are types A and B of this pattern.

The most common type B is actually not the four-syllable type of *ond hālig God,* but a five-syllable type with two unstressed syllables at the beginning:

> x   x   *́*  x      ′      Type B
> syððan ærest wearð  (6b)

Type A is also represented by many five-syllable verses, such as 8a (and 511 other instances of Pope's A5):

> ′   x   x   ′   x      Type A
> wēox under wolcnum  (8a)

These verses with extended dips (in type B running to as many as five syllables) allow the use of function words and a greater variety of syntactic patterns than would be possible in a purely syllabic meter. The extended dip—with its variable number of unstressed syllables—is also the feature that accounts for the strong-stress feel of Old English poetry. Oddly enough, weakly stressed syllables are more important than strongly stressed syllables in establishing a strong-stress meter. All poetry in English and the other Germanic languages has strong stresses; they cannot be avoided. What is special about strong-stress meter is the varying number of weakly stressed syllables between the heavy stresses—and the sense that the heavy stresses occur at equal intervals of time. It has been traditional to characterize both Old and Middle English alliterative meter as strong stress. Recent studies, however, have shown each of these traditions to be only *partially* strong stress, with constraints clearly applied to avoid complete strong-stress rhythm. The first half-*verse* in Old English poetry and the first half-*line* in Middle English poetry provide examples of strong-stress rhythms in as pure a form as we get:

> *́*  x   x      x   *́*  x
> wæpen ond gewædu  (*Beowulf* 292a)

> x x   x   ′   x   ′
> nū ic þus feorran cōm  (*Beowulf* 430b)

> x x   x  ′ x x   ′  x
> Hit is þe tytelet token  (*Gawain* 1515a)

It is of great interest that the stretches of more than one unstressed syllable on either side of and between the two stresses in the a-verse from *Gawain* do not occur in Old English poetry—nor do they occur in the b-verse of

*Gawain*, which must have one and only one extended dip, as we shall see in Chapter Four. Thus, the b-verse that completes the line just cited has an extended dip in the middle:

$$\overset{x}{\text{and}} \ \overset{\prime}{\text{tyxt}} \ \overset{x}{\text{of}} \ \overset{x}{\text{her}} \ \overset{\prime}{\text{werk}}\overset{x}{\text{kez}} \quad (\textit{Gawain} \ 1515\text{b})$$

And in many other verses the extended dip comes at the beginning:

$$\overset{x}{\text{bot}} \ \overset{x}{\text{on}} \ \overset{\prime}{\text{lit}}\overset{x}{\text{tel}} \ \overset{\prime}{\text{qui}}\overset{x}{\text{le}} \quad (\textit{Gawain} \ 30\text{b})$$

When we move to types C, D, and E, the rhythm immediately becomes more complex, because these types are not characterized by alternating rhythm. Instead, they are all, to some degree, characterized by clashing stress, or the *potential* for clashing stress. While clashing stress has long been a feature recognized in Old English meter, its significance in Modern English and in many other languages has become a central issue in phonological theory only since 1975. The extraordinary developments in various aspects of phonological theory—including tree, grid, and autosegmental phonology—would not have occurred had it not been for a serious consideration of stress clash, the conditions necessary to alleviate a clash, and the implications for general principles of rhythm that can be drawn from these specific structures.[23] Our reconsideration of Old English meter can profit from these developments.

When two fully stressed syllables occur in succession, the rhythmical pattern runs counter to an idealized norm. Elisabeth O. Selkirk has revived Henry Sweet's Principle of Rhythmic Alternation to analyze the periodicities of rhythm in English.[24] Patterns of alternation, indeed, seem to be relevant not only to English but to many languages, as recent studies have shown. The principles of general prosody and psychology that may be involved in the perception of patterns of alternation are beyond the scope of the present inquiry. The point to make is that clashing stress is the marked case, to which strategies for alleviating the clash may be brought.

In general there are two ways of alleviating a stress clash: by demoting one of the stresses to a level at which it does not clash (and perhaps also "shifting" that stress to another syllable at a more ideal distance away); or by spacing the two stresses by allowing a greater interval of time between them. When the second strategy is followed, the extended interval between the two stresses may be filled by either linguistic sound or silence (continued vocalization or pause, or some combination of the two).

Dwight Bolinger has presented numerous examples of these alternative strategies, one of which is cited by Bruce Hayes in his discussion of "eurhythmy."[25] Bolinger's tests show that subjects prefer "mad and senseless slaughter" to the clashing stress pattern of "senseless and mad slaughter"; and similarly "curt and hurried note" to "hurried and curt note." In nonsense monosyllables, subjects prefer "a plap and plam house" to "a plam and plap house," because of the length difference caused by the shortening of syllables closed by voiceless obstruents:

a plammmmm and plap house    a plap and plammmmm house

The point that is relevant for our concerns is that a temporal element—an extension of a syllable or a pause—is one way of alleviating clashing stress. The question that presents itself, then, is whether this solution to clashing stress was used in Old English poetry. In later chapters we shall also ask whether it was used in Old English prose, in Middle English alliterative poetry, and in the iambic pentameter from Chaucer to the present.

## 1.6   Old English: Stress-Timed or Syllable-Timed?

In order to determine whether temporal spacing was a regular element of Old English poetry, we must consider another closely related and well-known concept, the classification of languages as stress-timed or syllable-timed. Stress-timed languages have perceptually equal temporal intervals between stresses, regardless of the number of unstressed syllables. Syllable-timed languages have perceptually equal temporal intervals between syllables. Thus, a typically foreign-sounding pronunciation of English by a French speaker equalizes the spacing of syllables without regard to the stress pattern. (The more normal equalization of intervals between stresses causes a speeding up of unstressed syllables or the insertion of silent beats where necessary.)

In one influential treatment, David Abercrombie suggests that all languages of the world fall into one of the two categories.[26] Further research has shown that this view and some of the well-known comparative generalizations about speech timing have been overstated because of a bias from beginning with English, a language that has an unusual number of the phonetic, phonological, lexical, and syntactic features associated with stress-timing.[27] When the various features of timing are separated and analyzed, it becomes clear that there is a continuum of languages between the extremes of syllable-timing and stress-timing, depending on the mix of the features. English, which seems to have a "conspiracy" of stress-timing features, is at one extreme, and Spanish, which is often used as a contrast, is by no means at the other, syllable-timing extreme, but somewhere in the middle. R. M. Dauer, using the term "stress-based," finds the following continuum: [28]

Japanese    French    Spanish    Greek    Portuguese    English ⟶ Stress-based

It is natural to think of Old English as being at least as stress-based as Modern English. Fussell speaks of "our own Anglo-Saxon instinct to hear stress" (p. 7) and makes the kind of statement that appears regularly in the handbooks:

> The powerful Germanic accents of the Old English language provide a natural basis for a very heavily accentual prosody in which sense rhythm rather than any abstract metrical imperative tends to supply the meter. The standard poetic line in Old English consists of four strongly stressed syllables arranged, together with any number of unstressed syllables, in two hemistichs (or half-lines) of two stresses each (p. 63).

Yet when we look at the specific phonetic, phonological, and lexical structures that contribute to the impression of stress-timing, we see that Modern English is different from Old English on several counts. Indeed, the present stage of the language may be more truly stress-timed than the language of a thousand years ago, and our notion of the "powerful Germanic accents of the Old English language" may be anachronistic. The structures that are especially relevant are three:

(i) reduced syllables
(ii) polysyllabic, Romance lexical items
(iii) phonemic length

Modern English has an abundance of the first two of these features, which are relatively rare in Old English, but it does not have the third, which is a central part of Old English phonology. Exactly this combination of structures makes Modern English suited for stress-timing—or at least for the perception of stress-timing, in contrast with Old English. Let us consider each.

R. M. Dauer points out that the centralization of unstressed vowels to [ə]—as in English, Swedish, and Russian—contributes to the difference between stressed and unstressed syllables, which in turn contributes to the impression of stress-timing. This is true even though the durations of interstress intervals in English can be shown by instrumental measurements to be no more regular than those in Spanish. Thus, the impression of stress-timing in English, as compared with Spanish, is partly a result of the widespread reduction of vowels to [ə] in English. Processes of reduction in Spanish are more likely to reduce a sequence of adjacent vowels to a single vowel (syneresis) or to eliminate consonants (for example, /peskaðo/ 'fish' become [pɛkáo] in some accents). This elimination of consonants is rhythmically quite different from the result produced by English-type reduction rules: * [pəskáðə]. Similarly in French the impression of syllable-timing is sustained by the elimination of a vowel altogether—the elision of "e muet"—rather than reduction to [ə].

The influx of Romance words into the language increased the possibilities of reduction to [ə] within single lexical items. The French word *commemoratif* has five syllables, none of which is reduced: [kɔmɛmɔratif]. English *commemorative* has either three occurrences of [ə] or two occurrences with a resulting closed syllable, which also contributes to the impression of stress-timing: [kəmɛm(ə)rətɪv]. Hundreds of pairs of French and English words make the same point, with full vocalic value and syllable-timing in French, but reduction to [ə] and the impression of stress-timing in English:

recapitulation [rekapitülasyoⁿ]
recapitulation [rikəpìčəléšən]

impossibilite [iⁿposibilite]
impossibility [ɪmpùsəbíləti]

inseparable [iⁿseparabl]
inseparable [ɪnsép(ə)rəbəl]

president [prezidaⁿ]
president [prézədənt]

Because native words provide fewer contexts for multiple reductions to schwa within the word, the extent of this kind of reduction was not possible in Old English.

Finally, the relevance of phonemic length in making Old English more syllable-timed than Modern English can be seen in secondary stress. In *The Meter and Melody of* Beowulf I took issue with Otto Jespersen's analysis of certain lines of iambic pentameter, such as one he cites from *Richard III:* [29]

Grím-vìsag'd wárre hath smooth'd his wrinkled front  (I.i.9)

Secondary stress on *visag'd*, although a phonological fact, is by no means necessarily a metrical fact. I have argued that the metrical structure is the same as that in the following line by Pope:

Márk how it móunts, to Man's imperial race  (*Essay on Man* I.209)

As Wimsatt and Beardsley and others have made clear, the iambic pentameter is a binary, not a multileveled, system. The point of the comparison was to ask whether secondary stress in Old English meter might also be demoted to the level of nonictus to form a binary structure:

flōdȳþum féor   →   flōdȳþum féor

In order to prevent this demotion, I proposed melodic contours, which would keep separate the three levels of stress on the first three syllables.

My own analysis is probably typical of modern readings that impose conceptions of secondary stress inappropriately to a stage of the language that had phonemic length. However, it matters that the vowel in the first syllable of *-ȳþum* is long, and that the syllable itself is "long." There is less of a drop—in all of the correlates of linguistic prominence and of metrical ictus—between *flōd* and the first syllable of *ȳþum* than between *Grim* and the first syllable of *visag'd* in the line from *Richard III*. If we take into account the rhythmically retarding effects of phonemic length and secondary stress, melodic contours are not necessary. Dauer points out the importance of syllable structure in impressions of stress-timing and syllable-timing. He notes that in stress-timed languages there is considerable variation in syllable length. The occurrence in Old English of long and short vowels and the relevance of phonemic length help to moderate these differences, as in *flōdȳþum*, where the contour is not so much a drop from a peak to a valley, as from a peak to a foothill.

This analysis has a curious relationship to recent theories of the metrical phonology of ordinary spoken Modern English. The impetus for the theoretical activity was the recognition of the need to avoid "stress clash" in examples such as the one given above, *thirteen men,* which undergoes a shift in stress:

$$\text{thìrteen mén} \;\rightarrow\; \text{thìrteen mén}$$

Numerous other phrases follow a similar pattern: *Mississippi legislature, Cornell hockey, achromatic lens, Dundee marmalade, antique chair, Chinese industry,* etc. In citation form *Chinese* is stressed on the last syllable, but in the phrase *Chinese industry* the stress shifts to the left. The definition of "clash" and the mechanism for stress shift have been made more precise by means of a grid:

```
                x                        x
        x       x            x           x
    x   x       x            x   x       x
    thirteen men    →    thirteen men
```

Degrees of stress are indicated by heights of the columns of x's. A clash occurs when two columns have x's at the same height without an intervening column that has an x one level lower. This representation captures our intuitive sense of alternating rhythm. Thus, no stresses clash in the following sequence:

```
    x   x   x
    x x x x x x
    a b c d e f g
```

But stresses clash twice here:

```
    x       x - - - x
    x - x   x   x
    x x x x x x x
    a b c d e f g
```

The clash occurs not only between columns a and b, which are consecutive, but also between columns d and f, which have no intervening x one level down. By this definition of stress clash, there is a clash in *achromatic lens* even though -*mat*- and *lens* are not consecutive syllables (and thus a shift of stress to the first syllable of *achromatic*):

```
                x                        x
        x ------- x            x         x
    x       x   x            x     x     x
    x   x   x x   x          x   x   x x   x
    achromatic lens    →    achromatic lens
```

There has been much debate over whether these and similar rhythms are best captured by grids, or by branching trees, or by a combination of the two. My choice of the grid makes no claims about the issues in phonological theory. It is employed here as one phonological mechanism that usefully illustrates stress clash in poetic meter.

Jespersen's reading of the relevant syllables in "Grim-visag'd warre hath smooth'd his wrinkled front" can thus be represented by a grid:

Grim-visag'd warre hath smooth'd his wrinkled front

In this line there is only one stress clash—between *Grim* and the first syllable of *visag'd*. Between the first syllable of *visag'd* and *warre* there is an intervening syllable one level down, returning the rhythm to an even alternation. In Jespersen's terms, there is only one "disappointment" in the line, the clashing stress.

However, there is another, more traditional reading of structures such as these, one that gives a quite different sound from that of Jespersen's reading. The difference between *Grim* and *vis-* is made great enough so that *vis-* is relegated to the nonictus part of the meter, along with its second syllable, *-ag'd*. In other words, *visag'd* forms a two-syllable dip between stresses. Depending on the assumptions of one's theory, this differential could be accomplished by demoting *visag'd* or by promoting *Grim*. If we promote *Grim*, we get the following structure:

```
x ------------------------ x
x                          x
x        x                 x
x        x  x              x
```

Grim-visag'd warre hath smooth'd his wrinkled front

Now as regards the configuration of stress peaks, there is the possibility of clashing stress between *Grim* and *warre*. However, the stresses are spaced far enough (indeed possibly an ideal distance) so that the effect is not of clashing stress but of two stresses spaced in time—strong-stress rhythm. Chapter Five will argue that this is also the relevant structure when the even alternation of the iambic pentameter is interrupted by an "inverted first foot."

The pattern of stress on *Grim-visag'd*, with a two-level difference between the two root syllables raises an interesting parallel with conventional treatments of compound stress going back to structural phonology. In these, a two-level difference in the clashing stress of the root syllables of certain large classes of compounds (including the *Grim-visag'd* type) is taken as the normal pattern. Noam Chomsky and Morris Halle noted this reading, expressed uncertainty about its factual status, suggested a mechanism to produce it if necessary, and dismissed the problem as marginal. Mark Liberman and Alan Prince noted that the pattern had been effected in generative phonology by "various subsidiary rules," including a special rule of emendation and an otherwise vacuous application of the Compound Stress Rule.[30] In the line cited from Shakespeare, the present analysis ascribes the two-level difference to the tilting effect of poetic meter. If it turns out that the normal, nonpoetic intonation of the language has that pattern in any event, then the observation to make about the pattern in meter is simply that there is less "tension" (less divergence between the abstract pattern of meter and the abstract pattern of phonology). Furthermore, if it can be shown that the normal, nonpoetic pattern has this two-level difference, then we have a reason why there is usually no sense of a temporal beat between the elements of these compounds to compare with the beat that is widely perceived between the clashing stresses of a phrase. This difference between the rhythmical structure of stress clash in compounds and in phrases strikes me as correct, although the question certainly permits different answers. Heinz J. Giegerich, for example, argues for a temporal beat between the first two syllables of *well-funded bank*.[31]

The idea of spaced stresses raises the issue of isochrony—a topic that has been treated over the years in scores of studies by both literary metrists and phoneticians. In addition to observations about the "speeding up" and "compression" of unstressed syllables, various experiments have clocked the performance of utterances and measured their perceptual effects and acoustic correlates. Much of this is to one side of the problem that concerns us, because Old English meter does not allow the flexibility to make the full range of adjustments (of both promotion and demotion) that ordinary speech does. If in the verse *sægde him þæs lēanes þanc* (1809b) the first four syllables have to occupy a dip, it does not take acoustic instruments to tell us that even with considerable "speeding up" and "compression," *sægde him þæs* will take longer than the *-es* of the second dip. The point is that the speeding up of consecutive weak syllables is a widely recognized pattern of Modern English, whatever the clocked differences in perceived equalities might be. Marina Nespor and Irene Vogel observe that whereas Italian would create an alternating pattern on consecutive weak syllables, in English "the tendency would most likely be to speed up a bit and maintain

the string of weak syllables."[32] The example that they give includes the following grid:

```
    x                   x
    x                   x
    x                   x
    x   x x   x x   x   x
```

it wasn't happening if it was raining

We shall see when we get to the meters of Middle English and Modern
English that patterns of metrically unstressed syllables which require this
speeding up continue to figure prominently. The intrusion of what can be
called the "strong-stress mode" into more regularly alternating modes is
one of the most salient features of English poetic rhythm from its origins
to the present.

In my earlier theory of Old English meter, I argued that in *all* instances of clashing stress, whether type C or D, the first stress was heavier
than the second (as indeed other metrists had argued before). My exposition raised the possibility that the Nuclear Stress Rule (which throws
heaviest stress to the right in a phrase) was not a part of the language then.
A less radical explanation, however, seemed to be that the meter itself
caused the pattern, and it was this conclusion that the argument finally
urged. Now with a slightly different version of the meter, there are many
fewer unnatural patterns to explain. The more moderate view that results
is that nearly all type C verses do indeed follow compound stress, but that
many type D verses follow phrasal stress in the clash of the first two positions (at least in the first half-line, as we shall see in Chapter Six). This
clash raises the possibility of a metrical pause as a spacer:

$$\text{wearp} \overset{\prime}{\phantom{}} \overset{(x)}{\phantom{}} \overset{\prime}{\text{wælf}} \overset{\backslash}{\text{y}} \overset{x}{\text{re}} \quad (2582a)$$

When we eventually return to this matter (in section 6.4), we shall have
additional reasons for distinguishing compound and phrasal stress in the
earliest English poetry. These reasons involve some of the most basic questions in prosody, including "What is ictus?" and "Is there a place for time?"

## 1.7 The Derivativeness of Sievers' Five Types

When the metrical analysis involves the details of resolution and other
technicalities, as in the preceding sections, the mind yearns to step back
and perceive the overall picture, so as not to forget the place that the details

occupy. The process of stepping back and abstracting is of course central to metrics. The problem is that it is sometimes done as though there were a single linear direction of movement between the narrow focus and the broad focus. For example, the generalization of two heavy stresses to the half-line is often taken as a simplification of Sievers' Five Types. However, it may be that the abstraction of two heavy stresses is not an accurate simplification of the Five Types but a superficially similar phenomenon that is essentially unrelated. It may be a statement to one side of the problem. Similarly, the Five Types themselves may be a statement to one side of the most adequate paradigm. It is often assumed that the Five Types have a kind of factual status beyond theory, because they simply describe, neutrally, "what is there." By this assumption, theories can try to refine and simplify the Five Types, but they must always be tested by the hard core of facts that the Five Types represent.

The truth, of course, is that the Five Types themselves are a theory and an abstraction. They are at an intermediate level between alternative systems that are more concrete in one direction and more abstract in the other. A representation of Old English meter at an absurdly concrete level might read: "The set of patterns of Old English meter consists of the patterns of stress contained in the following words in the order that they occur within the following half-lines." The statement would be followed by a list of the 60,000 extant half-lines of Old English poetry. A representation of Old English meter at a more abstract level might be Sievers' theory of four *Glieder*. Sievers' Five Types might or might not be the most adequate statement at an intermediate level. For the normal half-line Bliss lists 130 patterns and Pope lists 279 patterns. Because in metrics little attention is ever given to general principles, simplicity and elegance are usually in the eye of the beholder (or the metrist).

For Sievers' Five Types the question comes down to whether those patterns are the paradigm itself or the epiphenomenal results of a simpler paradigm. Although the measurement of simplicity is anything but simple, here the answer is easy. The question is whether the mapping is (a) from the Five Types to the local interaction of syllables or (b) from the local interaction of syllables to the Five Types. It turns out that mapping (a) is more complex because it requires statements of all the details that mapping (b) requires (concerning long and short syllables, resolution, suspension of resolution, grammatical stress, alliteration, anacrusis, constraints on unstressed syllables in the second part of the half-line, etc.) plus a separate statement of the Five Types. Mapping (b) adds to the details of the local interactions between syllables simply the statement that these processes operate within a frame of four positions. Furthermore, because these positions can now be seen to tie directly to single syllables (with the allowance of one expansion), the relationship between Old English meter and other European meters has a saliency that the Five Types have never had.[33]

The contour theory that I presented in 1974 was arrived at by considering several independent problems in the various parts of the Old English line: anacrusis, clashing stress, secondary stress or intermediate ictus, resolution, suspension of resolution, etc. At the end it was shown that the interaction of all these separate constraints produced exactly Sievers' Five Types if they were forced to operate within a frame of four positions. Thus, instead of specifying Sievers' Five Types plus all these separate constraints, which have struck many observers as considerable machinery to produce as many exceptions as it does, one can list all the separate constraints, which are needed anyway, and then say: "Make them operate within four positions, where a position is identified locally as a change of ictus from the preceding position." This four-position paradigm is a more or less adequate way of considering Old English meter, although I would now put the emphasis on the single-syllable nature of most positions (seventeen of the twenty positions that are possible among Five Types consisting of four positions). Perspicuous as the paradigm may be, I obscured it by mapping it onto five concrete tunes.[34] The picture that resulted was more specific than the evidence warranted: a picture of the poet carrying around a stock of five melodic formulas to which he set words. The picture that emerges from the present study is that the contours are indeed real, at least for the overwhelming majority of verses, but, like the Five Types, they are derivative, not paradigmatic. To be sure, there is much that does not change in this shift of perspective. If the contours are real as surface facts, then many of the questions of meter and performance remain—for example, how these contours might fit with the contours of music. What is gained is a better insight into the fundamental principles of intonation and rhythm. This insight should help us understand similarities and differences within the development of a tradition, and between traditions.

The moral to draw, then, is this: in phonology—and perhaps in linguistic and musicological description generally—one should be wary of working at an intermediate level of representation, where the facts in a commonsensical, positivistic way seem to be most obvious. One should have instead a double vision of syllables interacting locally and also a simple explanatory generalization. The intermediate level will take care of itself. Instead of talking about contours as falling, or rising, or rising-falling, a more adequate theory describes the internal dynamics at the phonological level, states the parameters there, and then says: Do anything at all within the scope of the general principles. In Old English poetry the main general principle is a frame of four positions. It is now clear that a statement at the intermediate level of description that disallows three rising levels of stress is superfluous. Given the local constraint of clashing stress (whereby the second is subordinated to the first) and a hierarchy of lexical stress depending upon grammatical category, three rising levels are almost impossible.

# 2. Old English Rhythmical Prose and Early Middle English Meter

## 2.1 Disjunctions and Continuities in Metrical Style

Few principles of meter could be simpler, or more ancient, than a count of syllables.[1] Chapter One argued that Old English meter was based on four syllables to the half-line. We have seen that one natural modification of this simple scheme—and what has prevented metrists from perceiving the scheme itself—was the optional substitution of a stretch of unstressed syllables for one of the first two syllables. There is no obvious reason why the expansion should occur in the first half of the verse rather than in the second half, but the pattern is consistent with variation in numerous metrical traditions: in the iambic pentameter of Modern English, for example, the inverted first foot occurs most often at the beginning of the line, and the end of the verse returns to the regular pattern.

In any event, the simple provision for an optional expansion complicates the metrical pattern in rather unexpected ways. Syllables do not fill pre-existing structure but create structure. Because lifts and dips are not completely determined by grammatical category, a syllable that in one verse counts as a position by itself might in another verse be subsumed into a multisyllabic dip. Since the syllables themselves must define the dips, the count of syllables must be supplemented by a system of ictus based on stress and length—correlates of the syllable that brings the verse out of the dip. As we have seen, it becomes clear at a certain point in the verse that the variation is completed, and the verse returns to the simple count of syllables. From these principles, a bewildering array of patterns of stress and quantity results. Yet the paradigm itself can be stated succinctly as, "Count exactly four syllables (or the resolved equivalents) and allow an optional expansion for one of the first two syllables."

If we bring this Old English paradigm to the texts of the present chapter, we shall see that it fails utterly. This fact in itself is of interest, because it means that the paradigm succeeds in excluding patterns, as a paradigm should do. The many patterns that the paradigm cannot account for help us see what was excluded from classical Old English poetry. Because Early Middle English poetic texts share certain key rhythmical structures with Ælfric's rhythmical prose, it will be instructive to begin with Ælfric.

There are good reasons for locating the source of the later forms of poetry in a mode of composition closer to that of Ælfric's rhythmical prose than to that of the classical Old English poetry. It appears that in late Old English times there was a continuum of modes of composition, which modern investigators have divided into "poetry" and "prose," some of the prose being rhythmical. This simple division leads to such questions as, "Was Ælfric a poet?" and it tends to ignore the borderland between poetry and prose, to which N. F. Blake and others have brought a corrective focus.[2]

## 2.2 Ælfric's Rhythmical Prose

The general characteristics of Ælfric's rhythmical prose have received full and incisive treatment by John C. Pope.[3] The analysis that follows is an elaboration of part of Pope's discussion along the lines of studies that have been made by Angus McIntosh and by Sherman M. Kuhn.[4] The features that are focused on in detail may appear to be technical and minor. However, it should be clear from the direction that this study is taking that these technical features are diagnostic. Other metrists have analyzed the same features and have sometimes come to strikingly different conclusions from rather subtle differences in emphasis.

Part of the problem is lack of a metatheory for strong-stress meter: we tabulate similarities and differences without an explicit understanding of the weight of any feature. The adaptation of Sievers' Five Types for everything from Cædmon's *Hymn* to *Piers Plowman* is the clearest manifestation of a lack of theoretical coherence. To take it to an absurd end, any English meter could be described in terms of its correspondence to Sievers' Five Types, just as any English meter could ultimately be traced against the abstract pattern of iambic pentameter. But at some point one must question whether one has begun with the relevant paradigm.

Thus Pope's rejection of nineteenth-century efforts to describe Ælfric's rhythmical prose in terms of Sievers' Five Types is to the point (p. 107). His characterization of the metrical structure of Ælfric's line fits with impressions on reading the text: "The relatively firm patterns of the Sievers types, where secondary stresses have fixed positions and their presence limits the number and position of other syllables, are replaced by the more casual undulations of ordinary speech, in which the syllabic content of the lightly stressed portions varies unpredictably and is little regarded" (p. 117).

Furthermore, syllabic length, though still a part of the language, is not a part of the rhythmic structure. After scanning the *Life of St. Edmund* with attention to metrical length and resolution, I could not find an internally consistent pattern. Therefore, I scanned the text again without invoking resolution. Just as the regulation of lightly stressed syllables in Old English poetry depends on a firm framework, as Pope points out, so does the regulation of syllabic length. Pope's summary, in fact, is as succinct and accurate a statement as one can make: "In short, the syllabic weight and distinct rhythmic organization of the poetry are approached but rarely, and chiefly at moments of heightened feeling. . . . Distinctions between long and short syllables, though probably perceptible, could hardly have metrical significance in so relaxed a scheme; and certainly no one who accepts my theory of initial rests in the poetry will be tempted to introduce any here" (p. 118).

In light of these prefatory remarks it may seem odd that the discussions of rhythm in Ælfric, Lawman, and fourteenth-century alliterative poetry in this chapter and throughout the rest of the book will make use of a system of notation that is obviously derived from Sievers' Five Types. The reason is mainly mnemonic. Anyone with a passing familiarity with Old English will understand what is meant by type A, or type D, or the other types. To introduce a wholly different system would put an extra burden on both author and reader. There is of course a risk in implying more continuity than one intends. My modification of Sievers' system follows in certain respects J. P. Oakden's modification—for example, in the *rising-falling*, or BA type (x / x / x).[5] Oakden, however, takes this minor adjustment in notation to represent an equally minor adjustment in the overall metrical scheme. I take it as a crucial index to a transformation of the meter.

The system used for classifying half-lines throughout this study can be illustrated and explained by beginning with the fourteen most frequent patterns that occur in the 276 lines of Ælfric's *Life of St. Edmund* (see table). There is a systematic correlation between the name of the type and the number of syllables. The seventh pattern on the list is labeled 3A be-

*Life of St. Edmund*

|       | | a-verse | b-verse |
|-------|---------|---------|---------|
| B2A   | x / x x / x     | 19 | 23 |
| 2BA   | x x / x / x     | 25 | 13 |
| 2B2A  | x x / x x / x   | 14 | 21 |
| 3B2A  | x x x / x x / x | 7  | 12 |
| B3A   | x / x x x / x   | 10 | 9  |
| 2A    | / x x / x       | 5  | 14 |
| 3A    | / x x x / x     | 9  | 10 |
| 3BA   | x x x / x / x   | 11 | 7  |
| B2A2  | x / x x / x x   | 12 | 5  |
| 2A2   | / x x / x x     | 5  | 5  |
| 2B2   | x x / x x /     | 4  | 6  |
| 3B    | x x x / x /     | 3  | 7  |
| 2BA2  | x x / x / x x   | 6  | 4  |
| 2B3A  | x x / x x x / x | 3  | 7  |

cause it is Sievers' type A, and the first dip has three syllables. The number 3 before the letter indicates three syllables in the first dip whereas a number 3 after the letter would indicate three syllables in the second dip. No number after the letter A indicates the single syllable that is the minimum necessary in that position. The twelfth pattern in the list is labeled 2B2 because it has two syllables in each dip of Sievers' type B (x x / x x /). I follow Oakden in calling the rising-falling type BA, but again I classify the varieties of this type separately according to the number of syllables: B2A (x / x x / x) has two syllables in the second dip (shown by the number 2 after the B) and the minimum single syllable for both the first and the last dips (shown by no number before the B or after the A); 2BA (x x / x / x) has two syllables in the first dip and one in each of the last two. With a little use the system is easy to remember and apply.

The *Life of St. Edmund* has 99 types according to this system, and nearly all of them follow these general principles: one of Sievers' Five Types indicated by the letters A to E, alone or in combination, with numerals showing the position and count of weakly stressed syllables. Among all of the Old and Middle English texts that I have scanned, there is a total of 206 types, nearly all of which could be named without reference to a chart once the principles of classification are understood.[6]

A comparison of the distribution of metrical types in Ælfric's prose with the distribution in *Beowulf* is revealing both for the patterns that occur and for those that do not. All of the fourteen most common types in the *Life of St. Edmund* are varieties of A or B or combinations of A and B. Types C, D, and E do not occur among the most frequent patterns. A full list would show six verses of type 2C (x x / / x), six of 3C (x x x / / x), five of 2C2 (x x / / x x), three of 4C (x x x x / / x), and one each of C2 (x / / x x), 2C3 (x x / / x x x), 3C2 (x x x / / x x), and 4C (x x x x / / x). Thus, type C, although much less frequent than in *Beowulf*, is well enough represented to be a distinct type.

The situation is different with types D and E. In all of the *Life of St. Edmund*, there are no unambiguous examples of these two types. There are two verses labeled EA (/ \ x / x), but this five-member type would not have been allowed in the *Beowulf* meter. The lack of types D and E is significant in determining the rhythmical base that underlay Ælfric's rhythmical prose. A similar problem runs through our understanding of the essential rhythm of every text in strong-stress rhythm from Ælfric through the Alliterative Revival. The usual method of description has been to begin with Sievers' Five Types and, after discussion of varieties of types A, B, C, and BA, to include a note that types D and E do not occur. Such is the organization of Oakden's account and of Norman Davis's appendix on "Metre" in the Tolkien-Gordon edition of *Sir Gawain and the Green Knight*. Twenty-two pages into his Chapter 8 on "The Alliterative Revival," Oakden writes:

> D. and E. types are found in *The Description of Durham*, c. 1100, but not in any of the later pieces or early M.E. alliterative poetry. The C. type, however, is found in all the alliterative poems subsequent to 1100. . . . There is absolute continuity in rhythm from the O.E. period to the close of the M.E. period, despite a few important changes. (p. 174)

Because types D and E are so different from types A and B, and because their presence in classical Old English meter, even as minority types, raises such profound implications about the basis of the meter as a whole, "absolute continuity in rhythm" is meaningful only in the most superficial sense.

In comparison with Old English poetry, the texts that we are considering in this chapter (Ælfric's rhythmical prose and late Old English and early Middle English poetry) are characterized by alternating rhythms. Clashing stress and secondary stress are relatively rare. In order to understand the rhythmical significance of texts with a high proportion of alternating rhythms (types A, B, and combinations of A and B) and a low proportion of clashing stress (types C, D, and E), it is helpful to keep in mind the contrast drawn in Chapter One between syllabic rhythm and strong-stress rhythm. In syllabic rhythm, stresses often clash; in strong-stress rhythm some kind of alternation is the norm. A purely syllabic rhythm allows much less syntactic and lexical flexibility than a strong-stress rhythm, especially if the syllable count is set as low as four. This lack of flexibility accounts for the development of Old English meter as a *mixed* form—essentially syllabic but with a place in the first half of the half-line for one optional expansion.

Even with this allowance for expansion, the half-line of Old English poetry is notably self-contained and discrete. It must hook up, of course, with other half-lines to make a syntactic whole, although an obvious feature of the appositive style of Old English poetry is that the structure of composition is additive. In this sense the structure of the poetry may be said to be synthetic, in contrast with the analytic structure of the prose.

To show how Ælfric's prose has more of an analytic than a synthetic quality, we can compare texts of his nonrhythmical prose, such as the Christmas homily in the Second Series of *Catholic Homilies*, with examples of his rhythmical prose, such as the *Lives* of Edmund and Oswald. One has a sense with both types of prose that the syntax is not built up of small units, as in the poetry, but conceived whole. Both types of prose, of course, break into constituents, the difference being that the rhythmical prose breaks more easily into two-stress constituents of a certain length.

What does it mean to say that the poetry is built up of smaller units while the rhythmical prose breaks down into phrases? One way of rephrasing the question is to ask whether Old English rhythmical prose begins with Old English meter and undergoes a loosening—or begins with normal prose and undergoes a tightening. Let us consider specific syntactic structures.

A characteristic feature of syntax in nonrhythmical Ælfrician texts such as the "Catholicus Sermo de Natale Domini" is the tendency of whole clauses *not* to break readily into two-stress phrases with patterns such as those in the list above of the most common rhythmical types in *Edmund*. The clause, *þa ða he asende his agen bearn to slege for us*, might be divided into the following three constituents:

þa ða he asénde      his ágen béarn      to slége for ús [7]

The last phrase would be fine in rhythmical prose, and the first would be acceptable (because there are a number of apparently one-stress phrases in the prose). The middle phrase, however, has only four syllables. Although such a pattern is quite frequent in the poetry, it is rare enough in the prose to be suspect (only one four-stress half-line occurring in the 574 half-lines of *Oswald* and only one in the 552 half-lines of *Edmund*). However, if we attach the phrase to either the preceding or the following phrase, the resulting phrases are three-stress and four-stress, respectively:

þa ða he asénde his ágen béarn   to slége for ús

þa ða he asénde   his ágen béarn to slége for ús

Either phrase would be marginal at best in Ælfric's rhythmical prose. (We cannot say they would be flatly unacceptable until we have a better sense of the relevant principles.) This type of clause occurs frequently in the non-rhythmical prose, a clause that is too short or too long to break naturally into clear two-stress units of the kind that we find prevalent in the rhythmical prose. Many of these clauses contain discrete four-syllable units, which, as we have seen, occur in fewer than 0.2 of one percent of the lines in *Edmund* and *Oswald*.

Some clauses are simply too short:

He wæs æfre   of ðam fæder   acenned

Either grouping of the medial prepositional phrase leaves a fragment that is too short to occur in the rhythmical prose:

He wæs æfre of ðam fǽder   acénned

He wæs æfre   of ðam fǽder acénned

Even if a second stress were supplied for the phrase, *He wæs æfre*, the fact that it has only four syllables tells against it just as in the previous examples. For the rhythmical prose, a paradigm that would account for a considerable portion of attested patterns while screening out closely related unattested, and apparently unacceptable, patterns might read as follows:

*Rhythmical Prose*
A half-line of rhythmical prose is a syntactic constituent containing at least five syllables and exactly two stresses (as stresses are determined by the Hierarchy of Stress, section 1.4).

Additional examples will help to illustrate and refine this preliminary statement, as well as to give some substance to "syntactic constituent."

A noun phrase consisting of a determiner, adjective, noun, and appositive will naturally have three stresses, as in the prepositional phrase
that ends a clause in the Christmas homily, line 4:

$$\overset{x}{ }\ \overset{x}{ }\ \overset{x}{ }\overset{/}{ }\ \overset{x}{ }\overset{/}{ }\ \overset{x}{ }\ \overset{x}{ }\ \overset{x}{ }\overset{/}{ }\ \overset{x}{ }\ \overset{/}{ }\overset{x\ x}{ }\ \overset{/}{ }\overset{xx}{ }$$
He wæs todæg acenned   of ðam halgan mædene Marian

Because this phrase would be too long and heavy in the rhythmical prose,
the more typical pattern in *Edmund* and *Oswald* would simply have the
determiner, adjective, and noun. A preposition or conjunction before such
a noun phrase does not make the constituent too heavy. There are numerous examples of this syntactic pattern in the rhythmical prose; for example,
from *Oswald:*

> þurh his halgan geearnunge  (192b)
> þurh þone halgan wer   (203b)
> of þam halgan treowe  (263b)
> þæt se halga cynincg  (273b)
> Eft se halga cuðberht  (279a)
> þæs halgan bisceopes  (281a)
> þurh þone halgan wer  (286b)

And a representative sample from *Edmund:*

> þæs halgan eadmundes  (131b)
> and þæt halige heafod  (159a)
> to þam halgan bodige  (165a)
> þone halgan lichaman  (175a)
> æt þæs halgan byrgene  (190a)
> swa þæt se halga wer  (207a)
> and eac þa halgan canones  (220a)
> þone halgan sanct  (235a)
> and þam halgan gaste  (276b)

There are occasional exceptions to this general pattern—for example, *Oswald* 235b: *þæs halgan weres geearnunga.* The rhythmical prose, however,
was not written in a strict meter, and the comments in Chapter One regarding tendency statements and exceptions apply a fortiori to this form

that is intermediate between what we think of as poetry and what we think of as prose.

The treatment of weak verbs of class 2 in the three kinds of texts before us reveals an interesting similarity between the poetry and the non-rhythmical prose, on the one hand, and the rhythmical prose on the other. If one were to break the compound predicate in lines 15–16 of Ælfric's Christmas homily into half-lines, the closest approximation would be as follows:

> and his scyppendes bebod tobræc.

> and deofles lare    gehȳrsumode
> <br>(x / x x x over *gehyrsumode*)

The first constituent is instructive in itself because of the way it forces a three-stress unit (something that also happens in the rhythmical prose, although rarely). The second part of the compound predicate, however, is our focus. The class 2 weak verb *gehyrsumode* is set apart by itself, because to join it to the preceding constituent would create yet another three-stress unit. Such verbs occur easily in *Beowulf* as the only bearers of metrical stress in the half-line:[8]

> Swā rīxode  (144a)
> <br>(x / x x)

> ond þā gyddode  (630a)
> <br>(x   x / x x)

> Swā bealdode  (2177a)
> <br>(x / x x)

> ond ðā folgode  (2933a)
> <br>(x   x / x x)

But when weak verbs of class 2 occur in the rhythmical prose, there is nearly always a noun, adjective, verb, or adverb to provide a second stress. A selection from more than two dozen finite weak verbs of class 2 in *Oswald* illustrates the typical pattern:

> and to sceame tucode  (11b)
> <br>(x   x / x / x x)

> his cymes fægnode  (60b)
> <br>(x / x / x x)

He lufode forhæfednysse  (75a)

and munuclice leofode  (81a)

þe hine æfre wurðode  (108b)

and þus clypode on his fylle  (161a)

and geaxode his ban  (177a)

A similar distribution occurs in the *infinitive* of class 2 weak verbs. In the nonrhythmical prose and in *Beowulf*, in addition to occurring as one of two stresses in a unit, the infinitive can also occur as the only bearer of stress:

oferhīgian  (*Beowulf* 2766a)

But it is always one of two stresses in the rhythmical prose:

and bodian þam hæþenum  (*Oswald* 126a)

A plausible conclusion to draw is that a minimum of two stresses to the metrical unit is even more important in the rhythmical prose than in the poetry. This conclusion accords with the observations of Chapter One, where it was argued that a syllable-count theory of Old English meter is more adequate than a theory based on two stresses. The whole problem has to do with the underlying principles of rhythm, which appear clearly to be strong-stress principles in the rhythmical prose. Strong-stress meter requires a count of stresses and an indeterminate number of unstressed syllables. There is a *part* of the mixed meter of Old English poetry that is strong stress, but it is only the part in the optional expansion—in the first half of types A, B, and C. For the rest, Old English poetry can easily admit verses such as, *Swā bealdode,* because, although the verse has only one metrical stress, it has four syllables.

The characteristic difference in feel between Old English poetry and Ælfric's rhythmical prose has to do with reference to two different rhythmical principles, syllable count and strong stress, from among the small set of possible rhythmical principles. (Another possibility is evenly alternating rhythm, as in Chaucer's decasyllabic line, where the binary metrical categories, nonictus and ictus, tilt the variable levels of phonological stress.) We shall see that the poetic texts to be discussed in the rest of this chapter also make essential reference to strong-stress principles.

Our analysis gives support to the observation by Pope above of a change from the "relatively firm patterns of the Sievers types, where secondary stresses have fixed positions and their presence limits the number and position of other syllables" to a form that has "the more casual undulations of ordinary speech, in which the syllabic content of the lightly stressed portions varies unpredictably and is little regarded." A surprising development that we shall observe in fourteenth-century poetry is the reestablishment of considerable control over the weakly stressed syllables of the line (though not through secondary stress). First, however, it is possible to give a more precise account of the quality that Pope calls "the more casual undulations of ordinary speech," a quality that is to be found not only in Ælfric's rhythmical prose but also in alliterative poetry composed after the Conquest.

Nine of the fourteen most common patterns in the *Life of St. Edmund* are varieties of the rising-falling, or BA, type; for example:

x  x  x  /  x  /  x   3BA
þæt ic on feohte feolle  (66a)

x  /  x  x  / x   B2A
mid bearnum and wifum  (76b)

Altogether, 265 occurrences of twenty-seven different BA patterns account for 50 percent of the half-lines in the text. In the abstract form of the type, the varieties of BA resemble the pattern of the classical meter known as "type A with anacrusis":

x (x) / x (x) (x) (x) / x (x)

However, one of the most clearly established points of Old English meter in studies of the past decade is that "type A with anacrusis" cannot adequately be dealt with as an abstract pattern of stressed and unstressed syllables.[9] In the first place, morphological information (concerning, for example, verbal prefixes) is needed to account for the heavy constraints upon the pattern. Second, once the extent of the constraints is understood, it becomes obvious that a more general principle is at work. Old English meter proscribed a pattern that would have been extremely easy, syntactically and phonologically, to construct. Middle English meter, as we shall see, made this proscribed pattern the overwhelmingly favored one of the tradition. Perhaps more than any other single feature, this is the clue to understanding the transformation that occurred between Old English meter and Middle English meter. The point at which the transformation occurred, at least among extant texts, can be located more precisely than previous studies have done.

## 2.3  The End of the Classical Meter: *The Death of Edward* (1066) and *Durham* (c. 1100)

Most metrical accounts of the 21-line poem *Durham* (in MS. Ff.i.27 of University Library, Cambridge) see it as continuing the classical Old English meter. Indeed the majority of the verses considered in isolation would have been metrically acceptable in *Beowulf*. However, the late Old English author and audience did not consider the verses in isolation. They heard them as part of a single fabric, and although the fabric is composed of its parts, the parts are also shaped by the whole that they form—by their metrical context. This is especially true of ambiguous verses.

In an earlier study I argued that the poem about Durham is in a meter that bears a close superficial resemblance to the traditional Old English meter, but at base the meter is something different.[10] That study focused on the importance of secondary stress in types C, D, and E of the classical Old English meter and its relative scarcity in *Durham*. As explained in Chapter One, the handling of secondary stress in Old English meter can be seen as the result of other principles (the interaction of syllabism and strong-stress rhythm). Because the patterning of secondary stress is a quite direct reflex of these principles, many of the same generalizations emerge whichever phenomenon one chooses to analyze. Indeed, when we turn to the count of syllables that regulates the placing of secondary stress, we come to the same conclusion as when secondary stress is the criterion: the meter of *Durham* shows a clear break from the classical meter of Old English poetry.

In the 42 verses of the poem there is only one example each of types D and E:[11]

feóla físca kyn (5a)

wúdafæstern mícel (6b)

What does it mean to have only one example of each of these types that figured so prominently in giving the classical meter its characteristic feel? One answer, and a plausible one, is that only a scattering of types D and E would be expected at this time in a poem built on metrical principles quite different from those of traditional Old English poetry. A less plausible answer is that these two verses show a continuation of the Sievers Five Types.

The latter answer is less plausible because the Five Types depended on a clear, precise framework. However, when one turns from these two occurrences of the types that had accommodated the poetic compounds—types that should occur in the poem in some kind of critical quantity—to types that should not occur at all, the framework can be seen as anything but clear and precise. Six of the verses have three stresses in configurations that would not have been allowed in nonhypermetric Old English verses (4a, 7b, 8b, 12a, 15a, 20a). Four additional verses have rising-falling patterns that would have been suspect in Old English for not conforming to constraints on type A with anacrusis (5b, 8a, 15b, 16a).

Four verses appear to be normal types B (4a, 17b) and A (18a, 19a), until one remembers that the second dip of these types is restricted in the number of syllables it can contain. More than two unresolved syllables are not allowed in the *Beowulf* meter, and 17b has three:

and he his lára wel genóm (17b)

Two verses are so light as to have only three positions:

Ís in ðere býri eac (9a)

on gecheðe (16b)

The problem with 9a, which might appear to be Sievers' one-stress, type A3, pattern is that the last syllable is a monosyllabic word, which never ends an A3. The reason is clear enough: the phrasal stress rule would assign stress to an otherwise lightly stressed syllable, as in *Beowulf* 1683b:

ond his mōdor ēac (1683b)

Here one might object that this is cutting it all too fine and that the course to take is to suspend resolution on *byri* in the line from *Durham* and have a type B verse such as the one from *Beowulf*. However, the classical form does not permit suspension of resolution on the first stressed syllable of type B, for good reason. The intricate, interwoven rules of syllabic length, resolution, and suspension of resolution, along with the rules for primary stress, secondary stress, and alliteration produce a total pattern in a fabric, the parts of which are interdependent. If one part is removed the whole begins to unravel.

For example, if we tried to salvage 9a by omitting the rules of syllabic length, resolution, and suspension of resolution, there would be immediate problems (from the perspective of classical meter) with five other verses in which the metrical units have been reduced to the requirements of the paradigm through resolution. These include the single example of type D and of type E, noted above, 5a and 6b (and also 1a, 4b, and 12b). These verses would now have five members, or five positions, instead of the required four.

Indeed, the five-member scansion is arguably the right one for these verses in *Durham,* because the classical meter breaks down to the extent that syllabic length cannot be shown to be metrically relevant. Sustaining the classical meter requires an overall pattern that is firm enough to allow a consistent and predictable mapping between metrical units and linguistic units. One cannot pick and choose features of the classical meter and still have a poem in that meter. By my application of the classical rules, sixteen of the 42 verses in *Durham,* or 38.1 percent, are flatly unmetrical, and the distribution of metrical types is not close to that of *Beowulf.*

It is as though the author of *Durham* were familiar with earlier Old English poetic texts but misunderstood their metrical principles, and by formulating his own principles from this misreading produced a work in which a majority of verses are perfectly regular, some are dubious, and a considerable minority are unmetrical. The point here is not to question individual verses in *Durham* that conform to the classical meter. Overlapping metrical grammars could produce a considerable number of identical results. The agreement could approach 100 percent, and still the crucial question to ask is which principles are excluded from the overlap.

If *Durham* shows a misreading of metrical principles that had prevailed for four centuries, and a significant change in mode of composition and performance, what is the last extant poem in that mode? About thirty years earlier than the poem on Durham, a poem known as *The Death of Edward* in the *Chronicle* entry for 1065 conforms throughout nearly all of its 68 verses to the strictest requirements of the classical meter. The one unmetrical verse by my reading is 28a, *sopfæste sawle*, which is not, of course, analogous to a verse such as *Beowulf* 1271a, *gimfæste gife*, because of the long syllable in *sawle*. The point at which the occurrence of un-metrical verses in a poem is significant enough to signal a change in the metrical paradigm is a difficult judgment. I would say that despite the extra syllable in 28a, the poem as a whole can be said to be in the classical meter. (Indeed the metrical peculiarity of the verse appears to have gone un-noticed by editors in the past.) The distribution of types departs from that in *Beowulf* in the direction of the distribution in *The Battle of Maldon* for four of the five types (more types A and B, fewer types C and E), but *Edward* actually has a slightly higher percentage of type D verses than *Beowulf*. A comparison of distributions in *Beowulf*, *The Death of Edward*, and *Durham* confirms the impression that the *Chronicle* poem continues the four-century tradition but that *Durham* turns in a new direction (see table). The percentages in the table assume resolution of short stressed syl-lables in *Durham*, a doubtful feature because of the overall lack of strict-ness in the meter. If resolution does not in fact apply, the distribution of types diverges even further from that of *Beowulf*.

|  | *Beowulf* | *Death of Edward* | *Durham* |
|---|---|---|---|
| Metrical |  |  |  |
| A | 45.1% | 54.4% | 38.1% |
| B | 16.6% | 19.1% | 11.9% |
| C | 17.7% | 7.3% | 7.1% |
| D | 13.5% | 14.7% | 2.4% |
| E | 7.1% | 2.9% | 2.4% |
| Unmetrical |  |  |  |
| EA |  | 1.5% |  |
| 3-stress |  |  | 14.3% |
| Rising-falling |  |  | 9.5% |
| Strong 2nd dip |  |  | 9.5% |
| 3 positions |  |  | 4.8% |

The end of the Old English poetic tradition coincided, in a more pre-cise way than has been realized, with the most traumatic event in English history. From the composition of Cædmon's *Hymn* around 680 until the death of Edward the Confessor and the ensuing Conquest, the Anglo-Saxon verse form was transmitted in a highly regulated, technically precise, essentially monolithic, continuous tradition. The range of dates still proposed for the composition of *Beowulf* shows how little the varying features of style can be correlated with chronology. The metrical anomalies in *The Battle of Maldon* can be called "late," but they can also be read as superficial, idiosyncratic variations on the classical base. Oakden reads the metrical anomalies after the Conquest as still later and progressively more extensive variations. However, an analogy such as free variation vs. phonemic contrast might lead us to ask whether the point of reference is still the classical base, or whether a significant change has occurred.

## 2.4 *The Grave* (c. 1150)

One way of determining the meter of *Durham*, as most commentators have done, is by looking back to the Old English verse form. The analysis of the preceding section pointed out problems with this approach. Another way is by looking forward to see if later poems present a clearer manifestation of the incipient features of the new mode. Oakden continues to look back to Old English in describing *The Grave* (c. 1150), which he sees as continuing the Old English tradition. The only changes that he notes are the patterns of alliteration in six of its 24 lines. "The rhythmical types," he writes, "are quite traditional, there being 20 *A*. types, 13 *B*. types, 3 *C*. types, and 14 *A*. types 'mit auftakt'" (p. 137). The reasons why this conclusion is inadequate and misleading should be clear from the preceding section.

More interesting than the lack of D and E types, or the presence of "14 *A*. types 'mit auftakt,'" however, is the more subtle development of the ordinary type A without anacrusis, the most common of the Old English types. Again, it is helpful to have a list of the main types in the poem before us, which are given here with the *Durham* types, this time without resolution. (The reasoning above concerning resolution was essentially that the burden of proof for assuming its operation is on the metrist who sees it as forming a coherent system. There are good reasons for arguing for such a system in Old English but none for any poem after the Conquest.)

| | | The Grave | Durham |
|---|---|---|---|
| B3A | x / x x x / x | 7 | 0 |
| 2A | / x x / x | 5 | 7 |
| B2A | x / x x / x | 4 | 1 |
| 3A | / x x x / x | 4 | 1 |
| 2BA | x x / x / x | 3 | 1 |
| 3BA | x x x / x / x | 3 | 0 |

The six types shown in the table occur in *The Grave* in three or more verses. Four of them also show up in *Durham*. Type 2A, the most frequent type in *Durham* and the second most frequent type in *The Grave* is interesting because it is also a common type in *Beowulf*—as in *wēox under wolcnum*. An immediate conclusion might be that this type shows the continuation of the Old English patterns. However, quite different principles can produce overlapping results, and one reason for suspecting different principles at work here is the complete lack in *The Grave* of the four-syllable type A, / x / x, the most common of all types in Old English—as in *gomban gyldan*.

Indeed, the four-syllable type A, which is the one that all modern metrists begin with in discussing Old English prosody, is a rarity throughout Middle English. I am aware of only one instance in the *Gawain*-poet. This is a curious situation if the underlying principles of Middle English verse include the four-position, or four-member, paradigm that has been established for Old English verse. Instead, if one considers what the most frequent types in *The Grave* have in common, the pattern of two stresses separated by a variable number of unstressed syllables (preferably two or three) and ending with an unstressed syllable seems to establish the characteristic lilt, regardless of whether there is an unstressed syllable at the beginning: x / x x x / x, / x x / x, x / x x / x, / x x x / x, x x / x / x. When we turn to the next extant texts we find that this tendency is confirmed, and the basic framework of Middle English alliterative poetry is set for the next two centuries.

## 2.5  The Worcester Fragments (c. 1170)

The list shown in the table of the most frequent types in the *Soul's Address to the Body* of the Worcester Fragments includes all of the frequent types in the shorter poem *The Grave,* and it gives a fuller context for the development of the alliterative meter. More interesting than the metrical similarities with *The Grave,* however, are the metrical similarities with Ælfric's rhythmical prose, as can be seen immediately by a comparison of this list with the list for Ælfric above. Eight of the ten most common types occur in both lists, and they even approximate the same ordering. The rhythm of the Worcester Fragments is the rhythm of the *Life of St. Edmund,* not of *The Battle of Brunanburh.*[12] This background helps explain the next extant text, a key one in tracing the evolution of the tradition.

*Soul's Address to the Body*

|       |                         | a-verse | b-verse |
|-------|-------------------------|---------|---------|
| A-3   | x (x) (x) (x) / (x)     | 22      | 12      |
| B2A   | x / x x / x             | 15      | 19      |
| 3A    | / x x x / x             | 13      | 19      |
| B3A   | x / x x x / x           | 17      | 10      |
| 2A    | / x x / x               | 7       | 15      |
| 3BA   | x x x / x / x           | 11      | 8       |
| 2BA   | x x / x / x             | 6       | 12      |
| 2B2A  | x x / x x / x           | 10      | 7       |
| 3B2A  | x x x / x x / x         | 8       | 4       |
| BA    | x / x / x               | 8       | 4       |

## 2.6 Lawman's *Brut* (c. 1200)

For reasons of more than meter Lawman's *Brut* is an important link between the poetry of Old English and the alliterative poetry of the fourteenth century, but it is a difficult link. Arthur Wayne Glowka has demonstrated the uncertainties of scansion that confront the metrist in line after line of a text that is basically strong stress but sometimes regularly alternating, or apparently so; basically alliterative (irregularly alliterative), but sometimes rhyming; basically in lines of four stresses, but sometimes possibly in lines of five, six, or seven stresses, although there is always the possibility of subordinating one or more of these extra stresses.[13]

In scanning portions of this long poem, I have generally followed the rules of grammatical stress that applied in Old English, and I have tried at least to be consistent. Almost certainly I have not always succeeded, and there will be debatable points in many lines, more so doubtless than in any other poetic text of this study. Still, the hopeless feeling that no generalizations can be made about Lawman's meter gradually gives way to the sense of certain broad tendencies toward regularity. For example, in patterns of syllable count and the placing of stress, there is the same considerable overlap with Ælfric that we noted for the Worcester Fragments. It should be kept in mind that the 11 patterns shown are the most frequent out of a total of 101 patterns in *Brut*. Thus, it is of great interest that 10 of these 11 patterns are also the 10 most frequent patterns in Ælfric's *Life of St. Edmund* (out of a total of 99 patterns). The sample is 300 lines.

Lawman's *Brut*

|      |                     | a-verse | b-verse |
|------|---------------------|---------|---------|
| B3A  | x / x x x / x        | 10      | 18      |
| B2A  | x / x x / x          | 11      | 8       |
| 3A   | / x x x / x          | 6       | 12      |
| 3BA  | x x x / x / x        | 10      | 8       |
| 2B2A | x x / x x / x        | 8       | 8       |
| 2BA  | x x / x / x          | 10      | 4       |
| 2B2  | x x / x x /          | 8       | 5       |
| 3B2A | x x x / x x / x      | 2       | 10      |
| 2B3A | x x / x x x / x      | 5       | 6       |
| 2A   | / x x / x            | 0       | 10      |
| A-3  | x (x) (x) (x) / (x)  | 6       | 4       |

In Chapter Four we shall see that the 10 most frequent patterns in the *Gawain*-poet are also 10 of the 11 most frequent patterns in Lawman. From the information thus far presented, one might conclude that these patterns are somehow inevitably frequent in strong-stress poetry and that there must be an obvious explanation in the syntactic and phonological structure of the language. However, a quick comparison with the patterns that are usually listed to illustrate Old English meter reminds us that the explanation must lie in the meter. In the forms that are commonly (thought not quite accurately) thought to be basic, all five of the Sievers types are rare in the texts before us:

A    / x / x
B    x / x /
C    x / / x
D    / / \ x
E    / \ x /

We have already commented on the restrictions in Old English poetry. Five of the most frequent "rising-falling" types in Lawman's *Brut* are virtually nonexistent in *Beowulf*; the other two are admissible only under morphological constraints on anacrusis, which of course do not apply in Middle English.

In comparing the meter of *Brut* with the meter of *Beowulf*, however, there is another point to make that is both more subtle and more important than an account of missing patterns in one or the other poem. Whether or not an Old English metrical pattern is "missing" in Lawman's *Brut* depends on what the modern metrist's theory specifies as categorical in Old English meter. The "morphological constraints" mentioned in the preceding paragraph, for example, do not by any means appear in all modern theories of Old English meter. The grammatical and metrical categories that are hypothesized as relevant in modern theories of Old English meter vary widely from one metrist to the next, some of the categories showing up in several theories, some in only one, some in combinations that include categories missing from the next theory. There is a bewildering array of competing modern theories: the stress-based system of Sievers; the measure-based systems of Heusler, Pope, and Hieatt; the stress and breath group system of Bliss; my own earlier contour-based system; the phrasal-rhythm system of Luecke; the alliterative system of Hoover; the foot system of Russom; the stress and measure system of Obst; and in Chapter One of the present study a sketch of yet another theory, based on the intersecting systems of syllabism and strong stress.[14]

If modern scholars, with the benefit of each other's findings, can construct such mutually incompatible systems of Old English meter, it is reasonable to expect that this priest at King's Areley in Worcestershire would have had his own interpretation nearly a century and a half after the end of the classical tradition. Assuming for the sake of argument that the most adequate paradigm for Old English meter is that of Chapter One above (a set of syllabic principles intersected by a set of strong-stress principles: four syllables or syllable-equivalents except when one of the first two syllables is a strong dip), certain interesting implications follow for the meter of the *Brut*. Lawman could have fastened on the strong-stress element, which occurs only in the first half of the verse, and ignored the count of syllables (which indeed all modern scholars have ignored). Or, in a less obvious way, he could have paid close attention to the count of syllables in classical Old English meter and shaped his own meter accordingly.

It will clarify matters to focus on one simple empirical observation about the meter of the *Brut*. The theoretical context sketched above makes the observation both less curious and more revealing than it would be as an isolated fact: Half-lines of four syllables are very rare. In the list of the ten most frequent patterns in the *Brut*, four of the patterns have six syllables, four have seven syllables, and two have eight. Patterns with five syllables, such as / x x / x (2A) and x / x / x (BA), while not as frequent, are well represented. However, in the whole poem as it appears in the Caligula manuscript (16,095 long lines, 32,190 half-lines), there are only 102 half-lines written with fewer than five syllables (0.3 of one per cent). Sixty of these verses also appear in the Otho manuscript, where 43 of them are filled out to five syllables or more. For example:

gode knihtes (Caligula 681a)
wel gode cniþtes (Otho 681a)

Only 17 of the 32,190 verses in the poem have four or fewer syllables in both manuscripts (including two half-lines with three syllables).

Previous investigators, including Herbert Pilch and Ewald Standop have remarked upon the rarity of four-syllable verses but have accommodated them within their respective systems.[15] Examples are usually drawn from the first one hundred lines, where no fewer than seven verses are written with four syllables in the Caligula manuscript. However, these opening lines have by far the highest density of four-syllable verses in the poem; elsewhere there are hundreds of verses at a stretch without a single four-syllable pattern. My own count of four-syllable verses includes all verses as written, whether or not an inflectional syllable was expected in Lawman's dialect but omitted by the scribe.[16] Joseph Hall emends numerous verses, such as the following with a plural -e added to *ærest* and a dative -e to *Ælienor:*[17]

$\overset{\prime}{æ}\overset{x}{r}\overset{x}{e}st[e]\overset{\prime}{ah}\overset{x}{t}en$ (9b)

$\overset{\prime}{Æ}\overset{xx}{lienor}[e]$ (22b)

Both the Caligula and the Otho scribes clearly reflect Lawman's language better than fifteenth-century scribes reflect the language of the Alliterative Revival, but a detailed determination of the places where syllables are omitted in scribal transmission is beyond the scope of the present study.

If there is indeed a metrical constraint against half-lines of four syllables in Lawman's *Brut*, the relationship of this meter to classical Old English meter is complex. Four units figure prominently in the *Beowulf* meter, whether as the traditional four *Glieder* or, in the reinterpretation above, as four *Glieder* that are essentially four syllables or syllable-equivalents (except when one is a strong dip). One hypothesis that would account for these strange facts is that Lawman misunderstood the classical Old English meter and missed the significance of the four-unit structure of the verse. He would simply have gotten the meter wrong.

However, there is a degree to which a pattern is so rare that the rarity itself calls for an explanation. One might conclude that four-syllable verses were not merely neglected but actively avoided. Then the concept of "four-syllable verse" might well figure in the paradigm, albeit as a negative pattern. Could it be that Lawman understood the four-syllable norm of classical Old English meter and reacted against it? English Romantic poets understood the Augustan closed couplet and the regular placing of the caesura partly as norms to work against.

In English verse composed of phrasal hemistichs, there is every reason, syntactically and morphologically, to expect four-syllable phrases to occur with some frequency. If they do not occur, there must be a metrical constraint that skews the distribution of patterns. However, to complicate the matter further, the solution is not necessarily as simple as stating a proscription against patterns of four syllables or fewer. From the earlier discussion of basic principles and epiphenomena, it should be clear that the curious results we have observed could come from a completely different principle not yet considered. For example, it is possible that the proscription is not against verses of four or fewer syllables but against evenly alternating patterns: $x/x/$, $/x/x$, and $x/x/x$. Such a proscription would eliminate the minimal form of types A and B and would go a long way toward eliminating four-syllable verses. However, because the pattern $x/x/x$ occurs regularly enough to appear normal (as in 681a from the Otho manuscript quoted above), it does not seem likely that further investigation will establish this particular principle as the basic one.

The point to make is that the meters of all of the texts in question should be read through a wider range of hypotheses than have yet been proposed. Those meters must be analysed both internally and in comparison with the earlier and later meters before a history of the tradition can be written. The relevant texts include not only the poetry but also, as Angus McIntosh has made clear, Ælfric's rhythmical prose. A diachronic account depends on adequate synchronic analyses, but insights into an adequate synchronic analysis sometimes come from comparing other stages of the evolution. It was only in my scansion of Lawman's *Brut* that the essentially syllabic basis of Old English meter emerged by contrast.

## 2.7 The *Katherine* Group (c. 1200)

The rhythmical language of the *Ancrene Wisse* and the *Katherine* group (*Saint Katherine, Saint Juliana, Saint Margaret, Hali Meiðhad,* and *Sawles Warde*) has long been studied for its grammatical and stylistic features.[18] As with Ælfric's rhythmical prose, there has been a question whether the texts of the *Katherine* group are to be called poetry or prose, a question that perhaps reflects modern rather than medieval discriminations. The question of form, writes Roger Dahood, "has long been settled in favor of rhythmic prose."[19] Yet in a sample of 500 lines from *Saint Katherine* (following Einenkel's old division of the text into lines of poetry equivalent in length to hemistichs) we find the same most common patterns that we saw in Ælfric and in Lawman:

*Saint Katherine*

| | | |
|---|---|---|
| B2A | x / x x / x | 40 |
| B3A | x / x x x / x | 33 |
| 2A | / x x / x | 25 |
| 3BA | x x x / x / x | 19 |
| 2BA | x x / x / x | 19 |
| 3A | / x x x / x | 18 |
| 2B2A | x x / x x / x | 16 |
| B4A | x / x x x x / x | 15 |
| 2B2 | x x / x x / | 14 |
| 3B2A | x x x / x x / x | 10 |
| 4A | / x x x x / x | 9 |

There is the possibility that this recurring set of most common types reveals a flaw in the present method of analysis. Could it be that most English texts of every period will eventually divide up into two-stress phrases of the type listed above? Marjorie Daunt, in an often quoted description of Old English meter, suggested that the poetry was "the spoken language rather tidied up."[20] However, various metrists have shown that Daunt's view of Old English poetry was inadequate, and that Old English had an abstract meter. Similarly, it can be shown that there are principles of artifice—principles of *meter*—that regulate the rhythm of these texts in Middle English.

The key as always is to look for missing patterns. These are patterns that we would expect to occur were there not some kind of metrical paradigm screening them out. In order to determine how the *Katherine* group differs from unregulated prose, it would be useful to have examples of such prose for comparison. There are not many comparable prose texts of the period, but the Kentish Sermons of the thirteenth-century Bodleian MS. Laud Misc. 471 make the point clearly. The following passage illustrates the kinds of difficulty that one encounters in operating on the assumption that all prose divides naturally into two-stress phrases as that of *Saint Katherine* does. I have inserted possible phrasal divisions, which often come out too short or too long for a match of syntax and regular rhythm:

> Nu ihiereth wet signefieth / þet gold, þet stor, þet mirre; / and offre we gostliche / to ure Lorde / þet hi offrede flesliche. / Þet gold, þet is bricht / and glareth ine þo brichtnesse / of þo sunne, / signefieth þe gode beleaue / þet is bricht ine þe gode Cristenemannes herte: / si gode beleaue / licht and is bricht / ine þo herte / of þo gode manne ase gold. / Offre we þanne / God Almichti / god gold: / beleue we stedefastliche / þet Fader and Sune / and Holy Gost / is onlepi God.[21]

The difference in rhythm between this text and the texts of the *Katherine* group (including the *Ancrene Wisse*) is clear both impressionistically and in efforts at scansion. The rhythmical prose of *Saint Katherine* depends upon the regular coincidence of two-stress phrases and syntactic patterns. Three-stress phrases and one-stress phrases (Sievers' type A3) must be kept to a minimum; otherwise, too much is admissible; too many different kinds of movement are scannable. In order to impose a two-stress movement on the Kentish sermon, it is necessary to have frequent recourse to the licenses of rhythmical prose: one-stress verses (*ine þo herte*) and three-stress verses (*signefieth þe gode beleaue*); in addition, patterns occur that would have been unacceptable in Ælfric or in *Katherine: þet is bricht ine þe gode Cristenemannes herte* and *god gold*.

Finally, there is the matter of the four-syllable verses that could have occurred in Old English: *and Holy Gost*. As mentioned in the preceding section, these patterns were avoided in Middle English alliterative poetry. The reason, I shall argue, is that they are too close to the patterns of other meters (both Old English and iambic pentameter), and the Middle English poets were concerned to forge their own unambiguous meter. As we shall see in Chapter Four, this distinctively Middle English form combined both the even alternations of poetry and the cadences of prose, but it did so in a very precise way. There were appropriate, prescribed places in the line for each type of rhythm. In order to say anything about these patterns, however, it is necessary first to address the rhythmical central question of fourteenth-century final -*e*.

# 3. Fourteenth-Century Meter: Final -*e*

## 3.1 Surprising Facts

The early Middle English texts that we have examined to this point do not present the problem of final -*e* that has vexed the study of Chaucer and the Alliterative Revival. The usual assumption is that most inflectional and derivational syllables still counted in the metrical scheme of Lawman's *Brut*, but by the mid-fourteenth century we can be certain only that this feature of the language was in transition.

Modern approaches to solving the problem have suffered from the idea that Middle English alliterative meter represents a loosening of the Old English meter and a relaxation of rules so that it could not provide a rigid enough framework to determine the patterning of unstressed syllables. Norman Davis, for example, writes: "Though -*e* is very often written in words of most grammatical categories, the scribe's erratic practice, *the imprecision of the metre*, and the author's inconsistent use of it in rhyme . . . make it impossible to say how essential a part this was of the inflexional system of the original language" (italics supplied).[1]

The question of -*e* has traditionally been one of the two main problems in understanding the Middle English alliterative line, the other being the number of metrical stresses. The first problem is the subject of the present chapter; the second is part of the subject of the next. Throughout these two chapters we shall pay special attention to a third, generally unperceived problem, the patterning of unstressed syllables. Similar problems in *Beowulf* or in the *Canterbury Tales*, although also controversial, lend themselves to readier solutions because the meter is more clearly fixed. For *Beowulf* there has been little agreement over the past century and a half about the exact statement of that fixity beyond Sievers' Five Types, but unanimity among serious metrists that the precision is there. Similarly, in the case of Chaucer, the structure of the English iambic pentameter has provided a general context in which to work out the phonological and syntactic details, which in turn can be brought to bear on specific matters of meter in a way that is progressive without being circular.

In the *Gawain*-poet, however, all pieces of ground seem to move at once. As Marie Borroff writes: "In attempting to argue one way or the other about the lines in which the feminine ending would be constituted by the sounding of -*e*, one is all too likely to find oneself going in a circle. The poet sounded -*e* at the end of the long line because he preferred the feminine ending; the poet must have preferred the feminine ending, because he almost always uses words ending in -*e* at the end of the line."[2] It is not an overstatement to say that our present understanding of the meter of the *Gawain*-poet is no more advanced than Dryden's understanding of Chaucer's meter.

The results that I come to are somewhat different from those of Borroff, who recognizes the use of final -*e* in some of the wheels of *Gawain*, leaves open the possibility of final -*e* at the end of the long line, and disallows it within the long line. It is true, as Borroff points out, that the long lines and the wheels derive from two different traditions. Of final -*e* in the wheels she writes, "Its sporadic sounding is thus warranted by principles of rhyme and meter, and analogous principles must be established to warrant its sounding in the long alliterative lines" (p. 171). What follows is an attempt to establish some of those principles. The results suggest that the poet's phonological rules move easily between the two metrical traditions. As Angus McIntosh has pointed out, the main metrical categories that we impose on medieval poetry (alliterative vs. rhyming, accentual vs. syllabic, even prose vs. poetry) are modern polar terms that are often more misleading than helpful (although they can be helpful if they are taken to indicate roughly the line of a continuum).[3]

In the course of approaching the problem once again and trying to answer what I had thought was the central question about the Middle English alliterative long line (How many stresses?), I came upon what Charles S. Peirce would call "surprising facts" that required an explanation.[4] The more one works with these surprising facts the clearer it becomes that the configuration of unstressed syllables, and not the number of stresses, was most central to an understanding of the alliterative long line. Once an explanation is given for the surprising facts, the questions about the number of stresses in the long line and about final -*e* are answered as a matter of course.

If for some reason the explanation that is offered here proves unacceptable, there will still be a need for an explanation of this crucial fact: there is a correlation between the number of unstressed syllables that occurred in a word historically and the placing of the word in the long line.

For native English words the correlation depends, with few exceptions, on the number of syllables that the word had in Old English. For Old French and Old Norse loans, the correlation depends on the number of syllables that the word had in its uninflected form in the original language (in the accusative case for nouns of Old French origin). In increasing order of importance, we shall consider first Old Norse loans, then Old French loans, then native English words. We shall focus in this chapter on the end of the long line. The next chapter will show that the same principles hold for other specific positions in both the first half-line and the second half-line.

The discussion draws on a complete scansion and grammatical parsing of all 1,812 lines in *Cleanness*.[5] The analysis includes the etymology of every word in the poem and a marking of every syllable that would have occurred historically—as the word would have appeared in Old English, Old French, Old Norse, or Latin (the last category consisting mainly of a few Biblical names). This text, which I have analyzed and reanalyzed several times through, is part of a larger, similarly treated corpus of 6,100 long lines of Middle English alliterative poetry. While the immediate focus is on the final syllable in the lines of *Cleanness*, the conclusion can be generalized to the ends of lines in other poems, including *Sir Gawain and the Green Knight, Piers Plowman, Morte Arthure, The Parlement of the Thre Ages, William of Palerne, Alexander A,* and *The Wars of Alexander.* The same principles hold, with minor modifications depending on idiolect and individual style, for nearly all of the poems of the Alliterative Revival (*The Destruction of Troy* being an exception despite, or because of, its apparent regularity, and *Piers Plowman* requiring more modifications than most).

Some of the discussion that follows retraces ground covered by German philologists a century ago, especially Karl Luick, Julius Thomas, and Max Deutschbein.[6] Standing on their shoulders makes it possible to avoid problems that have caused criticism of their work. On several counts, the present study has benefited from progress in philology and linguistics during the past century. First, the empirical base is improved from a better understanding of the matches and mismatches between historical, grammatical categories and their manuscript representations. Also, the idea of "rule," as a means of organizing the empirical base, has been clarified by theoretical work in linguistic structure and language acquisition; the exceptions that remain are a normal part of linguistic description and of the indeterminacies of scribal transmission. The implications of stating a rule and tracing a poet's divergence from it are discussed in different ways throughout this study (sections 1.3, 3.7, 4.5, 4.6, and 4.7). Divergence from a rule is a key toward understanding the evolution of the tradition. Finally, the generalizations have improved over time. In more than one instance, the facts upon which a new generalization rests had been stated a hundred years earlier, but they were buried among other isolated facts. New facts often come from dealing with stubborn old facts, but more important, it is exactly in the problematic cases that a basis for a new generalization emerges. We can now state more coherent metrical principles for the two halves of the long line. These principles provide a clearer test for final -*e* than was possible before, and they supplement the patterns at the end of the line, to which we now turn under the rubrics "Old Norse Loans," "Old French Loans," and "Native Words."

## 3.2 Old Norse Loans

The distribution in *Cleanness* of loans from Old Norse is striking. Of the 3,624 hemistichs in the poem, 179 end with words borrowed into Middle English from Old Norse: 97 at the end of the a-verse, 82 at the end of the b-verse. The occurrences of the Old Norse loans at the end of the a-verse are split about equally between words that ended in a stressed syllable in Old Norse (52 instances) and those that ended in an unstressed syllable (45 instances); thus:

Wylde wormeȝ to her won   (< ON van) (533a)

Boþe to cayre at þe kart   (< ON kartr) (1259a)

Þat ilke skyl for no scaþe   (< ON skaði) (569a)

And Godde glydeȝ his gate   (< ON gate) (767a)

By contrast, 74 of the 82 occurrences of Old Norse loans in the b-verse ended with an unstressed syllable that reflects a historical syllable in Old Norse:

$\overset{\prime}{\text{ry}}\overset{\text{x}}{\text{3t}}\,\overset{\text{x}}{\text{to}}\,\overset{\text{x}}{\text{þe}}\,\overset{\prime}{\text{se}}\overset{\text{x}}{\text{te}}$   (< ON sæti)  (59b)

$\overset{\text{x}}{\text{and}}\,\overset{\prime}{\text{se}}\overset{\text{x}}{\text{tte}}\overset{\text{x}}{\text{3}}\,\overset{\text{x}}{\text{on}}\,\overset{\text{x}}{\text{þe}}\,\overset{\prime}{\text{do}}\overset{\text{x}}{\text{ue}}$   (< ON dufa)  (469b)

The remaining eight verses ended in one of three words that did not have
a final unstressed syllable in Old Norse: the postponed preposition *tylle*
(882b, 1064b, 1174b, 1752b), the adverbs *þertylle* (1509b) and *are*
(438b, 1128b), and the noun *scole* (1145b).

These facts require an explanation. Why is it that a-verses end freely in
words that had a final consonant in Old Norse? These words include *won*
(ON *van*), *tolke* (ON *tulkr*) *glam* (ON *glamm*), *layk* (ON *leikr*), *dam*
(ON *dammr*), *karle* (ON *karl*), *brest* (ON *brestr*), *ryfte* (ON *ript*), *skwe*
(ON *sky*), *syt* (ON *\*syt*), *3arm* (ON *jarmr*), *flot* (ON *flot*), *kest* (ON
*kast*), *tom* (ON *tom*), *kart* (ON *kartr*), *unþryfte* (ON *þrift*), *scylle* (ON
*skil*), *cal* noun (ON *kall*), *walt* (ON *val*), *wy3t* (ON *vigt*), *skelt* (?ON
*skellt*), *þro* (ON *þrar*), *alo3* (*a* + ON *lagr*), and *bayn* (ON *beinn*). Yet
none of these monosyllabic words appears at the end of the b-verse in
*Cleanness*. In the b-verse the only final Old Norse loans that were originally monosyllabic are a recurring preposition; two adverbs, which could
have acquired an analogical -*e*, as adverbs often did; and the noun *scole*.

My own explanation is to treat *tylle*, *are*, and *scole* as exceptional (either in their phonological development or in their metrical usage) and to
hypothesize three general principles:

(i) The second half-line must end on an unstressed syllable.
(ii) Old Norse loans that ended in a final vowel retain that vowel as -*e* in
the language of this fourteenth-century text.
(iii) Nouns from Old Norse do not have an inflectional syllable in the
dative case.

The point about the dative in (iii) is to limit the generalization in (ii) and
explain why objects of prepositions account for a substantial proportion of
the loans in both halves of the line. But in the a-verse, 20 of the singular
prepositional objects ended in a consonant in the nominative singular in
Old Norse. In the b-verse, all seven singular prepositional objects ended in
a vowel. A logical conclusion to draw is that those nouns that had a final
vowel in the nominative singular retained it in all cases in this text, and
those that did not have one did not add a vowel for the dative.

When faced with "surprising facts" (here the distribution of Old Norse loans in the two halves of the line), the idea is to develop a general explanation from which the facts would follow as a matter of course. The results of this hypothesized explanation, the formation of which Peirce terms "abduction," can then be tested inductively. The three-part hypothesis above is fairly general and complete except for a couple of ragged edges: an analogical -*e* must be assumed for two adverbs, and *scole* is simply an exception. However, the hypothesis can be accepted until a simpler and more general explanation is proposed. Such is the usual progress in paradigms of science. (The only other critical response is to show that the surprising facts are not surprising after all.)

As it turns out, the three-part hypothesis gains support from the much larger group of Old French loans. When both sets of loanwords are added to the still larger group of native English words at the end of verses, we can discern several pervasive principles of phonology and meter running through these texts.

## 3.3 Old French Loans

In the 1,812 lines of *Cleanness* there are 661 Old French loans at the ends of half-lines, 420 in the first half-line and 241 in the second. For example:

$$\overset{x\,x}{Þen}\ \overset{x}{þe}\ \overset{x}{har}\overset{\prime}{lot}\ \overset{x}{with}\ \overset{x}{has}\overset{\prime}{te}\overset{x}{}\quad (< \text{OF } haste)\ (39a)$$

$$\overset{x}{þat}\ \overset{x}{no}\ \overset{\prime}{wy}\overset{x\,x}{ʒe}\ \overset{\prime}{acha}\overset{x}{ped}\quad (< \text{OF } achaper)\ (970b)$$

$$\overset{x}{wat}\overset{\prime}{ʒ}\ \overset{x}{tow}\overset{x}{ched}\ \overset{x}{of}\ \overset{\prime}{þe}\ \overset{x}{feste}\quad (< \text{OF } feste)\ (1393b)$$

Of the 420 words at the end of the first half-line, 72 were monosyllabic or ended in a stressed syllable in Old French (or Anglo-Norman) and would not have had a final -*e* historically. For example:

$$\overset{x\,x}{He}\ \overset{x}{is}\ \overset{x}{so}\ \overset{\prime}{cle}\overset{x\,x}{ne}\ \overset{x}{in}\ \overset{x}{his}\ \overset{\prime}{courte}\quad (< \text{OF } court)\ (17a)$$

$$\overset{x}{Þe}\ \overset{x}{de}\overset{\prime}{fen}\overset{x}{ce}\ \overset{x}{wat}\overset{x}{ʒ}\ \overset{x}{þe}\ \overset{\prime}{fryt}\quad (< \text{OF } fruit)\ (245a)$$

$$\overset{x}{And}\ \overset{x}{þay}\ \overset{\prime}{sto}\overset{x}{ken}\ \overset{x}{so}\ \overset{\prime}{strayt}\quad (< \text{OF } estreit)\ (1199a)$$

By contrast, only nine b-verses end in Old French loans that would be read as monosyllabic.[7] What do not occur at the end of the b-verse are the numerous monosyllabic words that end the a-verse: *courte* (OF *cort*), *prys* (OF *pris*), *duk* (OF *duc*), *fryt* (OF *fruit*), *fayth* (OF *feid*), *soun* (OF *son*), *bost* (OF *bost*), *fol* (OF *fol*), *dece* (OF *deis*), *trot* (OF *trot*), *fete* (OF *fet*), *oste* (OF *ost*), *cry* noun (OF *cri*), *scorne* (OF *escarn*), *clos* (OF *clos*), *beke* (OF *bec*), *gyn* (OF *engin*), *grece* (OF *grez*), *gaye* (OF *gai*), *playn* (OF *plain*), *false* (OF *fals*), *fers* (OF *fers*), *chef* (OF *chef*), and *strayt* (OF *estreit*).

Again, these facts require an explanation in any theory of Middle English phonology and meter. Principles similar to those that I hypothesized for the Old Norse loans account for the conservative syllabic structure of words borrowed from Old French. A fairly detailed statement of the principles appears in section 3.6 below. However, it is the overall system that I wish to make clear at this point, and that system can best be seen by proceeding directly to the group of native English words.

## 3.4  Native Words

The distribution of syllabic patterns in loanwords at the ends of first and second half-lines has provided insights into phonology and meter at once. Now we come to the largest group of verses classified according to the final word—those ending in words descending from Old English. Here we have compelling evidence that historical final -e was an essential factor in the meter, and we can be quite specific. For example, a large number of the discriminations depended on a classification of nouns according to their grammatical gender.

By my count, 450, or 25 percent, of the first half-lines in *Cleanness* end with a stressed syllable in a native English word. Only 27, or 1.5 percent, of the second half-lines end with such a stressed syllable by my understanding of the grammatical principles as applied to the extant text. Of the words at the end of the first half-line a large number are monosyllabic masculine and neuter objects of prepositions; there are almost no occurrences of this category at the end of the second half-line—words such as *folk* (OE *folc*, n.), *dom* (OE *dom*, m.), *hous* (OE *hus*, n.), *wyf* (OE *wif*, n.), *wind* (OE *wind*, m.), *worde* (OE *word*, n.), *wyt* (OE *witt*, n.), *craft* (OE *cræft*, m.), *blod* (OE *blod*, n.), *ston* (OE *stan*, m.), *flesch* (OE *flæsc*, n.), *clop* (OE *clap*, m.), *bour* (OE *bur*, n.), *bak* (OE *bæc*, n.), *font* (OE *font*, m.), *mode* (OE *mod,* n.), *londe* (OE *land,* n.), *werk* (OE *weorc,* n.), *glem* (OE *glæm,* m.), *storme* (OE *storm,* m.), *clay* (OE *clæg,* m.), *wryt* (OE *writ,* n.), and dozens more.

At the end of the second half-line, however, there are many nouns that were feminine and also a number of masculine nouns that had a vowel in the nominative singular; for example: *hert* (OE *heorte,* f.), *blysse* (OE *bliss,* f.), *pryde* (OE *pryde,* f.), *synne* (OE *synn,* f.), *wille* (OE *willa,* m.), *lencþe* (OE *lengþu,* f.), *trawþe* (OE *treowþ,* f.), and *ende* (OE *ende,* m.).

Any explanation for these remarkable facts must address both metrical structure and historical phonology, for these are the two variables. The rules for final *-e* below are backward-looking, as are the rules for stress, and as indeed are some of the most salient literary qualities of the Alliterative Revival.

By my present understanding of the metrical paradigm, the general phonology of final *-e,* and the individual development of a few specific words, there are about two dozen exceptional lines in *Cleanness* ending with a native word. As we find out more about the interacting factors, we shall probably find some lines that should be added to this list of 27 and some in the list that should be taken out. The scribal *-e* that appears on some of the words is not justified by my present formulation of principles: the nouns *Cam* (299), *day* (494), *toune* (721), *lawe* (OE *hlæw,* 992), *ly3t* (1272), *wowe* (1531), *felde* (1750), and *Gode* (1730, the only exception among 99 occurrences of *God* in the *Gawain*-poet); the adjectives *blake* (747), *best* (913), *olde* (1123), and *wode* (1558); the imperative *bete* (627, where an inorganic final *-e* is common in Chaucer); the auxiliary *schal* (1571, which Israel Gollancz emends by adding *be* at the end); and a dozen lines with adverbs, many of which are uncertain because of the possibility of analogical *-e* or the variable stress on phrasal adverbs: *nere* (414, 1585), *þur3out* (1559), *aywhere* (1398, 1608), *þervpone* (1665), *away* (1241), *among* (1414), *þerof* (1499, 1507), *þerwyth* (1406, 1501).

Whether emendation is called for in 1571 or in any of the other verses is not the point of the present discussion, although the facts of this discussion might eventually lead to a consideration of certain principles of textual editing. In 1920, Robert J. Menner dismissed similar facts that had been noticed in 1908 by Julius Thomas: certain lines, said Menner, "where Thomas is obliged to resort to unlikely emendations, show that the weak ending cannot be accepted as a rule without exception."[8] The point for Menner was whether to emend specific lines in his edition. Although he made use of metrics, his aim was not the metrist's aim, and his questions and his emphasis were naturally different. The fact that a structure "cannot be accepted as a rule without exception" might settle one question for the editor (whether to emend on the basis of meter), but it raises a host of new questions for the metrist. To understand the meter one must ask why the structure occurs overwhelmingly as it does—in 92 percent of the lines according to Menner, or in 98 percent by my own count.

The argument of the chapter to this point has been that final -*e* was essential in fourteenth-century alliterative meter because the end of the first half-line allowed an unstressed syllable optionally, but the end of the second half-line had an unstressed syllable 98 percent of the time. Rule-minded people can say that the end of the second half-line required an unstressed syllable; a few exceptions must then be acknowledged (which eventually may be accounted for by unspecified conditions yet to be discovered). People who are not rule-minded, such as Menner, can say, as he does, that there was a very strong tendency. I find it not very useful to make general statements of "tendencies," because tendencies are the result of interacting principles and not the principles themselves. A summary statement of tendencies is a description of epiphenomena and not a very adequate one. It is only when the tendency statement is broken down into its component parts that we have a description that is useful empirically and theoretically (as discussed in section 1.3). Then we have a hypothesis to which evidence can be brought in support or refutation, and an indication of the direction in which to take further inquiry.

3.5 Double Feminine Endings

Now it is possible to take the argument a step further and show that the end of the first half-line allowed not only a single unstressed syllable, or none, but also two, and even three. In contrast, the second half-line allowed exactly one. This pattern of distribution not only reinforces the conclusion that final -*e* was phonologically present in otherwise monosyllabic words, but it also suggests that final -*e* was phonologically present in otherwise disyllabic words. Unless final -*e* in these longer words is recognized, one is left without an obvious explanation for the restriction to the first half-line of this particular set of words—those that end with an unstressed syllable plus an etymological -*e*.

Instead of examining only *Cleanness* we shall look at a slightly larger corpus of 2,200 lines, which includes samples from *Cleanness* (700 lines),

*Sir Gawain and the Green Knight* (350 lines), *The Parlement of the Thre Ages* (300 lines), *The Wars of Alexander* (200 lines), *Morte Arthure* (200 lines), *William of Palerne* (200 lines), and *Alexander A* (250 lines).

There are 69 verses in the corpus classified as B3A2, ending with two unstressed syllables at the end (x / x x x / x x). Sixty-six of the 69 are first half-lines. The occurrence of type B3A2 almost exclusively in the first half-line can be contrasted with the distribution of type B3A (x / x x x / x), which is one unstressed syllable shorter and occurs mainly in the second half-line. Of the 455 occurrences of B3A, 425, or 93.4 percent, are b-verses; for example, *Gawain* 1711b:

$$\overset{x}{\text{with}} \overset{\prime}{\text{w}\acute{\text{y}}\text{lez}} \overset{x}{\text{fro}} \overset{x}{\text{þe}} \overset{\prime}{\text{hou}\acute{\text{n}}\text{des}} \overset{x}{\quad} \text{B3A} \quad (1711\text{b})$$

Now the problem can be seen as more complex than simply whether the long line must have a feminine ending. That is part of it, but the evidence of these two types suggests that the long line must end on one and exactly one unstressed syllable (and the other types will bear this out). Furthermore, type B3A with one final unstressed syllable is avoided in the first half-line.

A rhythmical explanation for this striking contrast between two types differing by a single, final unstressed syllable will be proposed in Chapter Four. It is an explanation that goes beyond the technicalities of Middle English alliterative meter to the basic principles of rhythm in all periods of the English language.

For now, however, it is important to make clear the evidence for the reading of final -*e*. Of the 66 first half-lines of type B3A2, nine have the adverbial ending -*ly*, which is disyllabic according to the rules hypothesized in section 3.6 below; for example, from *William of Palerne:*[9]

$$\overset{x}{\text{and}} \overset{\prime}{\text{to}\acute{\text{l}}\text{d}} \overset{x}{\text{him}} \overset{x}{\text{al}} \overset{\prime}{\text{tre}\acute{\text{u}}\text{ly}} \overset{xx}{\quad} \quad (<\text{OE treowlice}) \quad \text{B3A2} \quad (558\text{a})$$

The adverbial ending is read as disyllabic because of the disyllabic structure of its two sources, OE -*lice* and ON -*liga*.

The present study diverges from traditional readings in proposing that the -*ly* adverbial ending is disyllabic in the fourteenth century. The explanation lies in the phonological and metrical arguments that run through this chapter. A survey of the distribution of metrical patterns shows that -*ly* adverbs show up often at the end of the first half-line but almost never at the end of the second half-line. Indeed, in the whole corpus that I have scanned, not a single long line ends with an -*ly* adverb. One way of crystallizing the arguments of the present chapter and of making clear the burden of opposing arguments is by asking the simple question, "Why don't -*ly* adverbs occur at the end of the long line?"

## 3.6 Phonological Rules

The double thesis underlying this and the next chapter can now be stated as the following: (1) the phonology of the West Midlands alliterative poetry is more conservative than the standard grammars indicate and (2) the fourteenth-century alliterative line is more highly regulated in its patterns of unstressed syllables than prosodists of the modern period have understood. These two propositions are linked in such a way that the kind of empirical evidence required to support or refute them is immediately clear.

The kind of evidence is clear, at least, once the structure of the problem is put into shape. In the sporadic activity of scanning thousands of these lines during the past decade, I had generally found myself in agreement with metrists who concluded that the form of the verse is too uncertain to allow much beyond stating general tendencies, with alternative possibilities for any given line. It was only within the past five years that I discovered patterns I had missed for years. The evidence that I have presented for the principles stated below is an exercise in mainstream historical metrics. We begin with patterns of occurrence and nonoccurrence and keep the usual questions in mind: "What structures do not occur that should occur? Are there structures missing that would be expected on normal phonological and syntactic grounds? Can consistent principles be formulated to explain these present and missing patterns? Can the principles be called 'metrical'? Do the 'metrical' principles contradict either themselves or independent evidence such as that provided by historical phonology?"

What follows is a full list of rules to the extent that I presently understand them on the basis of the methods described above. Modifications and additions, based on additional evidence from the same principles, will be necessary, but the overall shape of the rules will hold. Some of the rules are similar to descriptions in traditional grammars. Some have not been stated in exactly this form before. Some flatly contradict the most familiar grammars, but only because the grammars do not take into account different registers.

In general, these rules require final -*e* in more structures than most current authorities recognize. This apparent expansion of the line by my reading is checked by a new formulation of the meter, which conversely limits the number of unstressed syllables in certain contexts. Thus, there is a tension between the new phonological rules (which expand the line) and the new metrical rules (which constrain it), and there is the possibility for one set to contradict the other. To the extent that contradictions are avoided we have evidence in support of both sets of rules.

Finally it should be noted that some metrical studies have drawn a distinction between the use of final -*e* at the end of the long line (where it is considered more likely to have occurred if it occurred at all) and the use of final -*e* within the line (where its occurrence is considered more dubious).[10] All of the evidence in the present chapter has concerned final -*e* at the end of the long line. Should the rules that follow, then, be limited to words occurring in this position? Here it is useful to draw a distinction between phonological questions and metrical questions. The argument of the present chapter seeks to establish that the author of *Cleanness* had access to the traditional, historical correlation between certain syntactic and morphological categories and the phonological occurrence of final -*e*. The point is that this aspect of the linguistic history was still available to the fourteenth-century author. How he chose to use the phonological structure within the artifice of meter will be the question that Chapter Four addresses (parallel to the more familiar question of how Chaucer used the historical final -*e* within the iambic pentameter).

It is possible, for example, that the author chose to use final -*e* at the end of the line and within the rhyming wheels but to ignore it within the long line. The determination of this possibility, however, is a purely metrical question. If a syntactic description such as "monosyllabic adjectives from Old English occurring in traditional weak or plural contexts" is available for consideration of final -*e* at the end of the line, then it is also available for consideration within the line. The question becomes one of metrical structure (again, the problem of Chapter Four) and not of the historical survival of a linguistic structure. Other sets of assumptions are conceptually possible but are not very plausible. One might assume, for example, that the poet's metrical-formulaic grammar specified long lists of words that could occur at the end of the long line. Because such lists, aside from being unwieldy, would largely recapitulate the historical structures, the more plausible assumption is that in some registers, final -*e* was still "alive," in generally the same contexts that it always had been.

The rules that follow are a partial list of grammatical categories for final -*e* (those categories that have been tested explicitly and extensively):

*Phonology of final* -e

Nouns

1. Nouns from OE and ON that ended in a vowel in the nominative singular and nouns from OF that ended in a vowel in the accusative singular have final -*e* in non-genitive singular usage (e.g., *wyʒe* < OE *wiga; kyrke* < ON *kirkja; prynce* < OF *prince*).
2. Nouns from OE feminine declensions have a final -*e* in non-genitive singular usage (e.g., *þat styred synne* < OE *synn*, f., acc. sg. *synne*).

Adjectives

3. Adjectives from OE, ON, and OF that ended in a vowel in the uninflected form retain the vowel as -*e* (e.g., *clene* < OE *clæne; large* < OF *large*).
4. Monosyllabic adjectives from OE, ON, and OF have final -*e* in traditional weak contexts and in the plural:

þe dérk déde sée (*Cleanness* 1020; *derk* < OE *deorce; dede* < OE *deade*)

Verbs

5. Verbs from OE, ON, and OF have final -*e* in the infinitive.
6. Verbs from OE with preterites ending in -*ede, -edon*, and -*odon* have -*ede*. Verbs from OE with preterites ending in -*de* have -*de*. Verbs from OE with preterites ending in -*ode* (i.e., class 2 weak verbs in the preterite singular) have -*ed*.
7. Verbs from ON and OF form their preterites with -*ed* (without final -*e*).

Adverbs

8. Adverbs from OE with final -*e* retain the -*e*.
9. All adverbs ending in -*ly* retain the disyllabic structure of the two

sources of that ending (OE -*lice* and ON -*liga*). Where the fricative is lost, the ending is assumed to be [liə].

Exceptions

10. The following words diverge in their individual developments from the general principles stated above:

(a) Petrified datives: *on lyue, to grounde, to depe, on fete, on horse, of (in) gold.*[11]

(b) Disyllabic words from monosyllabic sources: *sope* < OE *soþ*; *burne* < OE *beorn*; *schryfte* < OE *scrift*; *hyʒt*, preterite sg., < OE *het*; *uche* < OE *ælc*; *there* < OE *þer*; *here* < OE *her*; *ofte* < OE *oft*; *lyte* < OE *lyt*.

(c) Monosyllabic words from disyllabic sources: *bot* < OE *butan*, *hir* (except before a pl. noun) < OE *hire*; *þan*, conj., < OE *þanne* (but *þan*, adv., is disyllabic).

(d) Disyllabic words from trisyllabic sources: *mony* before a pl. noun < OE *monige* (but trisyllabic *monye* < OE *monig* immediately before a sg. noun); *better* < OE *betera*; *herk(k)en* < OE *heorcnian*; *rekken* < OE *recenian* (a four-syllable source).

In all of my scansions, the various forms of "covered -*e*" are expanded to give more syllables than the spelling might indicate. *Wern* and *arn* are read as disyllabic when they are main verbs (but monosyllabic when they are auxiliaries). *Lorde* is read as disyllabic, as it was in Old English and in Middle English into the fourteenth century. The only words that I read with a variable number of syllables, depending on the meter of the verse, are *apel*, which has both disyllabic and trisyllabic forms in Old English (*æpel, æpele*) and *togeder*, which has both trisyllabic and quadrisyllabic forms in Old English (*to-gædre, to-gædere*).

Disallowing variable readings in the hypothesized categories for final -*e* is an important part of the argument. As the argument is set up, the evidence also must not violate a further hypothesis: that one part of the line requires no more than one unstressed syllable, another part requires exactly one unstressed syllable, and other parts require two or more unstressed syllables (see Chapter Four). It may be that various processes of elision operated in performance, but the advantages of disallowing elision in the formulation of a theory should be clear. If a perspicuous paradigm emerges even without the flexibility of elision, then one has a stronger theory because the data have been manipulated less. The syllables of the line have been less shaped to conform to the hypothesis.[12]

Just as the phonological rules stated above are conservative, so also are the rules of stress. With one important exception (the lack of metrically significant secondary stress), they recall the rules of stress for Old English poetry.

*Rules of Stress*

1. Nouns, adjectives (except indefinite and interrogative pronominal adjectives: *alle, many, any, fele, oþer, on, no, uche, ilk, what*), infinitives, and participles always receive metrical stress.[13]
2. Finite verbs and adverbs might or might not receive metrical stress. (The determining factors are complex, involving the rhythmical structure of the verse, the pattern of alliteration, semantic considerations, etc.)
3. Articles, prepositions, conjunctions, auxiliary verbs, linking verbs, the verb *have*, pronominal adjectives, and pronouns (personal, demonstrative, indefinite, relative, and interrogative) do not receive metrical stress unless they occur at the end of the half-line.[14]

Why should the reflexes of inflectional phonology and stress be so conservative, reflecting features of Old English? The historical grammars of Middle English state that final -e had disappeared from the spoken language of the North and Northwest Midlands at this time (although it must be remembered that the statements of the historical grammars were based in part on the same kind of evidence that we are examining here, and in many instances the evidence was less fully analyzed).[15]

To say that final -e was preserved in poetic texts is not, of course, to say that it was preserved in every instance in the spoken language. Doubtless there were varieties of the language (according to locality, time, individual speaker, and register) in which the syllable was lost. With reference to both Chaucer and Langland, M. L. Samuels has made the point that "in the late xiv century in southern England the use of -e depended on varying conditions of stress and register, and the individual usage of an author cannot be established simply on the evidence of when and where he lived."[16]

The spread of a sound change is a complex matter with conservative and innovative usages coexisting for a period. In other respects as well the texts of the Alliterative Revival are backward-looking, and if older forms were available, it is not surprising that the poets would have used them.[17]


## 3.7 The Structure of the Evidence and the Argument

The last three sections of Chapter Four will place the arguments of the present study within a general logical context. In anticipation of that meta-theoretical discussion, it is useful to recapitulate the particular structure of the evidence and argument of this chapter. The original frame within which I hypothesized the rules for -*e* was the final syllable at the end of each hemistich. The consistent patterns that began to materialize in this slot, during the course of scanning thousands of verses, led to conclusions about the other slots in the hemistich. The end of each half-line, in effect, cast a network of implicature leftwards. We can sketch the frame for the final syllable as follows:

First half-line                                                    Second half-line
_____/__ (x) (x)          _____/__ x

The parentheses around the two x's of the first half-line indicate that there can be one, or two, or no unstressed syllables in that position. The single x without parentheses in the second half-line indicates that there must be exactly one unstressed syllable at the end of the long line.

Let us, then, posit this pattern: the first half-line can end with no unstressed syllable, or with one or two unstressed syllables; the second half-line must end with exactly one unstressed syllable. If we examine the poems and find at the end of the first half-line words such as *men, halden,* and *parlement* (with, respectively, no unstressed syllable, one unstressed syllable, and two unstressed syllables), then we have evidence for the proposed first half-line pattern. If, further, we find at the end of the second half-line words such as *halden,* with one unstressed syllable, but no words such as *men* and also no words such as *parlement,* then we have evidence for the proposed pattern for the second half-line. The present chapter has followed exactly this method, grouping the various classes of words according to their origins.

As for -*e,* if the phonological rules specify no final unstressed syllable for a certain class of lexical items, and those items show up at the end of the second half-line, then we have evidence against either the phonological rules, the metrical pattern, or both. If it happens, for example, that Old Norse nouns with monosyllabic stems show up at the end of the second half-line, then we have to conclude that there is an error somewhere in our dual hypothesis. As we have seen, such nouns are carefully avoided in the final position of the fourteenth-century alliterative line. To come back to the beginning, then, the question to ask is "Why?" Any adequate theory of Middle English alliterative meter must answer this question. The choice between alternative theories depends upon the generality and economy of the answer.

The direction of the present theory accords with observations that A. T. E. Matonis has succinctly made: "The poets as a rule prefer a syllabically longer a-line; they allow a larger number of syllables in anacrusis in the a-line; many more a-lines end in double feminine endings; the a-line more frequently supports extended verses; and the a-lines are characteristically heavier in narrative value."[18] The patterns for final -*e* outlined above both confirm these observations and make them more definite.

They can be made more definite still. The proposed phonological rules are open to revision and supplementation, and the lines along which these adjustments can be made should be clear. The changes will involve details in the rules and statements about the development of individual words that are exceptions. For example, at one time I hypothesized that dative -*e* was productive in these texts, and I scanned all lines accordingly. On noticing that most of what I took to be dative -*e* occurred in feminine nouns, I changed the hypothesis to eliminate dative -*e* and posited instead a final -*e* on all nouns that were feminine in Old English. I then went back, as is necessary whenever assumptions are revised, and changed all the scansions of my working corpus to accord with the new hypothesis, which indeed accounts much more adequately for the facts. However, I would be surprised if *all* feminine nouns from Old English acquired a final -*e*. As the diagnostic contexts identify those nouns that did not (so far I have not identified any), further revisions in the rules, or additions to the specified exceptions will have to be made.

More important than the specific rules of this chapter, then, is the outline of a self-confirming method that will apply to some 60,000 lines of fourteenth-century Middle English. The process is time-consuming because of the need to revise earlier scansions as hypotheses are revised. However, the structure of the argument makes explicit the kind of empirical evidence that can be brought in support or refutation of the hypotheses. It establishes a firm piece of ground for studying the phonology of final -*e* and the meter of these West Midlands texts.


## 3.8 Systematic Final -*e*

The regularity in the occurrence of final -*e* which the present chapter has traced through a few structures (disyllabic and trisyllabic words at the end of each verse) will be seen in the next chapter to be even more general. This regularity brings into question some of the statements in the standard editions about the rhythm of specific lines. J. J. Anderson, for example, says of *Cleanness*, "The usual rhythmic pattern of the half-line is a rising one," and he cites verse 4a:

And in þe cóntrare kárk [19]

But *kark* derives from Anglo-Saxon *karke*, and therefore an -*e* would be expected, making the pattern a rising-falling one (3B2A). Beyond the specific example, Anderson's generalization deals with first and second half-lines without distinction. By my analysis some 23 percent of first half-lines end with a stress and to that extent could be characterized as "rising." However, fewer than 1.5 percent of the second half-lines, by the analysis above, have reason to be scanned with a final stressed syllable. A more accurate description of "the usual rhythmic pattern of the half-line" would be "falling instead of "rising," but it is best to avoid statements that attempt to characterize both the first and the second half-lines together.

There is a similar problem in Anderson's description of "clashing patterns." He quotes *Cleanness* 145b as an illustration:

in þat góun fébele

Although there are clashing patterns in *Cleanness*, the fact that *goun* derives from OF *goune* disqualifies it as a candidate. The verse would be a type 2BA, x x / x / x.

Finally, according to Anderson, "the dip may come before the two stressed syllables," and he gives as an example the verse, *and his sete ryche* (*Cleanness* 176b). He ignores the metrical significance of the fact that *sete* derives from ON *sæti* and *ryche* from OE *rice*, OF *riche*. The verse would have not one dip but three.

Underlying all these examples is Anderson's general statement: "Unstressed final -*e* is used unsystematically for the most part." The use might appear unsystematic until the system is searched out, but that appearance is a comment on our modern understanding of the line. Among the editors of *Cleanness*, Israel Gollancz pays the most careful attention to the meter and even provides an appendix with 360 "Suggested Metrical Emendations," nearly all of which the proposed rules stated above support.[20]

Marie Borroff does not find regular patterns in the long alliterative lines, although she does in the short rhyming lines of *Gawain*, where -*e* is sometimes required: "Its sporadic sounding is thus warranted by principles of rhyme and meter, and analogous principles must be established to warrant its sounding in the long alliterative lines. But there is no justification for assuming that the metrical principles of the short lines will hold true for the long lines as well. The two belong to different, and in certain respects opposed, traditions" (p. 171). Borroff's conclusion states a principle regarding final -*e* that I accept: that "analogous principles must be established to warrant its sounding in the long alliterative lines." The present chapter has tried to establish those principles. There is a second principle in her conclusion that I also accept: that the short rhyming lines and the long lines "belong to different, and in certain respects opposed traditions." Chapters Four and Five try to show the interaction of these two traditions in a way that points toward a general theory of English rhythm.

# 4. Fourteenth-Century Meter: The Abstract Pattern

## 4.1 The Count of Stresses and the Regulation of Dips

The phonological and metrical principles concerning final -*e* that were argued in Chapter Three now allow us to see other problems in fourteenth-century alliterative texts from a new perspective. Marie Borroff's chapter on the "extended" form of the alliterative long line is an admirably balanced account of the various approaches to the type of half-line that has three possible stresses instead of two.[1] She gives alternative readings to the structures in question and reasons in favor of the reading that she finds most plausible, a reading with two "major chief syllables" and one "minor chief syllable." She also acknowledges the possibility of assigning equal metrical ictus to three syllables instead of only two.

Joan Turville-Petre follows Borroff in scanning these half-lines with two stresses, and Thorlac Turville-Petre follows both metrists in his summary of the problem:

There has been much debate about how these so-called 'extended' half-lines should be analysed. They are of many types, and it may be the case that some should be read as half-lines of two metrical accents and others of three. However, a metrical pattern once established is not easily broken, and the context of the two-stress half-lines imposes its rhythm upon lines which might, out of that context, be interpreted in another way. It is logical, for this reason, to start out from the assumption that all 'extended' half-lines will conform to the standard pattern of the line, that is to say that only two of the three alliterating syllables will bear metrical stress. If it is at all possible to interpret the lines in this way it seems more satisfactory to do so.[2]

On independent grounds I had found the idea of an invariable two-stress half-line attractive. A dipodic structure such as Borroff suggests would reduce the stress on one of the three stressed syllables in the extended half-line and solve certain problems. In trying to apply the concept consistently, however, I found myself in contradictions that necessitated abandoning the dipodic theory and the invariable four-stress line. From the scansions of thousands of lines, including many alternative scansions based on different hypotheses, a set of patterns began to emerge. A systematic account of these patterns goes a long way toward solving most of the problems not only in the count of stresses but generally in the abstract paradigm of the fourteenth-century alliterative line.

Unexpectedly, the key to the solution lies in the patterning of the unstressed syllables, which have always been perceived as unregulated. The principles that govern the main tradition of late Middle English alliterative meter are stated as generalizations to which there are obvious exceptions. The status of the exceptions and the extent to which they are counterexamples to the generalizations will be discussed in section 4.6. (As in Old English, a strong dip is a run of two or more weakly stressed syllables. A minimal dip is one unstressed syllable or none.)

*General Principles*

1. The rhythmical patterns of the two halves of the line are mutually exclusive.
2. The first half-line is normally heavier than the second. It is heavier by virtue of having either two strong dips or three metrical stresses.
3. The second half-line must contain only two metrical stresses and rhythmical dissimilation (one strong dip and one minimal dip in either order) and a single, final unstressed syllable.[3]

A more formal statement of the theory appears in section 4.4 below.

*Piers Plowman* diverges from these principles more than nearly any other poem of the Alliterative Revival. *The Destruction of Troy* and *Joseph of Arimathie,* which diverge even further, can be shown to follow different rules. Further study may show Langland also to have fashioned a separate meter. Still, the norms of the tradition make the best point of departure even for Langland, and a few lines from *Piers Plowman* will illustrate the principles:[4]

$$\overset{\prime}{\text{Fe}}\overset{x}{\text{y}}\text{nen}\ \overset{x}{\text{hem}}\ \overset{\prime}{\text{fan}}\overset{x\ xx}{\text{tasies}} \qquad \overset{x}{\text{and}}\ \overset{\prime}{\text{fo}}\overset{x}{\text{les}}\ \overset{x}{\text{hem}}\ \overset{\prime}{\text{ma}}\overset{x}{\text{keth}}\ \text{(Prol. 36)}$$

$$\overset{x}{\text{For}}\ \overset{x}{\text{su}}\overset{x}{\text{che}}\ \overset{\prime}{\text{co}}\overset{x}{\text{meth}}\ \overset{x}{\text{to}}\ \overset{x}{\text{my}}\ \overset{\prime}{\text{croft}} \qquad \overset{x}{\text{and}}\ \overset{\prime}{\text{cro}}\overset{x}{\text{ppeth}}\ \overset{x}{\text{my}}\ \overset{\prime}{\text{whe}}\overset{x}{\text{te}}\ \text{(6.33)}$$

Because scribes are inconsistent in their writing of final *-e*, it is necessary to let the historical form of the words shine through the written form (according to the rules proposed in Chapter Three—exempting dative -*e*, etc.). Thus, in the following line *will* (from OE *willa*) has an -*e* that is not written:

x    x  x  x  x ⁄ x    x  ⁄  x     x ⁄  x  x  ⁄ x<br>
And also he bigileth þe gyuere     ageines his wil  (7.70)

## 4.2 Oakden's Evidence

Marie Borroff bases her account of the varying proportions of two-stress and three-stress half-lines in Middle English poems on J. P. Oakden's survey.[5] The first note of her Chapter Eight on "The Extended Form" is helpful both for its succinct summary of some of Oakden's data and also for an indication of why one might conclude that the three-stress pattern is a marginal one. The extended half-line appears more significant for the *Gawain*-poet than for other poets, and not very significant for the *Gawain*-poet:

> For a detailed discussion of the extended first half-lines, with a classification into types, see Oakden, *I*, 170–74. A table of percentages, showing the comparative frequency of occurrence of these half-lines in the poems of the Alliterative Revival, is presented on p. 171. From this table it is clear that the author of *Gawain* used the extended first half-line much more frequently than the other poets. In *Gawain*, *Purity*, *Patience*, and *St. Erkenwald* the percentages, as determined by Oakden, are 15.3, 15.8, 13.7, and 17.5 respectively, while in the other poems 12% is the maximum. *Wars Alex.* has 9.66, *Morte Arth.* has 4.3, and *Destr. Troy* has none. (p. 270 n 1)

Because Oakden is not explicit about the criteria that he uses for identifying extended half-lines, it is necessary to reconstruct his procedure by counting the lines anew.

The present analysis is based on a scansion of all the lines in *Cleanness* and a substantial number in *Sir Gawain and the Green Knight*, *Piers Plowman*, *William of Palerne*, *Morte Arthure*, *The Wars of Alexander*, *The Parlement of the Thre Ages*, and other poems. As noted in the previous chapter, the total corpus is 6,100 long lines. In all of these lines, ictus is assigned according to grammatical category as described in Chapter Three: metrical stress occurs always on nouns, adjectives, infinitives, and past participles; variably on finite verbs and adverbs, depending on the structure of the line and other factors; rarely on pronouns; and almost never on conjunctions, prepositions, articles, auxiliaries, and copulas (unless they come at the end of the verse).

My percentage for the number of three-stress first half-lines in *Cleanness* is considerably higher than Oakden's. Where he found 15.8 percent, I found 35 percent. By adding various numbers that Oakden gives, I have concluded that he counted both alliterating and nonalliterating stressed syllables in half-lines that clearly have only two stresses, but in half-lines with a possible third stress he generally counted three stressed syllables only if all three alliterate. For most poems, his figures amount to about one percentage point more than one would get from thus using alliteration as a strict guide. It appears that he added to the count of half-lines containing three stressed, alliterating syllables a few that he read as having three stresses even though no more than two alliterate.

In turning to other poems, my findings diverge even farther from Oakden's. Whereas he found 11 percent of the lines in *William of Palerne* to contain an extended half-line, I have found over half of them, 55 percent, to do so. For *The Wars of Alexander,* Oakden's figure is 9.7 percent, mine 38.2 percent. Here it is not a matter, as it often is in metrics, of different measuring sticks producing different statistics with a more or less systematic correspondence between them. My own results strikingly contradict Oakden's, and also those of Robert W. Sapora.[6] By my reading, the *Gawain*-poet has a higher number of these three-stress half-lines than other surveys find, but *William of Palerne* has a third more than *Gawain* has, not fewer. *The Wars of Alexander* and some of the other poems turn out to be closer to *William of Palerne* in this respect.

In lines as difficult as many of the ones in these poems, another person might disagree on some of my scansions. The point, however, is that, after testing various hypotheses, the present analysis applies a single system to various poems and arrives at consistent results that can be compared. The same is true of Oakden's survey, which follows alliteration closely, and Sapora's, which follows alliteration exclusively. When nonalliterating stressed syllables are taken into account, the meter of the *Gawain*-poet is by no means unusual in having a higher frequency of these extended half-lines than other poets. Borroff's interpretation of Oakden's data is valid, but his data are faulty. She writes: "Whether the extended first half-line is interpreted as a subclass of, or a real departure from, the normal two-part form, it is obvious that the *Gawain*-poet was more inclined than other poets of the alliterative tradition to load the long line with heavy syllables, both alliterating and nonalliterating" (p. 200). In fact, compared with most other Middle English poets, just the opposite is true.

Not only the comparative figures but also the absolute ones are important. If a type of verse occurs in various poems with a frequency between 20 percent and 55 percent, its significance is clearly greater than Oakden's statistics suggest (where the maximum frequency for the *Gawain*-poet was 15.8 percent, for *St. Erkenwald* 17.5 percent, and for other poems 12 percent). The arguments in favor of a necessary four-stress long line have rested largely on data that are faulty because of a bias in favor of alliteration. Moreover, the bias operates selectively, in possible three-stress half-lines but not in unambiguous two-stress half-lines. Thus, the criteria are both superficial, as patterns of alliteration often are when taken by themselves, and inconsistent.

## 4.3 Distributional Evidence from *Cleanness*

In one sense the alliterative long line is bewilderingly flexible. The configurations of stressed and unstressed syllables in *Cleanness* form 167 different half-line patterns. Yet a few general principles of rhythm give order and precision to the metrical variety. Although the principles are basically the same for most of the major poems in the Alliterative Revival, we shall consider a single text first and avoid certain distortions that come from conflating the data of several texts. On minor points where metrical styles differ among the poems, they often do so in opposite ways, so that an averaging of statistics can blur the differences by neutralizing and obscuring the features in question. This kind of conflation is one of the problems in Hoyt N. Duggan's analysis of alliterative poetry. Duggan rejects features identified in the style of a single poem, such as *Cleanness*, if contrary evidence can be found in another poem, such as *The Wars of Alexander*. However, if the frequency of a feature such as the extended first half-line can vary from 20 percent in one poem, to 35 percent in another poem, to 55 percent in yet another, the averaging of features from fifteen different poems may describe a style that no poet ever used. This is especially true if the tabulation includes, as Duggan's does, *The Destruction of Troy*. In its seemingly excessive regularity, *Troy* actually follows different rules of meter (see section 4.7 below).

All 167 patterns in *Cleanness* show a definite preference for one half of the line or the other. This distribution of patterns in the two halves of the line is clear in the fifteen most common patterns. It is even clearer in most of the less frequent types. Many a-verse patterns not listed here occur only in the a-verse: for example, x x x x / x x / x (15 verses), x x x / x / x x (4 verses), and dozens of other patterns. Again, the names of the types refer in obvious ways to Sievers' Five Types and the count of syllables. (For example, 2B2A means a combination of Sievers' B and A, with two syllables in the first dip and two in the second.)

The statistics shown in the table are drawn from the first 900 lines of *Cleanness*. The column of percentages indicates the frequency of the pattern in whichever half of the line it occurs in most. Because the percentages of these patterns range between 93.9 percent and 100 percent, it appears that a given pattern, for whatever reason, tends decisively toward one half of the line or the other.

Most Frequent Types in *Cleanness*

|  |  | First half-line | Second half-line | Percentage |
|---|---|---|---|---|
| B2A | x / x x / x | 3 | 244 | 98.9 |
| B3A | x / x x x / x | 6 | 174 | 96.7 |
| 2BA | x x / x / x | 3 | 98 | 97.0 |
| 2A | / x x / x | 0 | 94 | 100.0 |
| 3A | / x x x / x | 4 | 65 | 94.2 |
| 2B2A | x x / x x / x | 62 | 4 | 93.9 |
| 2B3A | x x / x x x / x | 57 | 2 | 96.6 |
| 3B2A | x x x / x x / x | 58 | 1 | 98.3 |
| 3BA | x x x / x / x | 3 | 53 | 94.6 |
| 3B3A | x x x / x x x / x | 39 | 0 | 100.0 |
| 2B2 | x x / x x / | 33 | 0 | 100.0 |
| 2B3 | x x / x x x / | 31 | 0 | 100.0 |
| 3B3 | x x x / x x x / | 30 | 0 | 100.0 |
| 2C | x x / / x | 0 | 30 | 100.0 |
| 3C | x x x / / x | 0 | 27 | 100.0 |

As it turns out, the tendency for the patterns of the two halves of the line to be mutually exclusive holds up for the other 152 types—in 93.2 percent of the half-lines by my present understanding of the grammar, the meter, and the development of individual words. Among first half-lines, 94 percent have a characteristic a-verse pattern; among second half-lines, 92.4 percent have a characteristic b-verse pattern. Sections 4.5 and 4.6 below discuss the significance of exceptions and the possibility of reducing or explaining them. What remains to be determined at this point is exactly what makes a pattern appropriate for one half of the line or the other.

It is well known that the first half-line is generally longer than the second. Overall length, however, is not the whole story: 3BA (x x x / x / x) and 2B2A (x x / x x / x) have exactly the same number of syllables, and they both end with an unstressed syllable (as required in the b-verse), but they have strikingly different distributions in the two halves of the line: 93.9 percent of 2B2A (x x / x x / x) patterns are in the first half-line; 94.6 percent of 3BA (x x x / x / x) patterns are in the second half-line. If we consider the arrangement of stressed and unstressed syllables within each type, it is clear that the more balanced pattern (x x / x x / x) occurs primarily in the a-verse; the unbalanced pattern (x x x / x / x), for whatever reason, occurs primarily in the b-verse. It appears that something in the internal rhythm of the pattern compels a type toward one half of the line or the other.

We can make the concept of balanced rhythm more precise by following the traditional idea that the texts before us are in strong-stress rhythm, a rhythm that stands in contrast with the regularly rising rhythm of the iambic pentameter. For a pattern to follow regularly rising rhythm strictly, there should be only one unstressed syllable before each stress. Therefore, let us define strong-stress rhythm as the obverse of this: any pattern that has two or more unstressed syllables before each stress. A metrical type is balanced as long as it stays in strong-stress rhythm. It becomes unbalanced if a regularly rising, or iambic, rhythm intrudes. This formulation allows us to state the mainstream meter of fourteenth-century alliterative poems succinctly.

## 4.4 A Theory of Middle English Alliterative Meter

The following rules overstate the regularity of the meter, because there are exceptions that must be explained, but this first approximation moves us toward understanding the general principles by which most of the extant fourteenth-century alliterative poetry was composed.

### Late Middle English Alliterative Meter

Definitions

Strong dip: A sequence of two or more metrically unstressed syllables.

Metrical stress: According to the principles in section 3.6.

First half-line

Normal verses: Two metrically stressed syllables and at least two strong dips.

Extended verses: Three stressed syllables with any pattern of dips.

Second half-line

Two metrically stressed syllables, one and only one of which is preceded by a strong dip. Exactly one metrically unstressed syllable at the end.

The paradigm for the normal (four-stress) line can be further abstracted and schematized as follows:

*First half-line*       *Second half-line*
$\sim/\sim/(-)\sim$       $\alpha\sim/-\alpha\sim/x$
            or
$\alpha\sim/-\alpha\sim/\sim$

The tilde represents the strong dip, a pattern of two or more weakly stressed syllables. The variable $\alpha$ represents the coefficient of the feature "strong dip," with a value of + or −. The combination of $+\alpha$ and $-\alpha$ in a single pattern functions as in segmental phonology to show a form of dissimilation. If the value of $\alpha$ is +, the values of tilde are $+(+)$ and $-(+)$; if the value of $\alpha$ is −, the values of tilde are $+(-)$ and $-(-)$. A minus value for tilde represents one syllable or no syllable, the normal dip of the iambic pentameter. Therefore, the iambic pattern ideally occurs before one (but not both) of the stressed syllables in the second half-line. However, it cannot occur before either stressed syllable of the first half-line unless, by compensation, the verse ends with a strong dip.

Let us illustrate these abstractions with examples from *William of Palerne*.[7] Line 486 has the necessary two strong dips in the first half-line and a weak and a strong dip in the second:

x   x   ′ x   x   x   x   ′ x       x   ′ x   x   ′ x
I wol breke out fram þat baret,    and blame my hert

This line would fit the pattern:

$\sim/\sim/--\sim$        $--\sim/+\sim/x$

The combination of *I* and *wol* form a strong dip, represented by the tilde; so also do the four unstressed syllables between the stresses in the a-verse.

The last syllable in the a-verse is represented by a minus sign and a tilde, indicating that the dip is not strong; that is, it contains one syllable or no syllable. Because the minus sign is in parentheses and thus optional, it would be ignored in a half-line that ended on two unstressed syllables.

To this point the notation may seem a needlessly abstract way of stating a pattern that could be described in numerous other ways, some of which would surely be clearer to some readers. It is in the second half-line that the alpha notation provides a simple and economical way of stating a generalization that goes to the heart of Middle English poetic rhythm: if the dip before the first stress is strong, the dip before the second stress is weak, and vice versa. Since alpha notation is familiar in phonology as a means of representing segmental dissimilation, it is natural to use it here to show rhythmical dissimilation. Thus, *and* in the first dip is minus strong, or minimal; therefore the second dip would be minus minus strong, or plus strong, as it is with the combination of -*e* and *my*.

Clearly, readers who have their own preferred systems of notation or who in any event do not care for the notation of theoretical phonology can find other ways of stating rhythmical dissimilation—as Hoyt Duggan did in his independent discovery of the phenomenon. The main case to be made for alpha notation is that it crystallizes and poses a question that can be held succinctly in the mind. What is rhythmically significant about a distinction between a strong dip and a dip that is something other than strong (a "minus strong dip")? Chapter Five will suggest that this distinction reaches all the way to the most basic distinction between the two chief metrical modes in English—strong-stress meter and foot meter.

For now, however, let us keep our focus on specific lines. Although Duggan's system requires rhythmical dissimilation, it has difficulty with the verse before us, since the assumptions by which he scanned the lines of his working corpus do not allow for final -*e* on infinitives. He would have to scan *William of Palerne* 486, *and blame my hert*, as x / x /, contrary to his own metrical rules. Furthermore, six lines later in 492, with the words reversed, he would have the same unmetrical pattern:

þus unhendly and hard    mi̇́ hérte tó bláme

The present theory takes the rhythm in both verses to be the most common b-verse pattern of all, B2A: x / x x / x. *Herte* (from OE *heorte*) and the infinitive *blame* would have final -*e* as a matter of course.

Verse 566a from *William of Palerne* shows what happens when the first dip of the a-verse is minimal:

$$\overset{x\ \ \ '\ \ \ x\ \ \ x\ \ \ '\ x\ \ \ x}{\text{what sorwes and sikingges}} \qquad \overset{x\ \ '\ \ x\ \ \ x\ \ \ x\ \ '\ x}{\text{I suffer for his sake}}$$

The second alternative for the first half-line (as given in the formalized rules above) fits the verse. Alpha is minus, and the two strong dips are in the second and third positions: $-\sim/\sim/\sim$.

It should be clear that the notation can also describe a-verses with strong dips in the first and third positions, as well as those with three strong dips. The most important point that the notation makes clear is the contrast in the rhythm of the two halves of the line. The a-verse rhythm is typically balanced by two strong dips; the b-verse rhythm is necessarily unbalanced by a strong dip and a minimal dip in either order, and a single unstressed syllable at the end. The implications of this unbalancing will be explored in the next chapter. Just as the iambic rhythm intrudes on the prevailing strong-stress rhythm in alliterative verse, so it can be shown that the strong-stress rhythm intrudes on the prevailing iambic rhythm of poetry written in the main English tradition since the time of Surrey.

## 4.5 The Structure of the Evidence and the Argument

As in Chapter Three it will be useful to recapitulate and make fully explicit the assumptions behind the evidence and the argument, and to distinguish the present method from other methods. The percentages from *Cleanness* in the table above are based on my present understanding of the principles regulating the rhythm of the alliterative long line, applied as consistently as I have been able. In aiming for consistency I have sometimes had to refrain from tilting a pattern in a direction that would be more favorable both to the statistics and to my own ear. The possibilities for tilting include promotion, demotion, and elision. As the examples that follow make clear, a considerable number of "exceptions" are counted as such because they are not in accord with the explicit statement of rules as it now stands.

The reason for being quite literal in compiling the data is not only heuristic (to avoid skewing the data in favor of the hypotheses) but also theoretical. If the tilting of ambiguous patterns in the direction of the paradigm is a legitimate aspect of meter (as one can argue that it is), then we need to have an idea of the frequency of verses that unambiguously conform to the paradigm. By my present understanding of the principles of meter and of the development of individual words, the verses of *Cleanness* follow the hypothesized rules over 93 percent of the time. This is to say that 93 percent of the half-lines, scanned according to the hypothesized rules for final -*e* and for stress as stated in Chapter Three support this general principle: the rhythmical patterns of the two halves of the alliterative long line belong to mutually exclusive sets. (The status of the 7 percent exceptions to this principle and thus the status of the principle are discussed in section 4.6 below.) Such a principle is a new way of considering "strong-stress meter," where the possibility of tilting in favor of the paradigm has always been undermined by the lack of a clear paradigm.

That the pardigm also holds for other poems in the tradition can be seen from a larger corpus of 4,400 half-lines; see table. Seven alliterative poems are represented.[8] Although the general point holds, we must keep in mind the problems that result from conflating statistics abstracted from poems that have their own individual style within the tradition. Again only the 15 most frequent patterns (out of a total of 207) are listed.

*Most Frequent Types in Seven Poems*

|  |  | First half-line | Second half-line | Percentage |
|---|---|---|---|---|
| B2A | x / x x / x | 17 | 501 | 96.7 |
| B3A | x / x x x / x | 30 | 425 | 93.4 |
| 2BA | x x / x / x | 5 | 216 | 97.7 |
| 2A | / x x / x | 7 | 199 | 96.6 |
| 3A | / x x x / x | 17 | 189 | 91.7 |
| 2B2A | x x / x x / x | 119 | 30 | 79.9 |
| 3B2A | x x x / x x / x | 129 | 7 | 94.9 |
| 3BA | x x x / x / x | 11 | 124 | 91.9 |
| 2B3A | x x / x x x / x | 103 | 19 | 84.4 |
| 3B3A | x x x / x x x / x | 101 | 0 | 100.0 |
| 2C | x x / / x | 0 | 91 | 100.0 |
| B4A | x / x x x x / x | 22 | 59 | 72.8 |
| 2B2 | x x / x x / | 80 | 0 | 100.0 |
| 3B3 | x x x / x x x / | 64 | 0 | 100.0 |
| 3B2 | x x x / x x / | 60 | 0 | 100.0 |

We can assume that some of the unmetrical verses result from errors in scribal transmission. *Cleanness* and most other poems of the Alliterative Revival are represented by a single manuscript. Except for *Piers Plowman, The Wars of Alexander, The Parlement of the Thre Ages,* and *The Siege of Jerusalem,* speculations on an archetypal manuscript by traditional methods of comparison are impossible. The idea of an archetype raises a question about the kinds of evidence to be considered and the line of division between evidence and theory.

Hoyt Duggan takes the view that an archetype reconstructed from multiple copies is more valuable as evidence than an unevaluated manuscript.[9] The view of the present study is that as soon as one reconstructs an archetype, one is no longer dealing with primary evidence but with one hypothesis in a total theory. In this case it is a hypothesis that projects backward from the fifteenth-century evidence that happens to have survived. For certain specific historical-phonological reasons in English (the loss of final *-e*), this kind of backward projection might not coincide at all with the opposite procedure that begins at a distant point in the past (as far back as necessary to find operative certainty) and projects forward.

My own projections forward involve an agnosticism about the exact words written down by the author but a certainty of constructing increasingly plausible hypotheses about the tradition as a whole, a tradition which includes the participation of the scribes. It is safe to assume that the scribes sometimes botched the meter of the text they were copying and sometimes revised to bring it into closer conformity with a widely shared norm. However, the full extent to which any scribe normalized or corrupted the meter of the authorial text—or even the meter of an archetype—is beyond determination. This skepticism about recovering the author's words and syllables, or even about the desirability of having that as an aim, has to do less with general assumptions about the relationship between an author (a complex concept in itself if we allow the possibility of a revising author) and a series of scribes than with what was happening in English during the fourteenth century. The whole picture is complicated by the fact that sometime during the period between the composition of the poems, or a period shortly before the composition of the poems, and the time of the fifteenth-century manuscripts, final *-e*, in various dialects and registers, at various times, was in some sense "lost."

We do not know the status of final *-e* in the informal spoken language of any poet; we do not know the relationship between that usage and a more formal, or conservative, or archaizing register; we do not know the attitude of scribes toward tinkering with the text in an effort to restore metrical regularity; and finally we do not know how far such scribal efforts would have been metrically misguided by a misunderstanding of the original meter—a misunderstanding brought about partly by the phonological changes just indicated. If the time, place, and register of the author's literary dialect retained final -e, and the time, place, and register of the scribe's reading dialect or copying dialect did not, then obviously a major disjunction is bracketed by the composition and the copy. The period in question is from the mid fourteenth to the mid fifteenth century.

For example, suppose that Robert Thornton, a Yorkshireman who copied the texts of *The Siege of Jerusalem, The Parlement of the Thre Ages,* and *Wynnere and Wastoure* in the middle of the fifteenth century, had lost final -e but nevertheless had an accurate understanding of the fourteenth-century meter and tended to "correct" lines to bring them into conformity with the meter. Such an assumption would be one explanation (among several possible explanations) why Thornton departed from the other six scribes of *The Siege of Jerusalem* in the third line of the poem: [10]

| MSS. Laud, etc. | Whyle Pylat was prouost . . . |
| Thornton | The while þat Pylat was prouost . . . |

If Thornton had lost final -e, then *Whyle* (from OE *hwile*) would no longer provide the strong dip needed in the a-verse. Thornton could get the strong dip by adding the two words that he did.

Similarly, there is much evidence that in fourteenth-century alliterative texts, adjectival past participles retained -e in the plural. Therefore, Thornton's departure from the other scribes in the following two b-verses would be consistent with the view of the present study (that the necessary strong dip originally depended on the final -e, which Thornton had lost):

| MSS. Laud, etc. | & pured stones |
| Thornton | & full proude stones  (472) |

| MSS. Laud, etc. | with grounden speres |
| Thornton | with scharpe grounden speres  (566) |

In line 472, MS. Ashburnham 130 also obtains the strong dip without reliance on -e: *& oþer ryche stones.* This kind of interaction of phonological and metrical grammars among poets and scribes makes archetypal reconstruction of dubious value for discovering metrical tradition.

There are, in short, several inescapable problems in using archetypal reconstructions for the recovery and analysis of meter. The distance in time and in the number of copies intervening between the archetype and the author's original is always uncertain. Also, the reconstruction itself is always uncertain, among other reasons because of convergent variation; thus the reconstruction is always a hypothesis and not primary data. And finally, if one uses as evidence for a metrical principle a reconstruction based on that metrical principle, the method becomes tautologous.

Because all scientific investigation is circular, it is necessary to distinguish between circularity and tautology.[11] Duggan's method turns out to be tautologous to the extent that he selects on the basis of meter the variants to count (where variants exist) and then uses the count of selected data to confirm his theory. Such a process changes the percentage of conformity to his rules from 85.8 percent of "raw" and "unevaluated" data to 99.5 percent of selected data.[12] Like any traditional editor, Duggan uses various kinds of considerations to select the variant that he posits as archetypal, including failure of sense and comparison with the source where the source exists, but the main point running through all his studies is that the metrical pattern as he conceives it can make the determination among variants when the sense or other considerations fail. To the extent that an archetypal line is hypothesized on the basis of a metrical theory and then that hypothesized line is counted in the statistics to confirm the metrical theory, the method dismisses data and adjusts evidence tautologically.[13]

The view of the present study is that there are two quite different kinds of linguistic structures to abstract from these poetic texts: structures which everyone agrees on (for example, the exact place in any line where the long line divides into half-lines) and structures which come into being through the hypothesized rules of a particular theory (for example, the occurrence of -e in a certain grammatical context). The goal is to superimpose these two kinds of structures so that the first will falsify the second. The construction of a theory involves a continuous, back-and-forth process of hypothesis, testing, and rejection. What should then remain are rules that are more plausible to assume than their negation, because their negation creates a set of strange facts that must be accounted for.

For example, if we hypothesize that -ly in pertly represents two syllables, then we are able to scan Gawain 1941a by the present theory, because the verse will have two strong dips:

x  x  /  xx  /  x    2B2A
As is pertly payed  (1941a)

Another working hypothesis is that *pertly* will have the same number of syllables wherever it occurs. Both hypotheses would be contradicted by the occurrence of *pertly* either at the end of the b-verse or in a position where the *-ly* would cause a second strong dip. We search the corpus for these contradictory contexts and find none. *Pertly* never occurs at the end of the line nor within the line where a weak dip would be required. The one instance of *pertly* in *Cleanness,* in fact, is in a position where disyllabic *-ly* is required by both my metrical theory and Duggan's:

x    /    xx    /    x    B2A<br>
and pertly halden  (244b)

More significantly, not just *pertly* but all *-ly* adverbs follow this pattern of distribution.[14] The rather remarkable distribution, then, fails to falsify the interacting hypotheses. Or, to put it another way: the distribution, which requires an explanation, is accounted for by the interacting hypotheses.

All the lexical and grammatical categories as well as the individual, exceptional words described in the rules of Chapter Three occur consistently in positions appropriate to their hypothesized syllabic structure, regardless of how many *-e*'s were omitted or added in the manuscripts: Old French nouns, weak adjectives, infinitives, petrified datives, and the rest. The concrete empirical test is the division of the line into two parts, a division that nearly always shines through the vagaries of the scribes. For each specific hypothesis presented above, the shape of the evidence in support or refutation of it is always simple and clear.

## 4.6 Generalizations and Exceptions

A final word on the use of statistics in this chapter and in the previous chapter may be useful. One possible objection is that after all the refinements, the statistics still show exceptions to the proposed rules. A rather different objection is that statistics are misleading at best and perhaps inappropriate in any case; in treating all lines alike the numbers ignore the fact that in this tradition more than in some other traditions each line in context has the possibility of varying from what is considered "metrical."

As for exceptions, a certain kind of textual editor might claim that poets by definition do not write unmetrical or deviant lines, and therefore a theory that allows unmetrical or deviant lines is faulty. From a quite different direction, a certain kind of linguistic metrist might claim that anything that the poet writes must be accounted for by rules—otherwise, how else would the lines get written? Rules, as rules are conceived, account for all the linguistic production of a poet, or of anyone else. The generative conception of "rule" is a robust and useful one, especially as it leads to the discovery of generalizations underlying what might otherwise appear to be lists of random, unassimilated facts. Generative metrics has traditionally included animadversions toward ad hoc lists of exceptions.

There comes a point, however, at which the incorporation of aberrant facts into the generalizations of a theory undermines the usefulness of the generalizations. For example, section II of *The Waste Land*, "A Game of Chess," opens with lines that were inspired by a famous passage of iambic pentameter:

> The Chair she sat in, like a burnished throne,
> Glowed on the marble, where the glass
> Held up by standards wrought with fruited vines
> From which a golden Cupidon peeped out                   80
> (Another hid his eyes behind his wing)
> Doubled the flames of sevenbranched candelabra
> Reflecting light upon the table as
> The glitter of her jewels rose to meet it,
> From satin cases poured in rich profusion.[15]

Even without knowledge of the source in *Antony and Cleopatra,* the reader knows by the fourth or fifth line that this parody itself is in iambic pentameter. The passage continues for another twenty-five lines, many of which are perfectly regular, unmistakable iambic pentameter, as are the first and third lines (77 and 79). Others, such as line 82, can be made to fit the pattern by familiar conventions long established in the English iambic pentameter tradition. However, some lines are not iambic pentameter by any traditional interpretation of the form. The second line in the passage, "Glowed on the marble, where the glass," has only eight syllables and at most four metrical stresses.

Given such a line, the metrist has several strategies to chose among. One would be to deny that iambic pentameter is even relevant in discussing this passage. Another would be to define the iambic pentameter so that it includes not only lines of five feet but also lines of four stresses. In fact, there are descriptions of the iambic pentameter which do just this, including a famous one by Northrop Frye. Frye's four-stress reading of Hamlet's soliloquy could be extended with no difficulty to include lines such as, "Glowed on the marble, where the glass." However, a compelling point that Wimsatt and Beardsley made was that a theory of the iambic pentameter *ought* to have difficulty with lines such as this, in that the basic principle of the form—five feet—is clearly violated.[16] It is a telling comment against a theory if such lines do *not* pose any difficulty for it. (This particular line was not one of their examples, although it illustrates their argument well.)

The simplest and most adequate generalization would describe the meter of the opening lines of "A Game of Chess" as iambic pentameter with five feet and would then acknowledge that this particular line falls out of the scheme. Here we come to a problem in terminology that often leads to confusion. In characterizing the line as "unmetrical" or "deviant" we simply mean that the line diverges from the most adequate generalizations that describe the metrical norm, including those generalizations that describe variations. It does not mean that the poet made an error or wrote an inferior line, or that there might be cause for editorial emendation.

The situation is complicated by the fact that in the description of some stricter traditions of prosody, "unmetrical" does indeed mean that the line is somehow corrupt, either in its composition or in some stage of its transmission. Thus, Wimsatt and Beardsley make the point that our knowledge of Pope's meter (and not our perfect memory of his poetry) tells us that the misquoted line, "Preserved in Milton's or Shakespeare's name," is wrong. Similarly, the meter of *Beowulf* is strict enough to cast into doubt line 747b, *ræhte ongēan*, and to prompt various emendations. However, Langland certainly and perhaps also the *Gawain*-poet appear to be closer to Eliot than to the *Beowulf*-poet in their freedom to diverge from the norm. Although Borroff and I do not always agree on the specifics of the basic pattern, we agree that there *is* a basic pattern and that it is not always adhered to. Borroff writes: "Though I concede that what I call the basic pattern is at times honored more in the breach than in the observance, I believe that it is in fact the 'basis,' or point of departure, for the other metrical patterns found in the poem."[17]

Now we can see a response to the objection that might be leveled against statistics in the first place. In compiling statistics, all lines indeed are treated alike, precisely in order to arrive at a norm. Then, with a norm established, we are able to make a set of descriptive statements that account for the great majority of verses and also to show exactly how the small minority of deviant lines vary from that norm. The norm, furthermore, is publically accessible—in John Hollander's terms, "a metrical contract." Once it is established, it takes on a life of its own that does not depend upon a single author. This is the very meaning of metrical tradition. The meter can be subscribed to and created by imitators, by scribes, and by anyone else who understands the paradigm. For purposes of determining the metrical tradition, a copy by a pedantic scribe can be more valuable than a holograph manuscript by an author who (like Eliot, perhaps like Langland) has the temperament and the confidence to take licenses with the conventions of the form.

The rules for final *-e* and for stress as stated in Chapter Three are approximations that require further refinements. In places they can be made more precise, and in other places supplementary rules can be added. As always, however, there will be a tradeoff between the simplicity of the generalization and the inclusiveness of its predictions. For example, the second rule for stress in section 3.6 states that verbs and adverbs "might or might not receive metrical stress," and it indicates some of the factors that bear upon the situation (the rhythmical structure of the verse, etc.). In *Cleanness* 547b the adverb *never* is scanned with metrical stress:

$$\overset{x}{\text{In the fyl}}\text{þe of þe flesch} \quad \overset{x}{\text{þat}} \ \overset{x}{\text{þou}} \ \overset{x}{\text{be}} \ \overset{\prime}{\text{foun}}\overset{x}{\text{den}} \ \overset{\prime}{\text{neu}}\overset{x}{\text{er}}$$

But in *Cleanness* 976b and 1720b the adverb is scanned without metrical stress:

$$\text{Trynande ay a hy3e trot} \quad \overset{x}{\text{þat}} \ \overset{\prime}{\text{tor}}\overset{x}{\text{ne}} \ \overset{x}{\text{neu}}\overset{x}{\text{er}} \ \overset{\prime}{\text{dor}}\overset{x}{\text{sten}}$$

$$\text{Made of stokkes and stone3} \quad \overset{x}{\text{þat}} \ \overset{x}{\text{neu}}\overset{x}{\text{er}} \ \overset{\prime}{\text{sty}}\overset{x}{\text{ry}} \ \overset{\prime}{\text{mo3t}}$$

A supplementary rule is clearly possible here to make more precise the contexts in which disyllabic adverbs such as *never* do and do not receive stress.

Similarly, there are contexts where words that are normally not stressed are promoted and other contexts where words that are normally stressed are demoted. Again, the third rule for stress in section 3.6 notes that function words do not receive metrical stress unless they occur at the end of the half-line. Thus, *dorsten* and *mo3t* in 976b and 1720b, above, bear ictus, as does *hade* in *Cleanness* 831b:

$$\overset{x}{\text{tyl}} \ \overset{x}{\text{þay}} \ \overset{\prime}{\text{was}}\overset{x}{\text{chen}} \ \overset{\prime}{\text{ha}}\overset{x}{\text{de}}$$

Just as function words can be promoted in certain contexts, so apparently can nouns and adjectives occasionally (though very rarely) be demoted, especially if strong stresses occur close together. In these cases, however, I have not yet tried to incorporate the special context into the generalization. For example, there is good reason to believe that *lyf* and *men* in *Cleanness* 325b and 787b should be demoted. However, they are counted in the tabulations among the three-stress BC types:

$$\overset{x}{\text{and }} \overset{\prime}{\text{gost}} \overset{x}{\text{of }} \overset{\prime}{\text{lyf}} \overset{\prime}{\text{habbe}}\overset{x}{_3} \quad (325\text{b})$$

$$\overset{x}{\text{þer }} \overset{\prime}{\text{stout}} \overset{x}{\text{men}} \overset{\prime}{\text{pla}}\overset{\prime}{\text{y}}\overset{x}{\text{ed}} \quad (787\text{b})$$

The obvious objection to the two-stress reading would be that demoting *lyf* and *men* in these b-verses but not demoting a third stress in similar a-verses loads the statistics in favor of the proposed theory. Partly for this reason, I have not read these verses as B2A, x/xx/x, but have simply counted them among the exceptions. Indeed no nouns are demoted anywhere in the corpus. A fair test of the theory depends on equal treatment of the two halves of the line. However, a very interesting fact emerges in this case: in the corpus of 4,400 verses, there are only ten verses of type BC, x/x//x, and all ten are in the b-verse. This fact strongly suggests that there is a general rhythm rule that demotes nouns and adjectives in this context and thus renders the verse appropriate only for the second half-line. In the next revision of the stress rules, I may try to incorporate this special context. Meanwhile, the results can stand as tabulated to emphasize that the rules are not final and that the scansions are made only in accordance with rules which have already been explicitly stated. This procedure helps to keep clear exactly what the statistics refer to and to flag contexts that may need to be made explicit in further refinements of the rules.[18]

## 4.7 Abduction

If the conclusions just stated seem tentative in certain respects, this impression is appropriate. The incremental process of observation, hypothesis, testing, and revision that has gone into formulating the rules of this particular theory of meter has its analogues in more general aspects of the study of language. Charles Sanders Peirce described a mode of inquiry which he termed *abduction* and which he distinguished from the more familiar processes of *deduction* and *induction*. Abduction, which Peirce also called *hypothesis,* is the only one of the three modes of reasoning that leads to new knowledge, and it is essential to scientific investigation. From knowledge quite separate from the facts at hand we create suppositions, or hypotheses, to explain the facts. Distinguishing between induction and abduction (or hypothesis), Peirce writes:

Induction is where we generalize from a number of cases of which something is true, and infer that the same thing is true of a whole class. Or, where we find a certain thing to be true of a certain proportion of cases and infer that it is true of the same proportion of the whole class. Hypothesis is where we find some very curious circumstance, which would be explained by the supposition that it was a case of a certain general rule, and thereupon adopt that supposition.[19]

Let us set out the differences between the three modes of reasoning as succinctly as possible:

Deduction:  Rule—All men are mortal.
            Case—Enoch and Elijah were men.
         ∴ Result—Enoch and Elijah were mortal.
Induction:  Case—Enoch and Elijah were men.
            Result—Enoch and Elijah were mortal.
         ∴ Rule—All men are mortal.
Abduction:  Rule—All men are mortal.
            Result—Enoch and Elijah were mortal.
         ∴ Case—Enoch and Elijah were men.

Of abduction, then, we can say the following: if we observe that Enoch and Elijah were mortal, we can try relating this fact to a general rule (which itself may be established independently or merely hypothesized) and draw a consistent though not a necessary conclusion that Enoch and Elijah were men. The new knowledge that we gained (in contrast with deduction and induction) comes from the matching of a case with a rule, which may or may not be the right matching. It takes only a few moments' contemplation to understand that abduction is a weaker argument that induction, which in turn is weaker than deduction—at least in terms of security. As Peirce said of abduction, "though its *security* is low, its *uberty* is high" (8.388) Or, as Henning Andersen states it:

The conclusions reached by abductive inference afford none of the security offered by induction and deduction. Since abductive inference goes beyond what is given to suggest that something may be the case, it is always a weak argument, sometimes a reasonable guess, but often a mere surmise. Still, abduction justly holds the prominent place in a theory of scientific method which Peirce accorded it, for it alone of the three modes of inference can originate new ideas; it alone gives us an understanding of things.[20]

The relevance of abduction to the present discussion is to point out that at a certain stage in the process of discovery—at the stage of hypothesis—the arguments of the present chapter and of Chapter Three are lacking in security. But this situation is true of every scientific investigation.[21] The hypotheses are tested by the later stage of induction, the examination of the individual members of a class. Having been determined true or false, the tested hypotheses (or propositions) are fitted into deductive arguments that can be characterized as valid or invalid, leading to true or false conclusions, as the case may be.

The idea of a weak point in the construction of a grammar—the point at which the "guessing" of hypotheses is made—allows insight not only into what the metrist does but also into what previous generations of poets did as the tradition evolved. Wrong hypotheses by language learners lead to language change. "Wrong" hypotheses by poets (intentionally or unintentionally in their fashioning of metricality as discussed above) lead to changes in the metrical tradition.

Linguists as different in theoretical orientation as Noam Chomsky and Henning Andersen have invoked Peirce's abduction as a model for language learning and language change.[22] The cyclical process that is true of the learner of a language is true also of the philologist. Andersen writes:

As he builds up his grammar, in his attempt to explain the utterances he has observed, the learner constantly tests its validity by use of both induction and deduction. He checks new utterances produced by his models against the relevant parts of his grammar, to see whether these new data ('results') can be reconciled with the linguistic structure he has formulated (the posited 'case') in conformity with the 'laws' of language; this is induction. If they cannot, there can be only one reason: his grammar is inadequate. He will then be prompted to make new abductions to make the grammar conform to all the observed facts. (p. 776)

In addition to the testable limits that the interacting hypotheses put upon themselves, there are certain fixed points within the Middle English long line that permit the objective, inductive verification of hypotheses.

These points include the overwhelming majority of instances of alliteration and also the overwhelming majority of instances of the mid-line break. Actually, of course, by a skeptical view, these features too can be said to depend upon subjective interpretation—as does *any* feature of the written line. Indeed for alliteration there are sometimes real questions about how to consider syllables with less than full stress. By contrast, the determination of the mid-line break, upon which some of the most important distributions of the arguments above depend, is virtually never a problem. I know of no instances where my own reading departs from that of Skeat or other editors who have marked it.

Let us take a specific example to see how the abductive process works for both the poet's construction of a grammar and our determination of that grammar. We read a text and form certain impressions. We make suppositions to explain those impressions. For adjectives the suppositions might run as follows:

> Rule—All adjectives that have a metrical -*e* in Middle English had a final vowel or -*an* in Old English.
> Result—These adjectives had a final vowel or -*an* in Old English.
> ∴ Case—These adjectives have a metrical -*e* in Middle English.

There are several points to notice about this reasoning. First, the rule, even if it is true, states a necessary but not a sufficient condition for metrical -*e* in Middle English. An Old English adjective might have had a vowel or an -*an* which did not become a metrical -*e* in Middle English. Even if Enoch and Elijah were mortal, they were not necessarily men. Thus, here is a place for a possibility of slippage, although not the only place. The "Result" is stated from our point of view as philologists armed with grammars and dictionaries. The parallel statement for the poet constructing a grammar would rest on a recognition that certain inflectional forms were a part of the language. This kind of recognition is exactly what Andersen describes as part of the normal process of learning a language. Because the poet did not have access to Old English grammars and dictionaries, these forms would necessarily be part of the living language—in some sense of "living." If all the linguistic structures could be captured faithfully in the internalized grammar of every speaker, then language change would be severely retarded. However, grammars are not replicated with the fidelity of DNA, and thus change takes place in human historical time rather than in evolutionary time.

We can infer a change in final -*e* generally and in adjectives specifically between the grammar of *Alexander A* (possibly mid fourteenth century) and *The Wars of Alexander* (possibly early to mid fifteenth century).[23] An impression on reading the two poems is that *Alexander A* has more trisyllabic words ending in -*e*. The specific cause of this tendency may not be easy to locate. For example, the category of present and past participles functioning adjectivally and also the category of adjectives ending in -*en* seem to have a final -*e* in *Wars*. Although the final -*e* is not written, we have seen that it is needed in this metrical context (according to both the present system and Duggan's). Many more examples could be added to the following list from *Wars:*

in drabland wedis  (232b)

a blesand table  (274b)

bitand lances  (788b, A)

bitand lancez  (788b, D)

in blasand wede  (2229b, A)

in blysnand wedes  (2229b, D)

of feȝtand folk  (2535b, A)

of fightand bernes  (2535b, D)

in starand maylis  (3615b)

of changand hewes  (3687b)

ne laȝand mirthis  (4367b)

& likand spices  (4606b)

of silkyn clathis  (236b)

bórden shíldis  (787b, A)

& bróuden shéldéz  (787b, D)

with sílken rápis  (1520b, A, D)

& gílten tómbis  (4451b)

It appears that the poet, though not the scribes, recognized and retained this older feature of the language.

In other poems of the Alliterative Revival other older features are retained. Fernand Mossé's grammar gives the standard paradigm for *-e* in weak and plural forms for monosyllabic adjectives, then adds: "also the same for *fast* 'firm', *ful* 'full', *lich* 'like' used alone or as suffixes and *-les* 'devoid of'."[24] If we focus on *full* as a suffix, we see that it is indeed used in a context where metrical *-e* is needed, as in these verses from *Alexander A*:

with rufúll dédes  (81b)

with caréful díntes  (147b)

ferefúll sóndes  (291b)

with bostefúll déedes  (390b)

þis ménskfull Quéene  (745b)

However, the same cannot be said for *The Wars of Alexander*, because words with *-full* are treated quite differently, and in this different treatment we can see the language (not the meter) in the process of change. In response to earlier presentations of this argument, Hoyt Duggan reconsidered the assumption on which he had scanned his whole corpus of Middle English alliterative poetry—the assumption that final *-e* was never sounded. He revised that assumption to propose that monosyllabic adjectives had doublet forms with and without final *-e* but that disyllabic adjectives such as *rufull* did not.[25] Instead, he suggested, under pressure of language change the meter itself changed to accommodate the pattern

(x) / (x) / (x) in this particular syntactic context. During the course of his discussion he considered a line with -*full* in two slightly different versions in the manuscripts:

þis miʒtifull prince (1201b, A)

þis mightfull prince (1201b, D)

Instead of assigning an -*e* to *mightfull* in D (which seems a plausible solution, though, as it turns out, probably wrong) or taking the trisyllabic form *miʒtifull* as archetypal (which is probably right), Duggan argues for the archetypal pattern (x) / (x) / (x) on the basis that "the b-verse combination of *miʒtful* + *noun* appears on several other occasions in the poem." He cites 1491 in A, *þe miʒtfull fadere* and "more regularly" in D, *& þat mightfull fadre*, as well as the plural form attested by both manuscripts at 2040 and 2789, *miʒtfull kniʒtis*. Duggan reasons as follows: "Had at any point both manuscripts agreed in *miʒtiful* or in *& þat*, the argument could be differently made, but there is pervasive evidence in both manuscripts of this kind of scribal interference" (p. 132).

Nothing could make clearer the contrast that I have been drawing between Duggan's positivism and the inferential process of abduction that goes into learning a language and into constructing an explicit grammar. Certainly there is scribal interference, but the specifics of that interference cannot be deduced from comparing scribal practice itself. There has to be a hypothesis of a norm for the scribes to have interfered with and to have varied from—just as the child in learning a language must make successive hypotheses to account for the bits of language (often in degraded form) that he or she happens to hear. The language is never given *tout cort*.

The avoidance of this kind of hypothesis and inference causes Duggan to miss the most revealing fact about adjectives in -*full*: the *miʒtifull/miʒtfull* alternation is the only adjective with -*full* to occur in the context x / x x / x in the whole of *The Wars of Alexander*. Other adjectives with -*full* occur in the poem: *blisfull* (5415), *bretfull* (1548, 4868), *carefull* (1815, 3869, 4106), *dredfull* (359), *ferdfull* (D750, 3036), *leuefull* (1674), *menskefull* (2953), *piʒt-full* (2284), *skilfull* (645), *spedfull* (971), *staffull* (1543, 4897), *synfull* (3663), *wrathfull* (3167). But these words are never used where an -*e* is possible syntactically and needed metrically—in contrast with the -*full* words in *Alexander A* above and in other poems.[26]

What, then, is the explanation? The poet who wrote *The Wars of Alex-*

*ander* had to learn a language during a period of extraordinary changes. Final *-e* was disappearing, but final *-e* did not disappear the way the members of an endangered species do, any one of which is alive or dead. It disappeared in changing configurations of grammatical categories from speaker to speaker. The evidence suggests that the poet's grammar retained *-e* on the present and past participles and on words with *-lich,* but there is no positive evidence (except *miȝtfull,* for which *miȝtifull* would be more plausible as authorial) that he retained *-e* in *-fulle.* The lack of positive evidence is evidence itself, though inferential, because positive evidence occurs in other poems. A plausible explanation, then, for what Peirce calls "strange facts" is that the poet of *The Wars of Alexander* constructed a grammar which in most of its details replicated the grammars of the earlier generation. On at least one small point, however, the poet as language learner missed a category that retained final *-e.* But this category was vulnerable in any event, because (as presented by Mossé) it was one of several additions to a generalization.

Duggan's method of manuscript comparison leads him to the conclusion that "scribal variation of an established formula" through scribal substitution of *miȝtifull* "is more probable . . . than that the poet was responsible for the variation" (p. 132). Yet he and Turville-Petre, as editors of the *Wars,* settle on *miȝtifull*—which is indeed, for reasons given above, the most plausible reading.[27] The fact that the editors' choice contradicts the method as explicitly laid out by Duggan underscores the inadequacy of the method and the metrical theory upon which it is based.

Our phonological rules as stated in Chapter Three do not presume to be a full grammar. Nor do they presume to be the same in every detail for every poet.[28] As the less systematic details are accounted for, the number of exceptions in the distribution of half-lines will be reduced, though perhaps never completely. The *Gawain*-poet may have written unmetrical verses just as Eliot did. On the verification of hypotheses, Peirce moved the discussion in the right direction:

> Positivism . . . is distinguished from other doctrines by the manner in which it regards hypotheses. . . . namely, "that no hypothesis is admissible which is not capable of verification by direct observation." The positivist regards an hypothesis, not as an inference, but as a device for stimulating and directing observation. But I have shown above that certain premises will render an hypothesis probable, so that there is such a thing as legitimate hypothetic inference. It may be replied that such conclusions are not hypotheses, but inductions. . . . The arguments which I term hypothetic are certainly not inductions, for induction is reasoning from particulars to generals, and this does not take place in these cases (2.511 n 1).

Duggan's criticism of the theory that I have proposed misses the point on two counts; he writes that "the evidence in support of the traditional view, compiled in dissertations and articles over a century and a half from a great variety of different sources, is voluminous and not to be overturned easily by a single set of largely inferential data." [29] First, it is a misreading of the studies of the past century and a half to think that they deny the possibility of a conservative linguistic register sustaining final -e in a conservative linguistic tradition. There is mainly a lack of evidence on this point. Lacking evidence, many philologists have expressed agnosticism; others have decided against reading a final -e until such evidence can be provided. The present study provides inferential evidence. But here is the other point that Duggan's criticism misses in his dismissive use of "inferential." The construction of a grammar is, by its very nature, inferential, as Henning Andersen reminds us in the passages quoted above.

How, then, is one theory to be chosen over another? We can make the question quite concrete by considering how the meter of *The Destruction of Troy* is treated in the theory of the present chapter in contrast with its treatment in standard accounts. *The Destruction of Troy* was not included in the tabulation of patterns from the set of seven poems in section 4.5. The usual view is that the meter of this poem is more regular than that of any other poem of the Alliterative Revival. Thorlac Turville-Petre says of the poet: "He was a writer who knew the standard patterns of alliterative verse, and for fourteen thousand lines he applied them rigidly and without much variation to his faithful translation." [30] But the point is precisely that the poet did not know the standard patterns of alliterative verse, or chose not to write in them. He wrote by a different set of rules—rules that allow the repetition of short b-verse patterns in the a-verse. By these rules the patterns for the two halves of the line are not in mutually exclusive sets. Thus, within the space of ten lines, the following seven first half-lines are of the b-verse type, or the b-verse type without the final syllable: [31]

$$\overset{x}{W}\overset{\prime}{a}s \overset{x}{pa}st \overset{x}{to} \overset{x}{the} \overset{\prime}{po}int \quad (12464a)$$

$$\overset{\prime}{H}\overset{x}{e}r\overset{x}{u}est, \overset{x}{with} \overset{x}{the} \overset{\prime}{he}\overset{x}{ite} \quad (12465a)$$

$$\overset{x}{W}\overset{\prime}{a}s \overset{x}{co}m\overset{x}{y}n \overset{x}{in}to \overset{x}{co}\overset{\prime}{l}de \quad (12466a)$$

$$\overset{x}{A}nd \overset{\prime}{br}i\overset{x}{d}des \overset{x}{a}b\overset{\prime}{a}t\overset{x}{i}d \quad (12468a)$$

The wÿnde óf thé wést (12469a)

With mÿstes fúll mérke (12472a)

fflódes wére félle (12473a)

This repetition of b-verse patterns in both halves of the line contributes significantly to the "eventually soporific" quality that Turville-Petre notes. Yet there is nothing in the metrical theories of either Turville-Petre or Duggan to disallow this patterning in the meter of *Sir Gawain and the Green Knight*. The generality of their descriptions characterizes the two poems as following the same set of metrical rules. The present theory claims that the difference between the meter of *The Destruction of Troy* and that of *Sir Gawain and the Green Knight* should be characterized by rules that establish a norm, rather than by vague reference to a difference in "metrical style."

By setting up explicit rules and a norm, it is instantly possible to identify exceptions. It is important to remember, however, that the present theory is not peculiar in having exceptions to the norm. The question of how to accommodate the so-called "extended verses" to a four-stress norm has been, as we have seen, one of the central problems in Middle English metrics. Marie Borroff has a chapter entitled, "The Alliterative Long Line: The Normal Form," followed by a chapter entitled, "The Alliterative Long Line: The Extended Form." By this traditional view, *The Destruction of Troy* is in a very regular meter, and many patterns of other poems (such as the eight described in the two tables in sections 4.3 and 4.5) diverge from the "normal form." The present theory builds this supposed divergence into the metrical paradigm itself: the first half-line should be different from the second half-line by having either three stresses or two strong dips. The 7 percent of divergencies from the norm that I presently calculate for my own theory are fewer than Oakden calculates—and far fewer than one must calculate after making the corrections that I have argued for his treatment of the data.

Obviously a choice between two theories cannot be made simply on the basis of fewest exceptions. To the extent that a metrical theory draws on principles of general prosody, it is possible to use it to show relationships among otherwise diverse and isolated phenomena. Thus far, the present study has tried to give some coherence to the notion of "strong-stress meter" in Old and Middle English. Chapter Five will extend the application of principles that have been discussed to a consideration of "foot meter" and "alternating meter." If English is a "stress-timed" language that employs these various modes of versification, an adequate theory should be able to relate them in a systematic way.

# 5. The Modes of English Meter

## 5.1 The Central Rift in English Prosody

In a landmark essay that clarified and crystallized some of the most important issues of metrics, W. K. Wimsatt, Jr. and Monroe C. Beardsley provided a historical rationale for the major English meters from the seventh century to the present.[1] The logic and symmetry of their explanation (which, as they pointed out, had been stated by others) no less than the force of their writing gave an imposing authority to the idea that there have been two central traditions: "the two main alternative principles of English meter . . . are actually two kinds of stress—strong stress (the Old English, the *Piers Plowman* tradition) and syllable stress (the Chaucer-Tennyson tradition)" (p. 588). The idea is one that gains strength from repetition throughout the essay until it seems almost self-evident to anyone who has read English poetry and reflected on it:

The important principle of stress or accent in English verse is, however, a rather ambiguous thing, for there are in fact two main kinds of stress meter in English: the very old (and recently revived) meter of strong stress with indeterminate or relatively indeterminate number of syllables between the stresses, and the other meter, of the great English art tradition (Chaucer to Tennyson), which is a syllable-stress meter, that is, a meter of counted syllables and of both major and minor stresses. (pp. 591–92)

The "recently revived" parenthesis refers to nineteenth and twentieth-century poets, especially Eliot, whose form in *Four Quartets* is something different from the syllable-stress meter that began with Chaucer. It should be clear from the previous chapters in this book that I do not find the analogy with Eliot relevant to the pre-Conquest verse-form. However, a comparison of Eliot's line, or Whitman's line, and the line of the fourteenth-century alliterative poets is another matter. That comparison will help us see certain similarities between the Middle English tradition and the Modern tradition, and certain important differences between the Middle English and the Old English. In the process we shall gain insights into all three.

Wimsatt and Beardsley's point of departure for their discussion of the two traditions of metrical stress is their denial of another commonly perceived opposition in English meter, that between "timers" and "stressers." Citing Karl Shapiro's remark that this rift reaches back to Sidney Lanier, Wimsatt and Beardsley argue that the temporal alternative is a spurious one. All elements of timing, by their view, concern the idiosyncrasies of performance, not the linguistic facts of the enduring poem, the meter of which, in any English tradition, can be stated only in terms of relative stress. Contrary to Wimsatt and Beardsley, recent developments in theoretical phonology will help us show that temporal elements are as much a part of predictable linguistic fact as relative stress is.[2]

## 5.2 Modern Manifestations of Strong Stress

Part of the argument of Chapter Four was that the "extended" half-line was not the problem that previous studies have found it to be. J. P. Oakden's evidence for reducing one of the three stresses in the half-line turns out to be faulty, and the distributional evidence of all the metrical types argues for a three-stress option. The full line in fourteenth-century Middle English poetry, then, usually has four stresses, but it often has five.

Eliot's *Four Quartets* illustrates clearly the smooth interplay between four and five-stress lines in Modern English. Usually the reader is not even aware of the variation (unless there is a conscious metrical reason for counting out the stresses). Helen Gardner points out that the metrical norm of much of Eliot's poetry is the four-stress line, with strong medial pause. Her comment speaks directly to the aesthetic effect of five-stress variations of a four-stress norm: "The ear accepts as perfectly natural the extension to five stresses in the third line."[3] Gardner compares the opening lines of Eliot's *Little Gidding* with the opening lines of *Piers Plowman*, and her scansion of the lines from Eliot is instructive:

Midwinter spring|is its own season

Sempiternal|though sodden towards sundown,

Suspended in time|between pole and tropic.

When the short day is brightest, | with frost and fire,

The brief sun flames the ice, | on pond and ditches,

In windless cold | that is the heart's heat,

Reflecting in a watery mirror

A glare that is blindness | in the early afternoon.

Beside this, Gardner puts her scansion of the first ten lines of *Piers Plowman*, which, except for the lack of stress on the alliterating verb *Went* in line 4 and an accent on *forwandred* that did not print, accords with my own as far as the stressed syllables are concerned:

In a somer seson   whan soft was the sonne,

I shope me in shroudes   as I a shepe were,

In habite as an heremite   vnholy of workes,

Went wyde in this world   wondres to here.

Ac on a May mornynge   on Maluerne hulles

Me byfel a ferly   of fairy me thoughte;

I was wery forwandred   and went me to reste

Vnder a brode banke   bi a bornes side,

And as I lay and lened   and loked in the wateres,

I slombred in a slepyng   it sweyved so merye.

In showing what is comparable and what is not, she writes: "The great defect of Langland's meter is its monotony. There is variety within the line, but the pace is too unvarying. Mr Eliot has freed the metre by exercising a far greater liberty within the line in the number of syllables, and by using the four-stress line as a norm to depart from and return to" (pp. 31–32).

The aesthetic judgment here bears on the descriptive statement that we have been formulating. One can acknowledge that in the ten lines quoted from *Piers Plowman* there is a prevailing, fairly unambiguous pattern of four stresses. If this pattern is perceived as monotonous, then one could say that we contribute to its monotony in scanning with four stresses the ambiguous lines that have five stresses. If the meter of *Piers Plowman* has as its norm the internal structure of strong and weak dips described in the preceding chapter, then Langland's departures from this norm make his verse anything but monotonous. The paradigm stated in Chapter Four is the point of reference, even for Langland, who conforms to it less than other poets. The lines from Eliot are useful for reminding us that the pattern imposed by four stresses is not a very forceful one. Certainly in Eliot there is a natural variation between four and five stresses, and many modern readers of Middle English alliterative poetry have found no problem in reading the extended a-verses with three stresses (and thus five stresses to the line).[4]

## 5.3 The Decasyllabic Meter of Chaucer and Gascoigne

The choice among competing metrical analyses of individual lines of poetry depends finally on the overall typology within which the analysis is set. The extent to which the typology is based on general principles of rhythm and the extent to which those principles are appropriate for the particular language determine the plausibility of the analysis. I shall argue that there are four simple elements of English meter from the beginnings to the present, plus a quantitative element only in Old English. These five elements are combined in various compound modes. All of the analyses thus far in the present study have dealt with three of the simple elements (both singly and in combination): syllabism, strong stress, and syllabic quantity. These three elements are uncontroversial as structures, although the role that Chapter One assigns to syllabism in Old English meter is unusual. The present study has described Old English meter as a compound meter based mainly on a count of syllables but modulated by strong stress and syllabic quantity.

The other two elements are foot meter and alternating meter, which in English prosody have usually been taken as competing metrical analyses of the same phenomenon, the iambic pentameter. For example, Otto Jespersen abstracts Shakespeare's meter to the continuous pattern a/b\a/b\a/b\a/b\a/b, while W. K. Wimsatt divides it into traditional feet, a/b a/b a/b a/b a/b.[5] (Both analyses accept syllabism as the other part of the compound mode, either directly by counting ten syllables to the line, or indirectly by counting two syllables to the foot and five feet to the line.) In this enduring controversy over whether the foot is a justifiable metrical abstraction of English prosody, neither side has considered the possibility that there are two quite different modes of the English iambic pentameter, one based on an alternating pattern, the other based on the foot.

The reason for hypothesizing two distinct traditions is that several metrical structures show significantly different distributions in Chaucer and Gascoigne, on the one hand, and in Sidney and Shakespeare, on the other. The two posited traditions, which at first glance appear to differ only subtly if at all, account rather straightforwardly for all these differences. The metrical structures in question are inverted first feet, stressed syllables in nonictus positions, and—most important for the present discussion—a rising pattern of stress through four consecutive syllables.

Historically, the *alternating* pattern is prior. It is Chaucer's decasyllabic meter, and also the sixteenth-century iambic pentameter of George Gascoigne, Barnabe Googe, and George Turberville. The newer mode of the iambic *foot* begins tentatively with Surrey, assuredly with Sir Philip Sidney, and it flourishes as the main meter of English poetry for the next three centuries.[6]

On a central point, the findings of the present study support those of Susanne Woods's work on English meter between Chaucer and Dryden: Chaucer's decasyllabic verse is a different meter from the iambic pentameter of Sidney, Shakespeare, and the rest of the mainstream British tradition into the twentieth century.[7] I diverge from Woods on what Chaucer's meter is exactly—except that it is not foot meter; and I identify certain mid-sixteenth century poets as writing in the same meter as Chaucer. (Fifteenth-century prosody, including that of Lydgate, remains a mystery. A plausible assumption is that Gascoigne arrived at his own alternating meter independently rather than through a continuation of a tradition from Chaucer.)

Woods's theory is a kind of compromise between the regularly alternating meter that Bernhard ten Brink describes and the four-stress "cadences" of James G. Southworth and Ian Robinson.[8] By her view, "Chaucer wrote a decasyllabic verse with four definite accents and a tendency always toward a fifth accent" (p. 45). Because of the expectation that there will be five stresses, Woods follows Wimsatt in drawing the distinction between linguistic stress and metrical accent, and thus she allows for promotion of syllables. The similarity of her system with four-stress systems is not so much in the count of stressed syllables as in the displacement of metrical ictus from the evenly alternating scheme. Woods presents two different scansions of the fifth line of the *General Prologue:*

Whan Zéphirus éek with hìs swéete bréeth

(X) Whán Zéphirus éek|with his swéete bréeth

What she does not consider is the reading that would make the verse evenly alternating:

Whan Zéphirus eek with his sweete breeth

The objection to this reading might be that it promotes two weak syllables to metrical ictus. We have the uneasy feeling that *any*thing could be made to conform to the meter, and thus the meter could not serve as a paradigm to filter out the nonmetrical. A minor manipulation of the line, however, shows that this is not true:

＊Whan eek Zephirus with his sweete breeth

If this line is unmetrical for Chaucer, as I consider it to be, then the fact that a theory of evenly alternating meter, a/b\a/b\a/b\a/b\a/b, *cannot* accommodate it is a point in favor of the theory. And the fact that theories which allow displacement of metrical ictus (such as Southworth's, Robinson's, or Woods's) *can* accommodate the line is a point against such theories. With reference to the Halle-Keyser theory, Wimsatt writes:

But to my mind it is significant that these possible minor stress maxima (i.e. secondary stress on polysyllables and stresses on minor words such as prepositions) should fall so readily, as Halle and Keyser point out, in the correct iambic positions. If we know where they *would* fall if they *did* fall, that is a linguistic given.[9]

Woods curiously groups the Halle-Keyser theory together with traditional theories as being too restrictive. However, close attention to the alter-

natives of the Halle-Keyser system will show that it allows virtually everything that Woods's theory allows and more.[10]

Much happens in English phonology between Chaucer and Gascoigne, including the loss of final *-e* and the Great Vowel Shift. In both
periods, however, a meter of evenly alternating stress is one of the limited
number of ways to organize a line of ten English syllables. It is not surprising that the discovery was made more than once. A few lines from Gascoigne establish the evenly alternating rhythm:

> Upon the stones a trampling steede we heard,
> Which came ful straight vnto our lodging doore,
> And straight therwith we heard how one enquirde,
> If such a Knight (as I describde before)
> Were lodged there: the Hoast withouten more,
> Sayd yes forsooth, and God he knowes (quod he)
> He is as sicke as any man maye bee.[11]
> (*Don Bartholmew of Bathe*, p. 510)

Because a theory of rising foot meter can describe all lines of alternating
meter (though as we shall see in the next section, the opposite is not true),
why do we not call Gascoigne's meter (and Chaucer's meter) nothing
more than rigorous, very regular iambic pentameter?

The problem is that there are "strange facts" (in C. S. Peirce's phrase)
that remained unexplained. These strange facts involve metrical patterns
that are missing or rare in alternating meter. Thus, a theory of rising foot
meter, although capable of describing all lines of alternating meter, is perhaps too weak for Chaucer. In terms of the familiar goals of grammar and
of meter—to describe all and only the acceptable patterns—a theory of
foot meter applied to alternating meter describes *all* but it does not describe *only*.

There are both theoretical and empirical aspects of the distinction between these two hypothesized meters. The theoretical aspect can be understood easily from contemplating the abstract form of the paradigms. If
Chaucer's meter is strictly of the alternating kind, then we should not find
sequences of four rising levels of stress; for example, $x \grave{x} \setminus /$. A strict alternating meter would require that the third syllable bear less metrical ictus
than the second: $a/b\setminus a/b$ . . . . There are indeed very few clear instances of
this pattern with four rising stresses in Chaucer.[12] Whether the pattern occurs in Shakespeare and other later poets will be the subject of the next

section. There we shall also ask whether a rising foot meter is capable of describing such patterns.

Both Chaucer and Gascoigne have a low proportion of inverted first feet compared with the later tradition. Inverted first feet, or initial trochees, can be accommodated naturally within a foot meter but not easily within an alternating meter that takes the contour of the full line as its paradigm.

Also, as Steven Guthrie points out, Chaucer's lines are lighter than Shakespeare's in their stress patterns. The relative lightness of Chaucer's line can be explained as follows: in an alternating meter (such as Chaucer's) it is more natural to promote stress on function words than to demote stress on nouns, adjectives, verbs, and adverbs; whereas in a foot meter (such as Shakespeare's) it is as natural to demote stress on nouns, adjectives, verbs, and adverbs in the nonictus part of the foot as to promote stress on prepositions in the ictus part. In an alternating meter, it must be remembered, stress is compared with stresses on both sides. In a string of weakly stressed syllables in a stressed-timed language, it is normal to promote syllables at evenly spaced intervals, even in nonmetered speech, and thus light sequences lend themselves naturally to even alternation. However, to stress a preposition over its following noun is not normal except in emphatic or contrastive stress. If a preposition and noun or a preposition and adjective fall in even and odd positions, where the odd position must be less heavily stressed, an awkwardness results. (See the discussion below of stress on *of* and *sweet* in "When to the sessions of sweet silent thought.") Thus alternating patterns (as opposed to foot patterns) may arise more naturally from lines that are on the average more lightly stressed. I do not intend to explore these possibilities here, but only to suggest the direction in which specific syntactic and phonological patterns might be found to correlate with a hypothesized meter. Instead, the main argument that we shall consider is the contrast of Chaucer's stress patterns with the rising (4-3-2-1) stress patterns of the Modern English iambic pentameter.

On the related questions of the number of stresses per line and the possibility of promoting and demoting syllables, my reading of Chaucer's meter is essentially that of Bernhard ten Brink and W. K. Wimsatt—a reading that has been criticized as "thumping" by metrists with a range of theoretical orientation and polemical tone, from genial wit (Alan Gaylord and Steven Guthrie) to strident sarcasm (James G. Southworth and Ian Robinson).[13] The only problem in accepting the characterization "De dum de dum de dum de dum de dum" for the base of Chaucer's meter is that the same characterization could be given for the base of Shakespeare's meter—aurally, at least. Visually, we can separate the mainstream iambic tradition with foot markers: De dum | de dum | de dum | de dum | de dum. Because of the theoretical claim that the silent foot division makes (that comparisons of stress are made only within feet, not between feet), a transformation occurs when the metrical template is brought into contact with the actual English language. The final effect is indeed aural—a fine-grained modulation of stress in foot meter that alternating meter does not achieve. Chaucer has his own artful modulations, but they do not primarily lie in the tension that results from matching the several degrees of linguistic stress to a binary meter. It is to this more complex kind of meter that we now turn.

## 5.4 The Iambic Pentameter of Modern English

Consider that the following three paradigms are arranged in order of decreasing restrictiveness:

| | |
|---|---|
| Jespersen: | a/b\a/b\a/b\a/b\a/b |
| Traditional foot: | a/b a/b a/b a/b a/b |
| Halle-Keyser: | W S W S W S W S W S |

It is often said that the foot adds superfluous structure to the paradigm. In comparison with Jespersen's alternating meter, however, it should be clear that the foot actually *reduces* structure. A meter composed of feet claims that the relative stress between the last unit of one foot and the first unit of the next foot is irrelevant in deciding the metricality of a line. A succession of English metrists—going back to Jespersen and including Derek Attridge—have proposed eliminating the binary relation that compares every two syllables in favor of comparing every successive syllable in the line.[14] Attridge characterizes feet as walls standing between syllables. However, the claim implicit in avoiding feet is that it is necessary to specify the relation between every successive syllable. If the foot meter can be described as "rising," and the meter of continuous comparisons as "alternating," then the alternating meter introduces 80 percent more structure and makes 80 percent more claims than the rising meter.

The objection to the foot based on its classical origins is a red herring, as is the often cited history of confusion by poets and metrists, who have always referred to feet in inconsistent terms. Great poets often write great poetry on the assumption that they are doing something other than what they are doing. If the poets could give an explicit account of their meter, there would be no need for those who come along afterwards and study the meter.

Consider the Halle-Keyser paradigm, which reduces structure even further than foot structure does. In a series of increasingly general options, its final claim is that a stress maximum cannot occur in a W position (where a stress maximum is defined as a fully stressed syllable that "occurs between two unstressed syllables in the same syntactic constituent within a line of verse"). Wimsatt and others have criticized the Halle-Keyser paradigm for being too permissive—specifically for allowing lines that are so light that they could not reasonably be considered iambic pentameter. These criticisms are a sufficient reason for rejecting a key part of the paradigm, the "stress maximum," and in any case they will not be our concern here. (In rejecting the "stress maximum," I should also affirm the great value of Halle and Keyser's generative prosody for clarifying the goals of meter.)

What is more interesting for general prosody is Wimsatt's criticism from the other direction, where he cites feet that are heavier than normal feet. These feet provide the key to the essence of the iambic pentameter in Modern English. As it turns out, the first two lines of Shakespeare's Sonnet 30 have been used repeatedly by metrists to make the point—so much so that one tends to think of the structure as a peculiarly marginal one, rather than the pervasive one that it is:

$$\overset{\text{x}}{\text{When to the ses}}\text{sions } \overset{\text{x\,|}}{\text{of}} \text{ sweet } \overset{\text{\textbackslash}}{\text{si}}\overset{\prime}{\text{lent}} \text{ thought}$$

$$\text{I summon up remem}\overset{\text{x}}{\text{brance }} \overset{\text{x\,|}}{\text{of}} \text{ things } \overset{\prime}{\text{past.}}{}^{[15]}$$

If we accept Wimsatt's reading that there is a "sequence of four escalating syllables, odd-even, odd-even" (p. 205), we have a clear argument for foot structure, and for a degree of restrictiveness intermediate between Jespersen's theory and Halle and Keyser's theory.

Within the generative prosody debate the example was originally Halle and Keyser's. Criticizing the "strict iambic theory," they write:

> In the first line . . . the strict iambic theory requires that the preposition *to* receive greater stress than *when*, and *of* receive greater stress than *sweet* in violation of the linguistic givens of spoken English. Moreover, it requires that in the phrase

*sweet, silent thought* the adjective *sweet* receive less stress than *silent*. But since this stress pattern is in direct violation of English, the line must be classed as deviant.[16]

They make a similar point about relative stress on *of* and *things* in the next line and conclude, "Evidently such a theory cannot be considered tenable." Wimsatt's response is worth quoting at length:

> But it is difficult to say whose theory this "strict" theory is supposed to be. And I must report (1) that in my own theory, which I have always considered mainly traditional, the preposition *of* in each line is a sufficient ictus of a foot (or a sufficiently strong syllable in an ictus position) because in each instance it is clearly stronger than the *preceding* syllable—-*sions*, -*brance*. And (2) that, contrary to their reading, the adjective *sweet* (though it receives more stress than *of*) does indeed receive less stress than the first syllable of *silent*—just as in the second line, *things* receives more stress than *of* but less than *past*. . . . In each of these lines then, we have an instance of a four-syllable stress sequence, two iambs, steadily rising, which is a characteristic tensional variant (but not a violation) in English iambic verse.

4  3   2   1     4  3   2     1       4  3   2    1

*-sions of sweet si-;  -brance of things past;  Hail! to thee, blithe spirit.*[17]

Wimsatt's description is profoundly suggestive, and his quotation of the final example from Shelley makes the point that should be emphasized—that the 4-3-2-1 pattern occurs throughout the iambic pentameter of Modern English.

Shakespeare's poetry is endlessly modulated by the pattern. Sonnet 23 alone has five lines that arguably have rising stress through four syllables:

4   3   | 2     1

Or some fierce thing replete with too much rage  (3)

4   3 | 2    1

Whose strength's abundance weakens his own heart  (4)

4 3 | 2    1

The perfect ceremony of love's rite  (6)

4  3 | 2    1

And dumb presagers of my speaking breast  (10)

4 3  | 2   1

To hear with eyes belongs to love's fine wit  (14)

And in two other lines of the same sonnet the pattern of rising stress plausibly extends through six syllables:

6  5 |  4   3 | 2    1

And in mine own love's strength seem to decay  (7)

$$\overset{6\quad5\ |\quad4\qquad3\ |\ 2\qquad1}{\text{O'ercharg'd with burden of mine own love's might}}\quad(8)$$

The words "arguably" and "plausibly" in my readings above set my interpretation apart from generative metrists who find the rules of stress to be "ironclad." While it is obvious that rules of word stress are largely fixed (except for rhythmical stress shifts that are well recognized throughout the history of English),[18] patterns of phrasal stress are much more sensitive to pressures of the context within which they are set. The standard response of linguists to this observation is to invoke more rules: to the extent that phrasal stress is sensitive to nuances of meaning, including emphatic and contrastive stress, then rules can be stated, and the rules are ironclad; there is no "violation of the linguistic givens for the sake of meter."[19]

While it is a good working strategy to assume that the syntactic and phonological aspects of language can in principle be stated fully and explicitly by rules, it is an error to exclude from consideration the interaction between the rules of literary meter and the rules of normal, unmetered discourse. The error is in the literary understanding, not the purely linguistic understanding. It is an error that derives from a failure to consider certain large, enduring questions of literary theory, including the validity of a particular interpretation and the locus of existence of the literary text. Assertions of parallels with low-level phonetic rules do not address these questions. In short, neither theoretical consideration nor empirical evidence militates against Wimsatt's view of the "tilting" power of meter. Halle and Keyser, to the contrary, conclude that "the linguistic rules of stress are every bit as ironclad as the linguistic rules of voicing, aspiration, or vowel lengthening":

Moreover, a metrical theory which allows the meter to coerce us into departing from "the linguistic rules of stress" and to tilt the linguistically given stress levels "in favor of the meter" is virtually contentless, for by recourse to such tilting in favor of the meter almost any arrangement of linguistically given stresses may be rendered metrically acceptable.[20]

The question, however, is not whether meter can completely reshape the stress patterns of unmetered language, but whether any tilting in the direction of the abstract meter is possible, and if so, where.

Sorting out the areas of interaction between the two systems is admittedly a difficult task. What follows is a sketch some of the relevant considerations with respect to a particular syntactic pattern: unstressed preposition or inflectional syllable, possessive pronoun, adjective, and noun, as in line four from Sonnet 23, quoted above:

$$\overset{4}{\text{Whose}} \overset{3\ \ \ |\ \ 2}{\text{strength's abundance weakens his}} \overset{1}{\text{own heart}}$$

This pattern and indeed all of the 4-3-2-1 patterns above are examples of what has traditionally been called "hovering accent." George R. Stewart, Jr. illustrates the phenomenon with the same syntactic pattern from Pope's *Rape of the Lock:*

$$\overset{4}{\text{On}} \overset{3\ \ \ |}{\text{her white}} \overset{2}{\text{breast a sparkling Cross she wore}} \quad (2.7)$$

Stewart uses the symbols "o" for an unstressed syllable in a position of nonictus; "O" for a stressed syllable in a position of nonictus; and "S" for a stressed syllable in a position of ictus.[21] He writes:

[I]f we consider *white* a mere conventional epithet, our reading might be:
    oS O S oSo S oS
But considering it really descriptive, we should read:
    ooS S oSo oS.    (p. 66)

The two readings, which are clearly distinct, are both plausible. In the notation that we have been using, the stress pattern of "On her white breast" could be represented as x x̀|\/ vs. x x \|/, or 4-3|2-1 vs. 4-4-2|1. The important question is not the exact degree of stress on *white,* secondary or primary, but whether *white* is perceived as bearing metrical ictus. Stewart writes: "These ambiguous cases have given rise to the term 'hovering accent,' *i.e.,* a metrical situation in which the stress seems to hover over two syllables, uncertain upon which it should alight" (p. 66).

One who is bent on preserving the "linguistic givens" might respond that ambiguity is a part of all natural language, and once the meaning is determined (whether *white* is a "conventional epithet" or "really descriptive"), the rules of phonological stress follow in their ironclad way. This, however, misses the point that the possibility of *white* as a rhythmical filler, and thus the promotion of *her,* does not even arise until the phrase is cast into metered discourse. Then the tilting effect of the meter is manifested in the very possibility of ambiguity. Unless *white* is possible filler material to separate the two metrical stresses, the stress rules applied to *on her white breast* simply give x x \/, 4-4-2-1.[22] Many of the best metrists over the years have heard this ambiguity, and yet no rules of ordinary linguistic stress (excluding emphatic or contrastive stress, by which *any* word can be promoted) provide for the promotion of *her* in this context. These facts argue for the interaction of literary meter and the normal rules of English stress.

It should be noted that subsequent to Halle and Keyser's early studies in generative metrics, rhythmical rules have become a part of mainstream phonology—indeed largely through the efforts of the work that Halle and Keyser and their students have done. Such work probably constitutes the most significant phonological scholarship during the past fifteen years. Most of the examples have involved stress shifts within words. There have been no proposals in generative prosody to promote minor category words such as *her* or *of* simply because they fall in a position of ictus in literary meter. The recognition of an interaction between the patterns of normal phonology and the patterns of the artifice of literary meter would be a phenomenologically natural extension of established rhythmical principles.

Jespersen recognized the difficulty that rising patterns of stress, especially those involving monosyllabic adjectives and nouns, posed for his alternating system of meter. His treatment of these patterns is a key to the contradictions within his system. Of the first four syllables of lines such as, "In the sweet pangs of it remember me," Jespersen writes:

> This figure is frequent in English verse, but not in other languages. I incline to read it with 1234 [where 1 is lightest and 4 heaviest, contrary to our usage above] and thus to say that the ascent is normal between the first and the second as well as between the third and the fourth syllable, so that there is only the one small anomaly of a slight ascent instead of a descent between the second and the third syllable. It is worth noting how frequently this figure contains an adjective (stressed 3) before a substantive (stressed 4).[23]

Later, with reference to an English example, Jespersen inconsistently says, "it will be extremely hard to find examples of the sequence 34 [i.e., 21 in our notation] as regularly occurring in any of the cognate languages" (p. 268).

In downplaying the pattern of rising phrasal stress, Jespersen gives prominence instead to falling stress, which occurs in all of the Germanic languages in compound words. Typically, he begins his discussion of specific patterns with lines such as "Sleek-headed men, and such as sleepe a-nights," or "Grim-visag'd warre hath smooth'd his wrinkled front," and then fits his treatment of adjective plus noun to the metrical pattern that he has established for "Sleek-headed men" and "Grim-visag'd warre." However, the compound stress pattern is much less typical than the adjective and noun pattern. The main point to make here is the reason for Jespersen's bias. In a theory that specifies falling ictus as well as rising ictus for the iambic pentameter (a/b\a/b\a/b\a/b\a/b), it is necessary for the theorist to emphasize the importance of compound stress and to slight phrasal stress, which is always there and available for the rising part of the pattern. Jespersen presents a view that seems plausible with the marginal and atypical patterns that he selects—except that the patterns are indeed marginal and atypical. I would argue that the iambic pentameter of Shakespeare specifies only rising ictus and that it accomplishes its modulations because of the fit of that meter with the rising patterns of English phrasal stress. The iambic pentameter of Chaucer, however, appears to be something different.

### 5.5 The Five Elements and Four Compound Modes of English Meter

The argument of the chapter to this point can be summarized by saying that historically the five elements of English meter have combined to produce the following mixed forms:

(1) Syllabism, strong stress, quantity: Old English.
(2) Strong stress and foot meter: Alliterative Revival.
(3) Alternating meter and syllabism: Chaucer, Gascoigne.
(4) Foot meter and syllabism: Sidney to Yeats.

The third of these compound modes may hold the key to certain central problems in traditional English prosody. Do Chaucer and Gascoigne share a meter that is similar in many respects to that of Sidney, Shakespeare, and Tennyson—but different at its base? The two fullest modern studies of early Renaissance English meter take the very line from Shakespeare that we have been pondering, "When to the sessions of sweet silent thought," as a kind of touchstone. Thompson writes, in his chapter on "Googe, Turberville, Gascoigne": "Another change in the understanding of the line had to take place, allowing both the metrical pattern and the pattern of speech to function, before lines like this were standard practice."[24] Susanne Woods makes repeated reference to the line in her opening chapter on "Terms and Approaches." The intuitions that accompany these references I certainly share. However, the pattern of the line is not as unusual as the line's popularity among metrists would suggest. It is important to make explicit the shift in paradigm that separates that line from an example Gascoigne cites, "I understanding your meanyng by your eye."

Gascoigne accompanies his example with a revealing contour: [25]

I understand your meanyng by your eye

This is visual evidence that Gascoigne thought of his meter as an alternating pattern of rises and falls. Poets, of course, can be mistaken about the paradigm they think that they use, just as speakers of language have naive understandings of their linguistic rules (to the extent that they are conscious of those rules at all). The difficulty is that out of context the line could be scanned as foot meter as well as alternating meter. What is the justification for considering Gascoigne's meter one or the other? The relevant paradigm must be established with reference to the distribution of patterns throughout a text, often by indirect means. For example, we might hypothesize that a higher frequency of "inverted first feet" would go with the second compound mode—feet and syllabism—than with alternating meter and syllabism. There would be a certain logic in the hypothesis, because foot meter allows disyllabic dips more naturally than an alternating meter does.[26] Indeed some foot meters, such as anapestic, are based on disyllabic dips. As it turns out, Gascoigne in the 1,241 iambic pentameter lines of *Don Bartholmew of Bathe* (which has passages of lines in other meters) uses only fifteen inverted first feet, by my count.

## 5.6 Strong-Stress Meter Again

Although strong-stress meter has been the main subject of the first four chapters of this book, more needs to be said to fit it into the typology and principles of general rhythm that we are developing here. The strong-stress element of Old and Middle English meter depends on the stress pattern of the language, which has been described as a "hierarchy of 'pulses' of different periodicities."[27]

The *Gawain* meter has traditionally been considered a development of the *Beowulf* meter, and both verse forms are said to belong to the "strong-stress tradition." They also obviously belong to an alliterative tradition, as the title of the present work acknowledges. Recent studies have shown the role of alliteration in the Old English metrical paradigm to be both more structural and more complex than the usual modern descriptions would have it.[28] This complexity in Old English alliteration as compared with the much less systematic alliteration in Middle English reinforces the break in the tradition after the eleventh century and casts doubt on attempts such as Oakden's to trace a continuing evolution in the patterns of alliteration.

Martin Halpern took the discussion in a promising direction in a 1962 article that was one of several responses to Wimsatt and Beardsley.[29] Halpern's classification set the iambic pentameter apart from all the other meters in English, which he collectively called "strong stress": anapestic, dactylic, trochaic, and the alliterative meters of Old and Middle English.

The essential element of the strong-stress mode is that metrical patterns are determined fairly rigidly by the stress patterns of the grammatical categories of words. In contrast with both the Old English mode and the Middle English alliterative mode, Shakespeare's iambic pentameter is the result of two patterns that work sometimes together, sometimes in opposition: the abstract metrical pattern and the pattern of linguistic stress. This characterization of Shakespeare's meter is familiar from its statement in terms similar to these over the years by metrists of widely different persuasions.

To say that the metrical patterns of the strong-stress mode are determined by linguistic stress patterns is to say that a metrical classification of the parts of speech is one of the first and most important statements to make about the meter. Every serious account of Old English meter includes a version of the Hierarchy of Stress given in section 1.4.[30] The hypothesis of a metrical pattern determined by grammatical categories may be compared with the hypothesis of a metrical pattern determined by four stresses invariably. If both patterns appear to exist, the question is which has priority. Thus, when Thorlac Turville-Petre writes, "a metrical pattern once established is not easily broken,"[31] the accurate observation does not dispense with possible five-stress lines. If the line has five possible stresses because of a metrical pattern determined by metrical categories (for example, metrical stress on nouns and adjectives), that pattern may be no more easily broken than the one that Turville-Petre has in mind (four stresses to the line). The question is an empirical one.

In brief, my argument is that Middle English alliterative meter shares with Old English meter a fairly strict determination of stress through grammatical categories—in contrast with Chaucer's meter, and with Shakespeare's still different meter. Middle English alliterative meter departs from Old English meter in its regulation of unstressed syllables so that there is a regular contrast within each b-verse between strong and non-strong dips.

Neither Chaucer's alternating meter nor Shakespeare's rising meter is tied to grammatical stress as closely as Old English meter is: in both kinds of "iambic pentameter," nouns and adjectives are often metrically unstressed; prepositions, conjunctions, and other minor category words are often metrically stressed.

Now that we have a theory of Middle English alliterative verse, we can use it to help make clear what Chaucer's meter is and is not. In the West Midlands alliterative tradition, the marking of a syllable as stressed or unstressed is categorial: nouns, adjectives, infinitives, and participles always receive stress; articles, prepositions, conjunctions, auxiliary verbs, linking verbs, the verb *have*, pronominal adjectives, and pronouns generally do not receive stress. The familiar binary division into "major category words" or "real" words (Selkirk's designation) and "function words" is a useful first approximation. Finite verbs and adverbs are major category words and usually receive stress, although, as in Old English, these parts of speech are not fully determined, and thus they introduce variation into the system.

The variation is negligible, however, compared with that in the iambic pentameter—both Chaucer's and Shakespeare's—where nouns and adjectives are often in metrically unstressed positions (forming heavy feet, or spondees), and conjunctions and prepositions are often in stressed positions (forming light feet, or pyrrhics). It is a crucial feature of iambic pentameter meter that normal patterns of stress are regularly tilted in one direction or another to conform with the abstract pattern. Without this tilting the verse would either be doggerel (because only regularly alternating syllables would occur) or would have no discernable pattern (because, in good poetry, the many gradations of linguistic stress would not have reference to a binary metrical system). Thus, it seems that linguistic categories are not mapped directly onto the metrical line, as in Middle English alliterative poetry, but are mediated by a binary relation of rising ictus, which compares successive syllables. The relation itself then becomes the pattern of modulated language that the meter accommodates.

# 6. Theoretical Implications

## 6.1 The English Alliterative Tradition

In varying degrees of completeness and detail, this book has presented theories and parts of theories of half a dozen different English metrical traditions: the meter of Old English poetry, of Lawman's *Brut,* of the Alliterative Revival, of Chaucer, of Gascoigne, and of the iambic pentameter from Sidney to the twentieth century; and Chapter Two has presented analyses of Old and Middle English rhythmical prose. Despite these descriptions of various stages in English metrical history, there is an important sense in which this whole study is not historical. It is not historical in the *diachronic* sense—in the dynamic sense of describing the principles of change. It is instead a series of synchronic analyses, arranged chronologically. As with the arrow in Zeno's Paradox the individual moments do not show us the language in motion, nor would a finer calibration of the moments. A different set of principles would be needed, more akin to those of dialectology. These would be principles such as were available to Oakden when he wrote *The Dialectal Survey,* or that are available to us now with the *Linguistic Atlas* by Angus McIntosh, M. L. Samuels, and Michael Benskin.[1]

Dialectology, like metrics, is an exercise in abstraction. The categories that one selects in asking questions determine the kind of answers one gets. It should now be clear that the three content words in the title of this book are all problematic. The word "alliterative" refers to a superficial feature, but one that selects the texts of the present study perhaps more efficiently than any other word. "Strong stress" would categorize most of what "alliterative" does (along with much else besides), but it would be even more misleading, for we have seen that certain parts of the verse in both Old English and Middle English specifically avoid the strong-stress rhythm. The present study, then, although it has had little to say about alliteration, has used "alliterative" as a useful classifying rubric.[2]

If alliteration is superficial, and much about meter can be described without discussing it, in what sense may it be said to define a "tradition"? What indeed is a "tradition"? Here we come to the heart of a recurring theme in the present work and in related studies. A tradition, though perceived as a single entity by those who join or define it, is upon closer examination a set of discontinuous parts, sequenced only by time. The tradition must be created anew, recapitulated, and sustained within each individual poet—perhaps with changes (intentional or otherwise). Hence the possibility of misreading and of evolution.

If this way of putting it sounds slightly mystical, we should remember that it is a standard way of describing language change. Thus the word "English" of our title raises questions such as: "In what sense is the language of *Beowulf* the same language that we speak now?" "In what sense is the language of Lawman the same as the language of Langland?" The abstractions of modern linguistics have proved useful on these matters in turning the focus of attention from comparing outputs of grammars to comparing the internalized grammars themselves.[3]

## 6.2 Meter in Modern Theory and in the Poet's Mind

Whatever mental representation the fourteenth-century alliterative poet had of his meter, we can be certain that it was not exactly the representation given anywhere in this book. This certainty is the kind that we have also of Old English meter: it is highly probable that no Anglo-Saxon poet ever referred to his five types as A, B, C, D, and E, or talked about subtype B48 or 1A*1a. Even for the living tradition of the iambic pentameter, every metrist probably has a different mental representation of a form that seems fairly simple. Not only the metrists but the poets as well, to the extent that they comment on their metrical practice, have sets of terms, symbols, and images that do not exactly match up with each other. Compare comments on the iambic pentameter by Sir Philip Sidney, Sidney Lanier, and John Hollander. It is unlikely in the extreme that any fourteenth-century poet thought of his meter in terms that included plus and minus $\alpha$, as in the paradigm presented in Chapter Four. The question of the identity of mental representation between poet and metrist, or poet and reader generally, connects at certain points with some of the main controversial themes of literary criticism—especially those involving authorial intention and reader response.[4]

A key assumption of the preceding chapters is that metrics is not about orthography and written texts apprehended by the eye but about mental structures. Another assumption is that neither the rhythms of the English language nor the structure of the human mind has changed enough in ten centuries or in six centuries to make patterns that were perceptible then inaccessible to us now.

The present study has focused on principles of general prosody that are necessary to rationalize the elements of norm and variation that are parts of both dialectology and meter. The effects of rhythmical structures take place in brains, and a good working hypothesis is that brains have not changed since the seventh century, or the fourteenth. Various developments in grammatical theory, including Chomsky's distinction between competence and performance, have now made familiar the idea that linguistics is about conceptual structures, not, as the American structuralists had it, "about noise and deposits of ink and graphite."[5] In historical linguistics, however, we must start with deposits of ink on vellum, and we have as yet no coherent methodology for proceeding from that evidence to a reconstruction of conceptual structures of the past. Elsewhere I have tried to show that there has been a natural oscillation between the literal study of the written record and the positing of abstract structures. This oscillation in philology can be traced from the *Buchstabenlehre* of Jacob Grimm, to the more abstract patterns of the structuralists, to a return to the literal written records in the work of current investigators (Angus McIntosh, Bruce Mitchell, the editors of the Toronto Dictionary of Old English, and others).[6] The study of Middle English meter has not enjoyed such an oscillation because the alliterative long line has never had a viable abstract description.

## 6.3 Meter, Performance, and Pause in Iambic Pentameter

It is hard to overemphasize the distinction between the written line and the spoken line, and yet because the distinction is so obvious and so familiar, it is also hard to appreciate its implications, even when agreeing on its importance. To get some distance on our own assumptions, we can ask questions such as, "What form of writing?" and "Whose way of speaking?"

To the second question Seymour Chatman once provided an answer in the form of tape recordings of eight readings of a short poem by Robert Frost, one of the readers being Frost himself.[7] Chatman's analysis provided W. K. Wimsatt, Jr. and Monroe C. Beardsley an occasion to draw a clear

and compelling distinction between the vagaries of individual performances and the permanence of the enduring text.[8] The meter, they argued,
was one of the permanent elements that endured.

Furthermore, Chatman's inclusion of phonetic transcription provided
Wimsatt and Beardsley the opportunity to distinguish between a detailed,
technical notation for a particular performance and the written line itself. Thus, they also addressed, in passing, the first question posed above,
"What form of writing?" The implicit answer was, "The printed text of
modern editions." Wimsatt and Beardsley did not discuss these implications as fully as the distinction between the performed line and the enduring line. To draw out the implications, one might ask, "Is it the same text
in Elizabethan spelling and in modern spelling?" and "Is it the same text in
Anglo-Saxon manuscripts, in which the poetry is not divided into lines but
written continuously, and in Klaeber's edition, in which not only lines but
half-lines are separated?"

The New Critical iconic view of the literary text has, of course, been
challenged from various directions during the past two decades. These include essays in reader-response criticism, such as those by Stanley Fish,
and essays in bibliography and the transmission of texts, such as those by
Jerome J. McGann. There are, however, specifically metrical problems that
crystallize some of these issues in a more precise and technical way than do
the broader issues in literary interpretation. Some of these problems pre-
date not only poststructuralism but New Criticism itself.

There is a traditional way of reading certain kinds of patterns in the
iambic pentameter that is clearly articulated in studies by Egerton Smith in
1923 and by George R. Stewart, Jr. in 1930, as well as by many other
metrists before and since.[9] These patterns involve a structural or metrical
pause that New Critics, including Wimsatt and Beardsley, generally failed
to distinguish from extrametrical or rhetorical pauses. The critics who hear
these pauses are most often among the group known as "timers." The
pauses occur clearly in lines where an unstressed syllable is missing and the
total number of syllables in the line is fewer than ten, as in the following
examples from Stewart: [10]

$$\overset{\prime}{\text{Stay!}}\ \overset{(x)}{\text{speak,}}\ \overset{\prime}{\text{speak!}}\ \overset{(x)}{\text{I}}\ \overset{\prime}{\text{charge}}\ \overset{x}{\text{thee,}}\ \overset{\prime}{\text{speak!}}\ (Hamlet,\ 1.1.51)$$

By extension the pauses can also be perceived in lines with the full comple-
ment of ten syllables but with an unstressed syllable missing in one part of
the line (compensated for by two syllables in another part):

x    x    /    (x)  /    x  /    x  /  x    /
And the pressed watch returned a silver sound
(*Rape of the Lock* 1.18)

Here the missing unstressed syllable between *pressed* and *watch* has already been supplied by an extra unstressed syllable at the beginning of the line. Finally, for temporal metrists who see the metrical unit as a *rising* foot, as well as for some phoneticians such as David Abercrombie, an initial pause that replaces a missing syllable is just as real as a medial pause; for example, structures with the "inverted first foot" can be read as an iambic foot plus an anapestic foot.[11]

Whether or not these readings are "correct," and in what sense "correct," are questions well beyond the scope of the present chapter.[12] In an often-quoted statement, Karl Shapiro observed that the division between timers and stressers has split the study of English prosody throughout its history.[13] Within the debate, no issue is more central than this apparently small and technical matter of a temporal pulse, or "metrical pause," which occurs somewhere other than on a syllable. We can see that the matter is also bound up with the status of the written line and the spoken line.

The standard orthographies of the European languages, unlike the standard system of European musical notation, include no precise markings for the various kinds of pause. The comma is hopelessly ambiguous compared with the eighth rest (ɤ) or the hold (ᴖ). Thus, it is natural when we refer to the "enduring line" to think only of the *words* of the line (in whatever spelling), and to relegate all temporal elements to the vague, elusive, and constantly shifting world of performance. However, it may be that our collective disposition to think in this way is a result of the particular history of the writing system, which diverges in this and in other crucial points from the history of music writing in the West.

The purpose here is not to justify these metrical pauses but to point out that sensitive metrists in one of the two main traditions of English prosody have always heard them; and other, equally sensitive metrists in the other main tradition have always denied that they exist as a systematic manifestation of the meter. This conflict raises several relevant questions. One question has to do with the locus of existence of the literary text. If, for the sake of argument, we assume that metrical pauses are correct, then it is obvious that the black marks on paper are not the text. These are only more or less adequate signs that point toward the text, which must be realized in time, and in a human brain. However, further contemplation reminds us that this state of affairs is true not just of the specific structure of metrical pause but also of many other kinds of structure, which are always indicated by a system of orthography and diacritics that is never completely adequate. In Chapter Three we saw reasons for pronouncing final -*e* in many places where the scribe had not written an -*e*. Thus, the apparently difficult questions of where the line exists and what endures are not so difficult after all. There is no enduring line *in toto*. Various elements of the line are perceived by large communities of readers, and there is always much overlap among the various readers, although always, inevitably, there is some degree of divergence. On a matter such as the metrical pause, readers as metrically acute as George R. Stewart, Jr. and W. K. Wimsatt, Jr. perceive different structures within the line. It may be said that they perceive different lines. Thus, we are brought directly to the large issues of interpretation addressed in reader-response criticism.

## 6.4  Pause and Ictus in Old English Meter

Just as in the iambic pentameter of Modern English the same sequence of written letters can point to different metrical lines (the line not being identical with its written indication), so in Old English poetry, perhaps even more so, the written form is ambiguous. One of the most familiar disjunctions between the written form and the hypothesized actual line is in John C. Pope's temporal theory of the Old English verse form.[14] In types B and C, Pope's theory makes systematic use of a rest (filled by a stroke of the harp). It is important to understand that Pope's theory is a description of the structure of the meter and of the line itself—not a score for performing an already existing line. Pope presents arguments, which may or may not convince, to the effect that the pauses are an integral part of the measured line, without which the line would be incomplete. Thus, he works within part of the general temporal tradition that includes Stewart and Smith, and which in America extends back to Sidney Lanier. Whatever the merits of Pope's particular theory, it cannot be relegated to the world of performance, as S. J. Keyser suggests that it should be.[15] The visual representation of the line causes Keyser to miss the structural status of the pauses in Pope's theory, just as it misled Wimsatt and Beardsley in their critique of Stewart's theory.

I would argue that the nature of metrical pause in Old English has not been adequately understood because the nature of metrical ictus in Old English has not been adequately understood. Ictus is usually one of those concepts that are easier to identify and illustrate than to define. (We generally know which syllables in the iambic pentameter receive metrical ictus, but it is hard to specify the exact phonetic correlates of ictus. Loudness? Pitch? The placement of the syllable where ictus is expected?) In Old English, however, aside from the difficulties of definition, there is the problem that we do not necessarily recognize ictus when we hear it (even if we hear it as the Anglo-Saxon audience did). This is because there are two different systems of stress that interact—categorial stress and rhythmic stress. Categorial stress has three clear levels, which we can call primary stress, secondary stress, and tertiary stress. Tertiary stress has been revealingly analyzed in current work by R. D. Fulk, who describes the structure in terms of syllabic quantity.[16] It appears that the distinctions between secondary stress and tertiary stress are less firm (or at least less understood at present) than the distinctions between primary stress and secondary stress. This whole area is an important one for future inquiry.

Indeed, the rest of this concluding chapter is mainly concerned with unsolved problems, and the analyses are tentative. Let us begin with rhythmic stress. Chapter One briefly noted the possibility of a metrical pause between the clashing stresses of some (but not all) type D verses; for example:

$$\overset{\prime \quad (x) \quad \prime \quad \backslash \quad x}{\text{wearp wælfyre}} \ (2582a)$$

Positing a beat between the clashing stresses of type D might appear to diverge radically from Pope's temporal theory, which posits a half note without a rest or pause:

$$| \ \overset{\prime\prime (\backslash)}{\text{♩}} \ | \ \overset{\prime\prime \quad \backslash\backslash}{\text{♩ ♪♪}} |$$
$$\text{wearp wælfyre} \ (2582a)$$

Yet the differences between the two readings are actually superficial. Both accord with recent findings in metrical phonology, as well as with older studies such as those by Dwight Bolinger, in which a beat, vocalized or not, separates clashing stresses. It is important to note that although there may seem to be two pairs of clashing stresses in this verse, between the first and second syllables and between the second and third, the second pair (in the stressed elements of the compound word) do not "clash" in the same way as the first, and do not have a temporal beat. This means that what we often think of as clashing stresses in types C and E do not, in the great majority of instances, actually clash. The normal structure is a compound word without a temporal beat. (This matter was discussed in Chapter One.) Now we can define rhythmic stress:

Rhythmic Stress: Occurs on any position that is heavier than the preceding position, either categorially or by promotion.

The most obvious position that bears rhythmic stress, then, is one that follows a dip. With the example of the iambic pentameter before us, where we saw silent beats separating clashing stresses and counting as metrical positions, we have a clue for the redefinition of "dip":

Dip: (i) a single metrically unstressed syllable; or (ii) more than one metrically unstressed syllable (a "strong" dip); or (iii) a silent beat.

This definition of *dip* removes the anomaly of excluding primary metrical stress from the beginning of the verse. Verse-initial primary metrical stress can be seen to rise from the dip of the preceding verse if the verse ends on a dip—or from the beat separating clashing stresses if the verse ends on a stress. Further refinement of these definitions might simply specify a verse boundary as a dip from which primary metrical stress can rise, but it is important not to obscure the way in which this context is not arbitrary. A similar analysis occurs in some traditional treatments of the "inverted first foot" in the English iambic pentameter.

When we turn to categorial stress, we find ourselves on more traditional ground. Setting verbs and adverbs aside for the moment, we can define the levels of categorial stress simply by grammatical category:

Primary Stress: The stressed syllable in nouns, adjectives, infinitives, and past participles.

Secondary stress: The subordinated second element of a lexical compound that immediately follows the stressed syllable (or resolved equivalent) of the first element.

Tertiary stress: Medial derivational syllables and the medial inflectional syllable of the present and past participle and the inflected infinitive (for example, *-ing-*, *-lic-*, *-end-*, *-en-*).

All of the structures that we have defined can be illustrated by verses from *Beowulf*. Thus, the marked syllables in the following verses bear secondary categorial stress:

gromheort gŭma  (1682a)

in gēardagum  (1b)

þanchycgende  (2235a)

sincfāge sel  (167a)

However, *-rinc* in 1307a does not bear secondary categorial stress by the definition, because it does not immediately follow the stressed syllable of the first element:

hār hilderinc  (1307a)

The relevant fact here is that *-rinc* rises out of a dip, and thus it bears rhythmic stress.

The following verses are usually considered to contain secondary stress on the third syllable. Following Bliss, we read these derivational and inflectional syllables with tertiary metrical stress:

ymbsittendra  (9b)

lindhæbbende  (245a)

eallirenne  (2338a)

Fulk goes a step further in an analysis that has rich implications for the whole system by replacing tertiary stress with syllabic length.

Using the distinctions that we have drawn between the systems of categorial and rhythmic stress in Old English, we can reformulate the requirements for resolution:

*A Condition for Resolution*
Resolution can occur only on a syllable bearing rhythmic stress.

The following verses fit various contexts for resolution:

   ´◡x  x     ⟋   x   A
monegum mægþum  (5a)

  x̱  x  x x  ´  x  ´◡x   B
næfre hē on aldordagum  (718a)

  ´  (x) ´◡x   \  x  D1
heall heorudrēore  (487a)

  ´    ´    x  ´◡x   D4
wōm wundorbebodum  (1747a)

  ´   \  x  ´◡x  E
Folcwaldan sunu  (1089b)

*Monegum* rises out of the inevitable dip (including the dip as silent beat) at the verse boundary. *Dagum,* although not bearing the main stress of the compound, does bear rhythmic stress, as does *-bodum. Heor-* follows the pause that separates it from the stress clash with *heall.* And the noun *sunu* simply rises out of a dip.

Verses of the type A pattern *frēowine folca* (430a) have traditionally been scanned with resolution of secondary stress:

  ´   \◡x ´  x
frēowine folca

Otherwise, the verse would seem to have five positions: / \ x / x. This use of resolution is odd. Resolution is ordinarily a means of giving more overall prominence to a short syllable bearing rhythmic stress. When the idea is applied to secondary stress in type A, however, the result is just the opposite. We inconsistently scan *frēowine folca* with resolution on *-wine* not to enhance that stress but to squeeze it into the position occupied by a single syllable, often an inflectional syllable. By the view argued here, the pattern / \x̆ / x (in which the second syllable has secondary stress and is short, and the third syllable is historically short) is simply type A with a disyllabic first dip that is heavier than usual but not so heavy as to break into two positions.

For any given type D verse, it is necessary to determine whether the first two syllables have the pattern with the silent beat and rhythmic stress, or the pattern in which the second syllable is subordinated. (The basis for these two essentially different readings was explored in Chapter One.) My 1974 theory simply subordinated the second syllable of all type D verses and noted in passing the possibility of a temporal beat. Now it appears that this reading is oversimplified and that the three basic categories of type D (aside from D4) need to be sorted out. The distribution of resolution and also of the "expanded," or D\*, type offers clues to the sorting. In turn, the sorting promises to rationalize the peculiarities of resolution and of the expanded D\* pattern (the only five-position pattern in Old English meter).

The three categories into which type D verses must be divided can be schematized as follows:

/ (x) / \ x
/ \ x̀ x
/ \ x x

The first pattern has a temporal beat, as in *heall (x) heorudrēore* above, or a temporal beat filled by an unstressed syllable, as in *sīde sǣnæssas* (223a). The second pattern is the continuously falling pattern without a temporal beat, which can be shown with a downstepping contour:

lindhæbbende  (245a)

The third pattern is of the type *fēond treddode* (725b).

Because resolution depends upon structural pauses in certain contexts, it would be good if those pauses could be systematically located through their alignment with other patterns. As it turns out, the great majority of compounds in type D verses that require resolution on the first element also contain a secondary stress (not a tertiary stress) on the immediately following second element. Some of these compounds are in regular type D patterns, and somewhat more are in D\* patterns:

heáll heórudréore  (487a)

swýlcra séaroníða  (582a)

Indeed nearly all D* patterns have a secondary metrical stress on the second element of the compound. They tend not to have derivative and inflectional syllables in that position. What this suggests is that consecutive heavy stresses "back up" from the end of the verse, so that at the beginning of the verse the normal way of alleviating the clash is with the insertion of a pause. Otherwise, the first syllable would have to subordinate the second syllable, which has already subordinated the third. If a pause occurs of necessity in these heavy verses, then, as Max Kaluza noted in 1909, little is changed rhythmically by filling the pause with an unstressed syllable.[17] A syllable can fill the pause created by stress clash in type D:

róndas régnhéarde  (326a)

Thus, the main anomaly in Sievers' Five Types, the *fünfgliedrig* D* type—expanded D with five positions—follows naturally from the asymmetrical patterning of temporal elements in the Old English verse. Type D with secondary stress has the only context in Old English meter for a metrical pause, and type D* has the only context for a fifth position. Types C and E do not have a metrical pause, even though they are sometimes said to have clashing stress. This is because the typical structure that is thought of as clashing stress in types C and E is simply compound stress. (Type C verses that have stresses in separate words also follow the compound stress pattern.) In type D, compound stress is the *prerequisite* for a preceding clashing stress and for the metrical pause that separates the stresses of the first two positions. The whole compound word abuts another word to the left.

The condition that resolution can occur only on a syllable bearing rhythmic stress produces a dozen or so possible exceptions in types C, D, and E in *Beowulf*.[18] Some of these verses are problematic in other systems as well. Pope notes that 1946a, *þæt hío léodbealewa*, might be read as *-bealwa*, and that 2921b, *milts ungyfeðe*, might be read as type A. Bliss reads *fyrdsearu fúslicu* (232a) as a type A, against Pope's reading of it as a type D*. Verse 1187a, *umborwesendum ǽr* is an exception to Kaluza's Law, and the two verses with *-eges-* may involve syncope: *glédegesa grim* (2650a),

*līgegesan wæg* (2780b). The purpose here is not to explain away the twelve
to fifteen verses in *Beowulf* that might possibly be read with resolution of
secondary categorial stress, but to point out that at most they amount to
very few verses compared with the approximately 1,400 verses that contain resolution of rhythmic stress. This difference in numbers indicates that
two quite different processes are lumped together as "resolution."

A more serious objection to disallowing resolution of secondary
stress is the distribution of quantities in the patterns /\x̆/x and //\x̄,
which A. J. Bliss noticed and which R. D. Fulk has examined in relation to
Kaluza's Law (see section 1.4 above). In the present discussion of theoretical implications, Bliss's work in general is interesting to contemplate because it is so determinedly *un*theoretical. The dozens of valuable insights
that Bliss presents are never linked to underlying principles, and the main
generalization that results is a list of 130 occurring patterns, to which
other patterns could easily be added. With no principle of exclusion, Bliss's
interpretation of his data often seems arbitrary. A slight shift of perspective
can lead to a quite different conclusion. For example, Bliss's discussion of
resolution begins with two lists of verses from *Beowulf*. In the first list,
containing 62 verses on the pattern of *frēowine folca* (430a), the third syllable of the verse is a historically short vowel; in the second list, containing
37 verses on the patterns of *lēof landfruma* (31a) and *bāt bānlocan* (742a),
the last syllable is either a historically long vowel or it ends in a consonant.
Bliss's line of reasoning to explain this distribution depends upon positing,
for the first list, resolution of the short syllable bearing secondary stress
and its following short vowel; and, for the second list, suspension of resolution of the short syllable bearing secondary stress and the following
"long" syllable. Thus, despite the inconsistency of the traditional *frēowine*
scansion discussed above, the possibility of resolution of secondary stress
seems at first sight to be necessary.

Although taking note of the remarkable fact of distribution of quantities, Bliss does not comment upon another remarkable fact: all but two
of the 99 verses in the two lists occur in the a-verse. These verses do show a
late reflex of Kaluza's Law, but they also show a difference in meter between the a-verse and the b-verse. This difference involves secondary and
tertiary stress, a difference that Bliss himself discussed in the preceding
chapter. However, Bliss's terse presentation seems to have obscured the
most interesting generalizations for subsequent readers and indeed for
Bliss himself. The difference between secondary and tertiary stress is part

of the explanation, but only as this difference causes the more tangible difference between verses of the D* type (with the extra beat) and nearly all other verses, including most type D's. The difference is so basic that Sievers has two main categories: *viergliedrige Verse* and *fünfgliedrige Verse*. The D* verses are restricted to the a-verse (with only a few dubious exceptions).

If the a-verse is distinct in having the expanded D* type, the b-verse is distinct in having almost no type D verses with secondary stress. These two facts are related. There are only two verses with secondary stress (by Bliss's criteria that distinguish secondary and tertiary stress) among the approximately 390 type D b-verses of *Beowulf,* 164b and 495b.[19] This indeed is a remarkable fact, since it means that only two b-verses in all of *Beowulf* fit the familiar, basic pattern for D: //\x. If, as argued above, a secondary stress (by a slightly different definition from that of Bliss) is needed for the metrical pause in D*, then we have a correlation between the lack of secondary stress in the b-verse and the restriction of D* to the a-verse.

Finally, the difference between the meter of the a-verse and the meter of the b-verse shows up in yet a third list that Bliss compiles in discussing resolution, but again without remarking on the most significant fact. Bliss finds 46 type D verses containing class 2 weak verbs. He presents these as unfortunate complications of Kaluza's Law, requiring a distinction between secondary stress and tertiary stress. The point to make, however, is that with the exception of *Weard maþelode* (286a), all of these verses occur in the second half-line; for example:

hlyn swynsode  (611b)

fēond treddode  (725b)

hild sweðrode  (901b)

sinc brytnade  (2383b)

wæl rēafode  (3027b)

Because *maþelode* is problematic elsewhere as well, we seem to have a strange distribution that requires explanation.

To account for all of these apparently diverse facts (and to rationalize Kaluza's Law), a simple distinction between the two halves of the long line seems to be necessary. One possible statement of that distinction is as follows:

*Implications of Kaluza's Law*
(i) Initial clashing stress in the b-verse cannot be followed by secondary metrical stress.
(ii) Initial clashing stress in the a-verse cannot be followed by two short positions.

These ideas are embedded in Bliss's discussion, but neither the relation between them nor their theoretical implications are made explicit. It is the idea of *metrical pause* that gives these two statements (and indirectly Kaluza's Law) a significance and an interest beyond their specific contexts. Clashing stress and secondary stress are the prerequisites for metrical pause. However, a metrical pause can occur only in the a-verse, not in the b-verse.

Three clear exceptions have to be recognized: *fēond mancynnes* (164b) and *hroden ealowǣge* (495b) in the b-verse, and *Weard maþelode* (286a) in the a-verse—along with a small number of ambiguous verses.[20] In return, the two generalizations account for the interacting similarities and differences among some 850 other type D verses, including examples that show some of the most basic contrasts in Old English meter. Schematically, the distribution of verses with initial clashing stress shows patterns that are appropriate only for one half of the line or the other, and a middle category for which the requirements of the two halves of the line overlap:

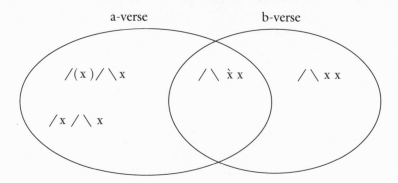

Thus, verses with tertiary stress occur in both half-lines:

gūðfremmendra (246a)

healsittendra (2015b)

hēardhícgénde  (394a, 799a)

sǽlīþénde  (377b)

Following Fulk, we could read the third syllable in each verse as unstressed, rather than with tertiary stress; but the syllable is also long, and it would thus still conform to the a-verse constraint, which disallows two short positions.

By that constraint, Bliss's list of D verses with class 2 weak verbs would be excluded from the a-verse. And by the b-verse constraint, those type D verses with a temporal beat caused ultimately by a secondary stress would occur only at the beginning of the long line. To the examples given above of regular D and D* verses in this category, one could add 250 more instances (all but two, as noted, in the a-verse):

betst beadorinca  (1109a)

rēþe renweardas  (770a)

burston bānlocan  (818a)

If we define "short position" in the a-verse exclusion to include historically short vowels, as Bliss following Kaluza does, then we have an explanation for the absence of hypothetical verses such as the following:

*frōd frēowine

The problem is not that resolved stress on -wine would shorten the verse to three positions, for we have already disallowed resolution of secondary stress as a general principle. Rather the problem is that the two positions after the clashing stress are too light for the a-verse (in being short) and too heavy for the b-verse (in having secondary stress).

This analysis must be tentative, because there are certain categories that remain as unexplained exceptions. The two constraints taken together make the strong claim that the kind of compound that occurs in type D* should not occur in the b-verse, and vice versa. However, the class of compounds that begin with a prefix like un-, oð-, or-, in- seems to occur freely in both contexts:

elne unflitme  (1097a)

Wiht unhǣlo  (120b)

These patterns are problematic also for Bliss, whose explanation ("the prefix normally bears full stress and the primary element loses its stress,"
p. 26) is unconvincing for not connecting with other principles. Another
problem is the occurrence of inflected *Scylding* in all type D contexts. If
inflected proper names are read with tertiary stress on the middle syllable,
we have an explanation for why inflected *Bēowulf, Hrōðgār, Ecgþēow,* etc.
never occur in D * verses. However, among D * verses are four instances of
*Scyldinga* (913a, 1154a, 1675a, 1871a), and also, with a short third syllable, *Ēast-Dena* (392a, 616a) and *Ecgwelan* (1710a). Finally, there are 25
instances of *maþelode* in D * verses: *Bēowulf maþelode, Wulfgār maþelode,*
etc. All of these possible exceptions have caused problems in one theory or
another over the years.[21]

In splitting the level that is usually thought of as secondary stress into
three levels of metrical stress—primary, secondary, and tertiary—we are
able to work toward an explanation of these facts of Old English meter,
which had no coherent explanation before, and other facts that might appear unrelated. For example, the asymmetry between the pattern of *hār
hilderinc* (1307a), which occurs often, and that of * *hilderinc hār,* which
does not occur and appears to be unmetrical:

　／　／　×　＼
hār hilderinc

　／　×　＼　　／
* hilderinc hār

In a contour theory (such as my 1974 theory), the absence of verses like
* *hilderinc hār* can be accounted for by a proscription against three rising
levels of stress:

　／　×　＼　　／
hilderinc hār

At one level of representation this statement is surely true, and it also happens to account for the two other logically possible, but unmetrical,
patterns in which stress rises through three of the four positions:

However, there must be a deeper explanation for this seemingly arbitrary proscription. Geoffrey Russom's theory, which ties possible metrical patterns to possible word shapes, is precisely that deeper explanation: no words in Old English have the stress pattern x\/.[22]

There are two different ways of using Russom's insight. The simplest would be to say that the possible Old English word patterns serve as a filter, a paradigm to rule out *hilderinc hār* as unmetrical. This way retains the flavor of a contour theory because it looks for a match between the unified contour of the metrical template (specifically, feet and the combination of feet). In this particular instance there is no match, and the tested verse is ruled out. A less obvious way is to consider the local interaction between successive syllables and syllable-equivalents. It may be that independent constraints regulating this local interaction preclude verses from being produced which do not match word shapes and which would be unmetrical.

Something of the sort seems to happen in this pattern. The unmetrical construction *hilderinc hār* contains a stress clash in the last two positions, but the context does not permit removal of the clash by either of the two processes that are normal in Old English meter. The principle of demoting the second of two stresses, as in compounds, clearly does not apply to the combination of *-rinc* (itself the second element of a compound) and *hār* (the alliterating final syllable of the verse). Nor is a metrical pause plausible as a spacer for the two stresses. In the tightly constrained patterns of the Old English half-line we have been able to identify a metrical pause only between the first two stresses of type D, and only then when the second of those stresses is pumped up by yet another stress to the right—a primary or secondary stress, not a tertiary stress. Thus, *hilderinc hār* appears to be excluded as a pattern, not because of its failure to fit an overall contour, but because of the clash of irreconcilable principles at a specific point.

There are analogies here with at least three topics in theoretical phonology that have been the sites of vast amounts of research during the past two decades. The solution sketched for *hilderinc hār,* as well as the reconsiderations of Old English meter generally in this chapter and in Chapter One, imply a model similar to the "Tone Sequence" model in the study of intonational phonology. This view is a shift away from the emphasis in my 1974 study, which also has an analogue in intonational phonology, the "Contour Interaction" model. Briefly, the Contour Interaction model treats "sentence intonation" as a phonological primitive in itself, usually expressed graphically as a solid, curving line tracing the various rising and falling tones. The Tone Sequence view, in D. Robert Ladd's words, "assumes that those pitch movements are simply concatenated to *make up* the tune, so that 'sentence intonation' is merely the sum of its accent-related parts."[23]

Related to the way tunes are made up are two topics that have received attention in autosegmental phonology and which may prove relevant to Old English meter: the Obligatory Contour Principle and downstep. Both phenomena were originally studied in tone languages, but they have been given much wider application. For example, the Obligatory Contour Principle, which states, "At the melodic level, adjacent identical elements are prohibited," has been applied to the familiar phenomenon of stress clash in Modern English and to the removal of clash by the Rhythm Rule.[24] The considerations here are of obvious interest for patterns such as type D, which is usually represented as /|/\x. Downstep, with its falling contours, gives a *direction* for avoiding adjacent identical elements.[25] It may be that the falling contours of Old English meter can be related to these more general phonological processes.

A final reason for preferring a model that specifies interacting parts over one that specifies overall contours concerns one of the most basic perceptual questions about literary texts. In Old English verse how do we know what the verse and line units are? We have been dealing with these verses and lines as they are given in modern editions with white spaces at the left and right margins and a generous space between the half-lines. Barbara Strang addresses the question and provides an answer: "as in later English, there is more than one feature which acts as a line-end marker. The end of a half-line is always determinate in syllabic structure; if it is occupied by a lift this goes without saying, but if it is occupied by a drop there is the special restriction that the drop must there be monosyllabic."[26] Again the question to ask is what determines what? If the analyses of second-class weak verbs in the present theory and in Russom's theory are right, then a verse such as *Swā rīxode* (144a) does indeed end on two metrically unstressed syllables. By the present theory, the verse is acceptable in the second half-line simply because it has four syllables without an extended dip in the first two positions. If all verses were as simple, there would be no problem. For verses that have a strong dip in one of the first two positions, however, the question of where the verse ends can be answered only by answering the question of where the dip ends—or vice versa. Can the questions be answered strictly by proceeding from left to right? Or is a determination of the end of the verse necessary in order to determine the domain of the dip (as in the Antepenultimate Rules of Chapter One)? Or does the determination of some verses depend upon scanning both left and right? This is an area in which the formal properties of finite-state automata and of context-free grammars, which have figured prominently in recent linguistic theory, could clarify both the theoretical questions that need to be asked and also the kinds of empirical evidence that need to be supplied.[27]

## 6.5 The Modes of English Meter in Their Temporal Setting

The typological summary of the compound modes of English meter appeared in Chapter Five as follows:

(1) Syllabism, strong stress, quantity:  Old English.
(2) Strong stress and foot meter:  Alliterative Revival.
(3) Alternating meter and syllabism:  Chaucer, Gascoigne.
(4) Foot meter and syllabism:  Sidney to Yeats.

From the discussion of pauses in the present chapter, it should be clear that these modes are also compounded with a temporal element. The preceding two sections considered pauses in the first and fourth compound modes, Old English meter and the iambic pentameter of Modern English. We saw in Chapter One that the meaning of "strong stress" is bound up with matters of timing in stress-based languages, and so the second compound mode, Middle English alliterative meter, must also have temporal elements in both its strong-stress and foot components. An examination of the alternating, syllable-count meter of Chaucer and Gascoigne would show temporal elements in that mode as well, specifically in those lines where the pattern diverges from strict alternation. Thus, an element of timing is a part of the meter in all of these modes. This element is in addition to the quantitative element in Old English that is intrinsic to the syllable.

It is important to emphasize the place of timing in specific metrical structures, because the ubiquitousness of time tends to render it discountable in some views. If time is the background and setting for all language, indeed all human activity, then one might consider taking it as a given and looking for the more limited features that make a paradigmatic difference. This was the view of Wimsatt and Beardsley in their influential essay that has been cited several times in the present study. The point that has been made here is that certain precise temporal patterns are paradigmatically significant, just as certain patterns of stress are. Time and stress are among the specifiable suprasegmentals of language. Following our earlier reasoning, metrically significant variations in patterns of suprasegmentals would mean not "the same verse performed different ways" but "different verses." Establishing the metrically significant suprasegmentals is a part of establishing the text.

## 6.6 Multiple Mental Texts

In criticizing what he calls "the ideology of final intentions," Jerome J. McGann sketches the changing status of authorial intentions in modern textual criticism.[28] By McGann's reading of the scholarly tradition, Fredson Bowers introduced the idea into W. W. Greg's rationale of copy-text. Greg's famous essay made a distinction between "accidentals" (such as punctuation) and "substantive readings" and prescribed that the editor follow the copy-text on accidentals but should be prepared to deviate from the copy-text in the matter of substantive readings. Whereas Greg did not deal with the choice between substantive readings, later bibliographers such as Bowers and G. Thomas Tanselle faced the issue squarely and turned inevitably to consider the author's intentions. They saw the author as an autonomous authority. McGann demurs from this conception and argues for placing the literary text in its social context, even for purposes of textual editing. He emphasizes the authority not simply of the author but of the author in relationship to amanuensis, publisher, editor, printer, various audiences at various stages, and reviewers.

Although the tradition that McGann describes is mainly concerned with printed texts, his general emphasis is useful in considering the transmission of a metrical tradition by scribes. The tradition flows into the individual author from a social context of other authors and audiences, where one can speak of a shared social construct—a metrical contract, as John Hollander puts it.[29] This tradition and other traditions—of poets, world knowledge, politics, belief, etc.—come to a momentary convergence and interaction in the brain of the author. Exactly what happens in the brain remains mysterious, but it is certain that the event will vary from author to author and, within a single author, from moment to moment. Perhaps at a given moment in the process of composition, three different syntactic possibilities will flicker, and perhaps later the revising poet will return to the text to substitute a word that was originally considered and dismissed. In the normal course of things, only one way of expressing a line among the competing possibilities gets written down at any one time. The written line then leaves the poet to join the social context. A reader in that context can abstract any portion of this linguistic entity, which originated in complex sources, for any particular purpose. A pedantic scribe might choose to tinker with the meter.

Derek Pearsall describes such a scribe. Huntington Library MS. HM 137 was the manuscript of the C text of *Piers Plowman* used by Skeat—"a masterpiece of medieval editing," in Pearsall's phrase, who continues: "What Skeat wanted—a clean, full, careful text, purged of error, awkwardness, and obscurity, and systematic in metrical practice (even to the extent of splitting excessively long lines into two and padding them out with inert material)—is exactly what the editor of Huntington 137 provided."[30] A main point of Pearsall's essay is that contemporary readers, audiences, and scribes provide valuable clues to understanding aspects of a tradition that by its very nature is social. Certainly for the specific, technical problems of meter, "improvements" by the right kind of scribe can provide clearer clues to the paradigm within which the author worked than the best informed and most sensitive modern reconstruction.

At the moment of poetic composition there existed multiple syntactic texts, usually only one of which got written down. Some of the other potential written texts might or might not have been thought by the poet. In *Piers Plowman*, in its various texts and manuscripts, some of the arrangements of words are by Langland, and some are by the scribes. Certain gross scribal changes can be identified, but many are forever unassignable between scribe and author. We can assume that some of these changes would have been unassignable by Langland himself after his text grew cold, because the part of the scribal grammar that produced them overlaps with part of Langland's grammar. With this realization the urgent first question of the textual editor (What did the author write?) suddenly becomes less urgent.

# Appendix

1. *Beowulf,* 1401b–1411b. From Frederick Klaeber, ed., *Beowulf and the Fight at Finnsburg,* 3rd ed. (Boston: Heath, 1950).

```
                    1   2  3   4
                    /   \  x   /
                 gumfēþa stōp
```

```
  1    2    3   4      1  2   3  4
  /    \    x̆   x      /  x   ⌣  x
lindhæbbendra.     Lāstas wæron
```

```
   1     2     3  4      1   2   3  4
   x  x    /    \  x      /  x   x  /  x
 æfter waldswaþum     wīde gesȳne,
```

```
  1     2    3    4       1   2   3   4
  /    x  x   /    x        x   /   x   /
gang ofer grundas,     [swā] gegnum fōr
```

```
  1  2  3    4         1    2    3   4
  x  x   /    x    /       /⌣x  \   x   /
ofer myrcan mōr,     magoþegna bær            1405
```

```
  1   2 3 4        1  2  3    4
  x  x  /  x̆  x     /   x  /    x
þone sēlestan     sāwollēasne
```

```
  1           2   3  4      1    2   3  4
  x  x   x    x     /   \  x     /    /   x  x
þāra þe mid Hrōðgāre     hām eahtode.
```

```
  1  2   3   4      1    2    3   4
  x  x   /    x   /     /⌣x  x̆    x   /
Oferēode þā     æþelinga bearn
```

```
  1   2   3    4   5      1  2   3    4
  /  (x)  /    \   x      /   x  /    x
stēap stānhliðo,     stīge nearwe,
```

```
  1   2 3   4   5      1  2    3 4
  /   x  /   \   x      /   \   x /
enge ānpaðas,     uncūð gelād,                1410
```

```
  1    2   3   4      1     2 3   4
  /    x   /   x      /⌣x  \  x  /⌣x
neowle næssas,     nicorhūsa fela.
```

Of the 21 verses, 10 have exactly four syllables without counting syllable equivalents. The passage includes the four types of D from the Venn diagram in section 6.4: *lindhæbbendra* (1402a) could have occurred in either half-line; *hām eahtode* (1407b) is restricted to the b-verse; *stēap stānhliðo* (1409a), with secondary categorial stress, is restricted to the a-verse and is scanned with five positions, one of which is a metrical pause. In the next line, the same context for metrical pause is filled by the second syllable of *enge*, making the verse a traditional D* type. These two verses are the only five-position verses in the passage. The third syllable of *sāwollēasne*, although the second element of a compound, bears rhythmic stress, because it rises out of a dip.

2. Ælfric, Edmund, 119–26. From Walter W. Skeat, ed., *Ælfric's Lives of Saints*, Early English Text Society, OS No. 114 (Oxford: Oxford UP, 1900), p. 322.

x  x /    /     x          x /  x  x   /    x
Þa geseah hingwar     se arlease flot-man.

x   x / x x  / x            x  x  /  x   x  / x
þæt se æþela cyning     nolde criste wið-sacan.          120

x    x  /  x  x    x / x         x x / x   / x  x
ac mid anrædum geleafan     hine æfre clypode.

/     x x   x   x /   xx        x    x  / x x    x / x
het hine þa beheafdian     and þa hæðenan swa dydon.

x   x    /    x  x / x x        x   / x  x /
Betwux þam þe he clypode     to criste þagit

x  / x   x  / x x        x x  /  x   x   / x
þa tugon þa hæþenan     þone halgan to slæge.

x    x  / x     /    x       / x  x  x   x  / x
and mid anum swencge     slogon him of þæt heafod.          125

x    x  /   /  x x        x / x   x  / x
and his sawl siþode     gesælig to criste.

The curious thing about Ælfric's rhythmical prose is that it comes closer to what the standard modern sources describe as strong-stress meter than any other selection in this Appendix. The pattern consists of two fairly readily identifiable stresses per half-line and an indeterminate number of metrically unstressed syllables before, between, and after the two stresses. Because secondary and tertiary phonological stress does not form part of the metrical pattern, the scansion is binary. Stress on the second

syllable of words such as *hingwar, arlease, flot-man,* and *anrædum,* though
real phonologically, is not registered at the metrical level of description.

3. Lawman, *Brut,* 1470–74. Printed from BL MS. Cotton Caligula A. ix
   by G. L. Brook and R. F. Leslie, eds., *Laʒamon: Brut,* 2 vols., Early
   English Text Society, OS Nos. 250, 277 (Oxford: Oxford UP, 1963,
   1978), I, p. 76.

```
  x  /   x  x   x  /         x    /  x x x   /  x x
Þa ældede þe king :      & wakede an aðelan.

  x   x  x  x  x  /  x        x   x   /    /  x
& he hine bi-þohte :     wet he don mahte.

  x   x   /  x /  x        x  x   x   / x
of his kineriche :     æfter his deie.

  x  /  x  x   x   /  x        x   x  / x    /
He seide to himsuluen :     þat þat vuel wes :          1470

  x   x x   x x  /  x  x  /        /  x   x x    /   x
Ic wlle mine riche to-don.     allen minen dohtren :

  x  /  x   x    x x  /  x  /  x        x   /  x   x x  /  x
& ʒeuen hem mine kine-þeode :     & twemen mine bearnen.

  x  /  x x   x x  /   xx        x   x x  x   x  /  x  /
Ac ærst ic wille fondien :     whulchere beo mi beste freond.

  x    ?   x  /  x  x  / x  /       x   x x   /  x  x  /
and heo scal habbe þat beste del :     of mine drih-lichen lon[d].
```

Typically in this passage neither the Caligula nor the Otho manuscript
contains a half-line of fewer than five syllables, a minimum length that
seems to be a metrical requirement (met in 99.7% of the Caligula verses).
The reduced stress on the second elements of the compounds *kineriche*
(1469) and *kine-þeode* (1472) rises out of a dip and functions as rhythmic
stress. Although the Old English inflectional system has broken down to
some extent, nearly all the words in this passage seem to have the same
number of syllables as their earlier forms would have had in the same syntactic contexts in Old English. The dative case is still productive: for example, *deie* as the object of the preposition *after* in 1469. That same verse
is an example of the metrical type that I take to be one-stress, as in 1468,
although the meter is so flexible that this pattern is one of many uncertainties in scanning Lawman's poetry.

4. *Cleanness*, 213–23. From J. J. Anderson, ed., *Cleanness* (Manchester: Manchester UP, 1977).

With þis worde þat he warp    þe wrake on hym lyȝt;

Dryȝtyn with his dere dom    hym drof to þe abyme.

In þe mesure of his mode    his metȝ neuer þe lasse;    215

Bot þer he tynt þe tyþe dool    of his tour ryche.

Þaȝ þe feloun were so fers    for his fayre wedeȝ,

And his glorious glem    þat glent so bryȝt,

As sone as dryȝtyneȝ dome    drof to hymseluen,

Þikke þowsandeȝ þro    þrwen þeroute;    220

Fellen fro þe fyrmament    fendeȝ ful blake,

Sweued at þe fyrst swap    as þe snaw þikke,

Hurled into helle-hole    as þe hyue swarmeȝ.

The patterns of the two halves of the line are mutually exclusive. The a-verses either have two strong dips (in six lines, as marked with tildes) or three stresses (the extended form, in the remaining five lines). Of the b-verses, six have the sequence minus strong dip, strong dip ($-\sim / \sim$), and four have the sequence strong, minus strong dip ($\sim$ / $-\sim$). All lines end with a single unstressed syllable. The scribe omitted final *-e* on the preterite *ly3t* (OE *lihte*) in 213 and on the adverb *bry3t* (OE *beorhte*) in 218, and inserted an *-e* in 215 on *mode* (OE *mod*, neuter), where the dative case is no longer productive. Verse 218b, which as scanned is unmetrical for either half of the line, has a question mark to indicate that more needs to be known about the past tense of verbs borrowed from ON. A final *-e* would make the verse conform to the b-verse pattern, but I have scanned it according to the rules as they now stand. This is the only unmetrical verse in the passage of 22 verses, a fairly representative sample. In the poem as a whole, the a-verses conform to the posited meter slightly more than the b-verses do. Because the scansion is based on a phonological representation and not a specific phonetic representation, the various elisions that might occur in individual performances are not marked (for example, dropping the *-e* in *mesure of*, line 215). The extent to which it is possible to reconstruct elision is uncertain. Even to make the attempt, however, it is necessary to start with the full phonological representation. A similar difficulty holds for the marking of metrically significant secondary and tertiary stress (which can be identified more readily in both Old English meter and in the iambic pentameter). The significant categorial distinctions of metrical stress are binary.

5. Chaucer, *The Nun's Priest's Tale*, 3001–08. From Larry D. Benson et al., eds., *The Riverside Chaucer*, 3rd ed. (Boston: Houghton Mifflin, 1987).

And so bifel that, longe er it were day,

This man mette in his bed, ther as he lay,

How that his felawe gan upon hym calle,

And seyde, 'Allas. for in an oxes stalle

This nyght I shal be mordred ther I lye!          3005

Now help me, deere brother, or I dye.

In alle haste com to me!' he sayde.

This man out of his sleep for feere abrayde.

The firm structure of the iambic pentameter makes it possible to identify elisions within the line more certainly than in alliterative meter. Thus, the -e on *seyde* in 3004 is not pronounced. Because an unstressed syllable is simply an option at the end of the line, it is actually harder to determine the status of line-final -e than to do so in the alliterative meter. One can infer that *sayde* in 3007 has the -e, since Chaucer had the option in the next line of rhyming with the strong form *abrayd*, but apparently chose the newer, weak form *abrayde* instead. In 3002, the subordination of *mette* to the preposition *in* strikes modern ears as artificial, but this is Chaucer's alternating meter. It is also the reason some metrists object (wrongly, I have argued) to what they hear as thumping readings. Any other scansion would involve an inverted foot in second position, the rarest position for an inverted foot. The same consideration determines the stress on *out of* in 3008.

6. Shakespeare, from Sonnet 104. From David Bevington, ed., *The Complete Works of Shakespeare*, 3rd ed. (Glenview, IL: Scott Foresman, 1980).

To me, fair friend, you never can be old,

For, as you were when first your eye I ey'd,

Such seems your beauty still. Three winters cold

Have from the forests shook three summers' pride,

Three beauteous springs to yellow autumn turn'd     5

In process of the seasons have I seen,

Three April perfumes in three hot Junes burn'd,

Since first I saw you fresh, which yet are green.

The identification of relative stress within feet is easier than tracing the overall intonation, which is partly a matter of the literary interpretation. In addition to the usual four levels of stress (x, x̀, ˋ, ˊ), I have added a fifth, extra high, level (ʺ). In contrast with Chaucer, Shakespeare offers frequent possibilities for four consecutive rising levels of stress. I find them in *To me, fair friend* (1), *-ty still. Three wint-* (3), *-ests shook three sum-* (4), *-fumes in three hot*. Other readings are, of course, possible, including additional sequences of four rising levels, as in line 2. The heavy foot, in any case, is a definite feature of Shakespeare's meter: *fair friend, Three wint-, three sum-, Junes burn'd,* etc.

# Notes

*Introduction*
   1. Eduard Sievers, *Altgermanische Metrik* (Halle: Niemeyer, 1893); Thomas Cable, *The Meter and Melody of* Beowulf (Urbana: U of Illinois Press, 1974).
   2. J. P. Oakden, *Alliterative Poetry in Middle English*, 2 vols. (Manchester: Manchester UP, 1930–35).
   3. See, for example, Noam Chomsky, *Knowledge of Language: Its Nature, Origin, and Use* (New York: Praeger, 1986).
   4. See Charles S. Peirce, *Collected Papers*, I. ed. Charles Hartshorne and Paul Weiss (Cambridge, MA: Harvard UP, 1931), p. 31.
   5. See Stephen G. Nichols, ed., *The New Philology*, spec. issue of *Speculum*, 65.1 (1990), 1–108.
   6. Geoffrey Russom, *Old English Meter and Linguistic Theory* (Cambridge: Cambridge UP, 1987).
   7. Mark Liberman, "The Intonational System of English," diss., MIT, 1975; Mark Liberman and Alan Prince, "On Stress and Linguistic Rhythm," *Linguistic Inquiry*, 8 (1977), 249–336; Elisabeth O. Selkirk, *Phonology and Syntax: The Relation between Sound and Structure* (Cambridge, MA: MIT Press, 1984).

*Chapter One*
   1. W. K. Wimsatt, Jr. and Monroe C. Beardsley, "The Concept of Meter: An Exercise in Abstraction," *PMLA*, 74 (1959), 592.
   2. Thomas Cable, *The Meter and Melody of* Beowulf (Urbana: U of Illinois Press, 1974).
   3. Eduard Sievers, *Altgermanische Metrik* (Halle: Niemeyer, 1893).
   4. Lines cited from *Beowulf* are from the edition by Frederick Klaeber, *Beowulf and the Fight at Finnsburg*, 3rd ed. (Boston: Heath, 1950). All verses of Old English poetry in this chapter are from *Beowulf* (and thus references to "Old English Meter" are, in fact, more narrowly to "the *Beowulf* meter"). Lines cited from *Sir Gawain and the Green Knight* are from the edition by J. R. R. Tolkien and E. V. Gordon, 2nd ed. rev. Norman Davis (Oxford: Clarendon, 1967).
   5. On the reasons for exempting verbal prefixes, see my "Constraints on Anacrusis in Old English Meter," *Modern Philology*, 69 (1971), 97–104; rpt. in *The Meter and Melody of* Beowulf, pp. 32–44.
   6. See Geoffrey Russom, *Old English Meter and Linguistic Theory* (Cambridge: Cambridge UP, 1987); see also Hoyt N. Duggan, "The Shape of the B-Verse in Middle English Alliterative Poetry," *Speculum*, 61 (1986), 564–92. Russom argues for an abstract pattern of two metrical feet based on word patterns. The count of two words in his theory and the count of four syllables in the present

theory clearly have much in common. The present revisions of my 1974 theory are due in part to evidence and arguments that Russom has presented.

7. Type D* is exceptional in having five positions. See the discussion of this expanded type in section 6.4.

8. On tendency rules, see R. B. Braithwaite, *Scientific Explanation: A Study of the Function of Theory, Probability and Law in Science* (Cambridge: Cambridge UP, 1953).

9. Edwin W. Duncan, "Stress, Meter, and Alliteration in Old English Poetry," diss., U of Texas at Austin, 1985.

10. Daniel Donoghue, "On the Classification of B-Verses with Anacrusis in *Beowulf* and *Andreas*," *Notes and Queries*, 232 (1987), 1–6.

11. In some verses, of course, a verbal prefix must count as a metrical position; for example, *on hand gehwearf* (2208a). Recognizing this variability in the mapping of linguistic and metrical units is no more of a theoretical inconsistency than, say, recognizing the variability of metrical stress on finite verbs.

poetry is especially helpful on this subject. Among numerous studies by him, see especially "On Quantity and Quantitative Verse," in *In Honour of Daniel Jones*, ed. David Abercrombie, et al. (London: Longmans, 1964), pp. 3–15; and *Accent and Rhythm: Prosodic Features of Latin and Greek: A Study in Theory and Reconstruction* (Cambridge: Cambridge UP, 1973), pp. 335–59, et passim.

13. See A. J. Bliss, *The Metre of* Beowulf, 2nd ed. rev. (Oxford: Blackwell, 1967), pp. 27–35. R. D. Fulk has recently revived Bliss's insights and applied them to the dating of texts—as summarized in a paper at the 1989 annual convention of the Modern Language Association, "Redating *Beowulf*: The Evidence of Kaluza's Law."

14. It is not feasible to give a definition of "rhythmic stress" until certain ideas involving temporal units are developed in Chapters Five and Six. Until then we shall have to rely on an intuitive notion of rhythmic stress, which includes most of what is thought of as primary metrical stress, but not secondary metrical stress.

15. After the present study was copyedited and ready for the printer, I received from R. D. Fulk a draft of a book, "A History of Old English Meter," which describes his independent discovery of these phenomena. Fulk's findings are of great importance because he applies his Rule of the Coda to Old English texts beyond *Beowulf* and to the meters of Old Norse and Old Saxon. Although Fulk's full and meticulous study arrived too late for me to integrate fully into the present work, I have added comments at the end of this section on matters of terminology and on the domains of his rule and my own (which turn out, as far as I can tell, to be exactly the same). I have also made some significant changes in Chapter Six.

16. Hans Kuhn, "Zur Wortstellung und -betonung im Altgermanischen," *Beiträge zur Geschichte der deutschen Sprache und Literatur*, 57 (1933), 1–109.

17. In Mary Blockley and Thomas Cable, "Kuhn's Laws, Old English Poetry, and the New Philology," forthcoming.

18. Robert P. Creed, *Reconstructing the Rhythm of* Beowulf (Columbia: University of Missouri Press, 1990). This very recently published work arrived too late for a full consideration in the present study.

19. See, for example, Bruce Hayes, "Extrametricality and English Stress," *Linguistic Inquiry*, 13 (1982), 227–76.

20. C. B. McCully and R. M. Hogg, "An Account of Old English Stress," *Journal of Linguistics*, 26 (1990), 315–39.

21. A. Campbell, *Old English Grammar*, rev. ed. (Oxford: Clarendon, 1962), pp. 34–35. For a critique of traditional views, see C. B. McCully, "The Phonology of Resolution in Old English Word-Stress and Metre," *Edinburgh Studies in English Language*, 2 (1990), forthcoming.

22. Paul Fussell, *Poetic Meter and Poetic Form*, rev. ed. (New York: Random House, 1979), p. 7.

23. Especially important in establishing the issues of recent metrical phonology have been Mark Liberman, "The Intonational System of English" diss., MIT, 1975; and Mark Liberman and Alan Prince, "On Stress and Linguistic Rhythm," *Linguistic Inquiry*, 8 (1977), 249–336. For a clear account of these and related theories, see Richard Hogg and C. B. McCully, *Metrical Phonology: A Coursebook* (Cambridge: Cambridge UP, 1987).

24. Elisabeth O. Selkirk, *Phonology and Syntax: The Relation between Sound and Structure* (Cambridge, MA: MIT Press, 1984), p. 12.

25. See Dwight Bolinger, "Binomials and Pitch Accent," *Lingua*, 11 (1962), 34–44. See also Bruce Hayes, "The Phonology of Rhythm in English," *Linguistic Inquiry*, 15 (1984), 70–73.

26. See David Abercrombie, "A Phonetician's View of Verse Structure," in his *Studies in Phonetics and Linguistics* (London: Oxford UP, 1965), pp. 16–25, and other studies by Abercrombie.

27. See Ilse Lehiste, "Isochrony Reconsidered," *Journal of Phonetics*, 5 (1977), 253–63. See also Peter Roach, "On the Distinction between 'Stress-timed' and 'Syllable-timed' Languages," in *Linguistic Controversies: Essays in Linguistic Theory and Practice in Honour of F. R. Palmer*, ed. David Crystal (London: Arnold, 1982), pp. 73–79.

28. R. M. Dauer, "Stress-timing and Syllable-timing Reanalyzed," *Journal of Phonetics*, 11 (1983), 51–62.

29. Otto Jespersen, "Notes on Metre (1913)," in *Linguistica: Selected Papers in English, French and German* (Copenhagen: Levin & Munksgaard, 1933), p. 259.

30. See Noam Chomsky and Morris Halle, *The Sound Pattern of English* (New York: Harper & Row, 1968), pp. 93, 109; see also Liberman and Prince, p. 255.

31. Heinz J. Giegerich, *Metrical Phonology and Phonological Structure: German and English* (Cambridge: Cambridge UP, 1985), pp. 15, 216.

32. Marina Nespor and Irene Vogel, "On Clashes and Lapses," *Phonology*, 6 (1989), 102–103.

33. On the syllabic nature of meters in various Indo-European languages (including Vedic, Greek, Russian, and Irish) and of the reconstructed Indo-European meter itself, see A. Meillet, *Les Origines Indo-Européennes des mètres Grecs* (Paris: Presses Universitaires de France, 1923); Roman Jakobson, "Studies in Com-

parative Slavic Metrics," *Oxford Slavonic Papers,* 3 (1952), 21–66; and Calvert Watkins, "Indo-European Metrics and Archaic Irish Verse," *Celtica,* 6 (1963), 194–249.

34. These are much like the tunes of the Contour Interaction model in phonological theory (to which the Tone Sequence model is opposed). The weaknesses in assumptions and analysis are similar. See my "Old English Meter and Its Musical Implications," in *The Union of Words and Music in Medieval Poetry,* ed. Rebecca A. Baltzer, Thomas Cable, and James I. Wimsatt (Austin: U of Texas Press, forthcoming). A clear explanation of the purely phonological problem is by D. Robert Ladd, "Phonological Features of Intonational Peaks," *Language,* 59 (1983), 721–59.

*Chapter Two*

1. See A. Meillet, *Les Origines Indo-Européennes des mètres Grecs* (Paris: Presses Universitaires de France, 1923); Roman Jakobson, "Studies in Comparative Slavic Metrics," *Oxford Slavonic Papers,* 3 (1952), 21–66; and Calvert Watkins, "Indo-European Metrics and Archaic Irish Verse," *Celtica,* 6 (1963), 194–249.

2. See N. F. Blake, "Rhythmical Alliteration," *Modern Philology,* 67 (1969), 118–24.

3. John C. Pope, ed., *Homilies of Ælfric: A Supplementary Collection,* 2 vols., Early English Text Society, OS Nos. 259, 260 (London: Oxford UP, 1967–68). See the section "Ælfric's Rhythmical Prose" in vol. 1, pp. 105–36.

4. Angus McIntosh, "Wulfstan's Prose," *Proceedings of the British Academy,* 35 (1949), 109–42; see also McIntosh's "Early Middle English Alliterative Verse," in *Middle English Alliterative Poetry,* ed. David Lawton (Cambridge: Brewer, 1982), pp. 20–33; see also Sherman M. Kuhn, "Was Ælfric a Poet?" *Philological Quarterly,* 52 (1973), 643–62.

5. J. P. Oakden, *Alliterative Poetry in Middle English,* 2 vols. (Manchester: Manchester UP, 1930, 1935).

6. The main exception is the A-3 type, which corresponds to the A3 subclass of Sievers' system, a well-known and fairly controversial subtype that has only one heavy stress. I have retained the original name (with a hyphen to distinguish Sievers' A3 from my A3) because it is one of the most familiar of the Sievers categories, and a new name would simply increase the difficulty of reference for most readers. Thus I have grouped together all single-stress verses regardless of length as A-3. A final, rare category, F, refers to two stressed syllables separated by two weakly stressed syllables ( / x x / ); F3 has three weakly stressed syllables in the mid position ( / x x x / ). It goes without saying that a list of 206 types is not the meter but a result of the meter. The metrical paradigm, or the set of general principles that accounts for the list of types, is the subject of Chapter Four.

7. Lines cited from the "Catholicus Sermo de Natale Domini" are from the edition by Malcolm Godden, *Ælfric's Catholic Homilies, The Second Series: Text,* Early English Text Society, SS No. 5 (Oxford: Oxford UP, 1979). Lines cited from *St. Oswald* and *St. Edmund* are from the edition by Walter W. Skeat, *Ælfric's Lives of Saints,* Early English Text Society, OS No. 114 (Oxford: Oxford UP, 1900).

8. Lines cited from *Beowulf* are from the edition by Frederick Klaeber, *Beowulf and the Fight at Finnsburg*, 3rd ed. (Boston: Heath, 1950).

9. See Chapter 3 of my *Meter and Melody of* Beowulf. See also Edwin W. Duncan, "Stress, Meter, and Alliteration in Old English Poetry," diss., U of Texas at Austin, 1985, Chapter 2; and Geoffrey Russom, *Old English Meter and Linguistic Theory* (Cambridge: Cambridge UP, 1987), Chapter 3.

10. Thomas Cable, "Metrical Style as Evidence for the Date of *Beowulf*," in *The Dating of* Beowulf, ed. Colin Chase (Toronto: U of Toronto Press, 1981), pp. 77–82.

11. The text cited is the edition by Elliott V. K. Dobbie, *The Anglo-Saxon Minor Poems*, Anglo-Saxon Poetic Records, vol. 6 (New York: Columbia UP, 1942), p. 27.

12. This point is made by the most recent editor of the fragments, Douglas Moffat, ed., *The Soul's Address to the Body: The Worcester Fragments* (East Lansing, MI: Colleagues Press, 1987), pp. 25–26.

13. Arthur Wayne Glowka, "Prosodic Decorum in Layamon's *Brut*," *Poetica*, 18 (1984), 40–53. See also James Noble, "The Four-Stress Hemistich in Layamon's *Brut*," *Neuphilologische Mitteilungen*, 87 (1986), 545–49.

14. See Eduard Sievers, "Zur Rhythmik des germanischen Alliterationsverses," *Beiträge zur Geschichte der deutschen Sprache und Literatur*, 10 (1885), 209–314, 451–545; Andreas Heusler, *Deutsche Versgeschichte, mit Einschluss des altenglischen und altnordischen Stabreimverses*, vol. 1 (Berlin: de Gruyter, 1925); John C. Pope, *The Rhythm of* Beowulf, 2nd ed. (New Haven: Yale UP, 1966); Constance B. Hieatt, "A New Theory of Triple Rhythm in the Hypermetric Lines of Old English Verse," *Modern Philology*, 66 (1969), 1–8; A. J. Bliss, *The Metre of* Beowulf, 2nd ed. rev. (Oxford: Blackwell, 1967); Jane-Marie Luecke, *Measuring Old English Rhythm* (Madison: U of Wisconsin Press, 1978); David L. Hoover, *A New Theory of Old English Meter* (New York: Lang, 1985); Geoffrey Russom, *Old English Meter and Linguistic Theory* (Cambridge: Cambridge UP, 1987); Wolfgang Obst, *Der Rhythmus des* Beowulf: *Eine Akzent- und Takttheorie* (Heidelberg: Winter, 1987).

15. See Herbert Pilch, *Layamons* Brut: *Eine literarische Studie* (Heidelberg: Winter, 1960), pp. 136 ff.; and Ewald Standop, "Der Rhythmus des Layamon-Verses," *Anglia*, 79 (1962), 267–86.

16. The one exception to following the orthography of the manuscript was to take the word *þusende*, which occurs both with and without a final *-e*, as trisyllabic in all instances. The edition used is by G. L. Brook and R. F. Leslie, *Laȝamon: Brut*, 2 vols., Early English Text Society, OS Nos. 250, 277 (Oxford: Oxford UP, 1963, 1978).

17. Joseph Hall, ed., *Layamon's* Brut: *Selections* (Oxford: Clarendon, 1924), p. 1.

18. See, for example, Dorothy Bethurum, "The Connection of the Katherine Group with Old English Prose," *Journal of English and Germanic Philology*, 34 (1935), 553–64.

19. Roger Dahood, "*Ancrene Wisse*, the Katherine Group, and the *Wohunge*," in *Middle English Prose: A Critical Guide to Major Authors and Genres*, ed. A. S. G. Edwards (New Brunswick, NJ: Rutgers UP, 1984), p. 16.

20. Marjorie Daunt, "Old English Verse and English Speech Rhythm," *Transactions of the Philological Society* (1946), 56.

21. J. A. W. Bennett and G. V. Smithers, eds., *Early Middle English Verse and Prose* (Oxford: Clarendon, 1966), p. 215.

### Chapter Three

1. J. R. R. Tolkien and E. V. Gordon, eds., *Sir Gawain and the Green Knight,* 2nd ed. rev. Norman Davis (Oxford: Clarendon, 1967), p. 143. Citations of lines from *Gawain* are from this edition.

2. Marie Borroff, *Sir Gawain and the Green Knight: A Stylistic and Metrical Study* (New Haven: Yale UP, 1962), p. 188.

3. Angus McIntosh, "Early Middle English Alliterative Verse," in *Middle English Alliterative Poetry,* ed. David Lawton (Cambridge: Brewer, 1982), pp. 20–33.

4. Charles S. Peirce, *Collected Papers,* V, ed. Charles Hartshorne and Paul Weiss (Cambridge, MA: Harvard UP, 1934), p. 117. In discussing "the operation of adopting an explanatory hypothesis—which is just what abduction is," Peirce states the form of inference as follows:

> The surprising fact, C, is observed;
> But if A were true, C would be a matter of course,
> Hence, there is reason to suspect that A is true.

5. Lines cited are from the edition by J. J. Anderson, *Cleanness* (Manchester: Manchester UP, 1977).

6. See Max Deutschbein, *Zur Entwicklung des englischen Alliterationsverses* (Halle: Karras, 1902), and Julius Thomas, *Die alliterierende Langzeile des Gawayn-Dichters,* diss., U Jena, 1908 (Coburg: Rossteutscher, 1908). See references to Luick in note 15 below.

7. Two of these are the word *(h)ayre* (OF *(h)eir*), which was clearly disyllabic in Early Middle English and into the fourteenth century (see the citations in the *MED*). The others are *vale* (673), *dyspyt* (821), *rounde* (1121), *pere* (1336), *palle* (1384), *clere* (1456), and *state* (1708).

8. Robert J. Menner, ed., *Purity: A Middle English Poem* (New Haven: Yale UP, 1920), p. lv n 1.

9. The edition is by G. H. V. Bunt, *William of Palerne: An Alliterative Romance* (Groningen: Bouma's Boekhuis, 1985).

10. See, for example, Borroff, pp. 187–88.

11. In *Chaucer's Irregular -E* (New York: King's Crown, 1942), Ruth B. Mc-Jimsey treats the first five of these phrases as petrified datives in Chaucer and *of gold* as uncertain.

12. For a broader consideration of the statement of metrical rules at the phonological level rather than the phonetic level, see the excellent discussion by Paul Kiparsky, "Metrics and Morphophonemics in the *Rigveda,*" in *Contributions to Generative Phonology,* ed. M. K. Brame (Austin: U of Texas Press, 1972), pp. 171–200.

13. My stressing of Romance words follows Borroff, pp. 164–71.

14. On alliterating function words, my reading accords with that of A. T. E. Matonis, "A Reexamination of the Middle English Alliterative Long Line," *Modern Philology*, 81 (1984), 342, 347–51, who finds that alliteration alone is not sufficient to promote a normally unstressed word over a nonalliterating major category word. See also Borroff, pp. 170–71.

15. See, for example, Karl Luick, *Historische Grammatik der englischen Sprache*, I (Leipzig: Tauchnitz, 1921), §473; see also Richard Jordan, *Handbook of Middle English Grammar: Phonology*, trans. and rev. Eugene J. Crook (The Hague: Mouton, 1974), §§138–41. The conclusions of the present study are closer to Luick's earlier and more conservative presentation of the phonology in "Die englische Stabreimzeile im XIV., XV., und XVI. Jahrhundert," *Anglia*, 11 (1889), 392–443, 553–618.

16. M. L. Samuels, "Langland's Dialect," *Medium Ævum*, 54 (1985), 243. See also his "Chaucerian Final '-e,'" *Notes and Queries*, 217 (1972), 445–48. See also E. Talbot Donaldson, "Chaucer's Final -*e*," *PMLA*, 63 (1948), 1101–24.

17. In an important series of articles, Donka Minkova takes into account the interacting factors and hierarchy of conditions that affected final -*e*, and she does so within a linguistic framework that the present study has also found revealing (one based on rhythmical grid theories of Selkirk and Hayes). Although she arrives at early dates for the loss of -*e* in various categories and contexts, her findings are not incompatible with retention of -*e* in the categories that the present study has found for the literarily conservative tradition of the Alliterative Revival. See the following articles by Donka Minkova: "Early Middle English Metric Elision and Schwa Deletion," in *English Historical Linguistics: Studies in Development*, ed. N. F. Blake and Charles Jones (Sheffield: CECTAL, U of Sheffield, 1984), 56–66; "On the Hierarchy of Factors Causing Schwa Loss in Middle English," *Neuphilologische Mitteilungen*, 85 (1984), 445–53; "The Prosodic Character of Early Schwa Deletion in English," in *Papers from the Seventh International Conference on Historical Linguistics*, ed. Anna Giacalone Ramat et al. (Amsterdam/Philadelphia: Benjamins, 1987), 445–57; and "Adjectival Inflexion Relics and Speech Rhythm in Late Middle and Early Modern English," in *Papers from the Fifth International Conference on English Historical Linguistics, Cambridge, England, April 1987*, ed. V. Law and S. Wright (Amsterdam/Philadelphia: Benjamins, forthcoming).

18. Matonis, p. 346.

19. Anderson, p. 112.

20. Israel Gollancz, ed., *Cleanness*, trans. D. S. Brewer (1921 orig. ed. without trans.; Cambridge: Brewer, 1974).

*Chapter Four*

1. Marie Borroff, *Sir Gawain and the Green Knight: A Stylistic and Metrical Study* (New Haven: Yale UP, 1962).

2. Thorlac Turville-Petre, *The Alliterative Revival* (Cambridge: Brewer, 1977), p. 54. See also Joan Turville-Petre, "The Metre of *Sir Gawain and the Green Knight*," *English Studies*, 57 (1976), 310–28.

3. The regulation of unstressed syllables in the first part of the b-verse, but not including the final syllable, was found independently by Hoyt N. Duggan; see

his "The Shape of the B-Verse in Middle English Alliterative Poetry," *Speculum*, 61 (1986), 564–92. Julius Thomas had also noticed a regulation of unstressed sylla- bles in the b-verse, but in stating the constraint as a minor detail regarding ana- crusis in type A (and then suspending it for a stressed ending in the a-verse), the generality of the principle was lost. See Thomas, *Die alliterierende Langzeile des Gawayn-Dichters*, diss., U Jena, 1908 (Coburg: Rossteutscher, 1908), p. 45.

4. Lines cited are from the text edited by J. A. W. Bennett, *Langland, Piers Plowman: The Prologue and Passus I–VII of the B text as found in Bodleian MS. Laud 581* (Oxford: Clarendon, 1972).

5. J. P. Oakden, *Alliterative Poetry in Middle English*, 2 vols. (Manchester: Manchester UP, 1930, 1935).

6. The count by Robert W. Sapora, Jr., *A Theory of Middle English Alliterative Meter with Critical Applications* (Cambridge, MA: Medieval Academy, 1977) is not significantly different from Oakden's. Extended lines in *Cleanness* amount to 17.5 percent by his tabulation (compared with Oakden's 15.8 percent). Sapora's analy- sis is explicitly based on alliteration.

7. Lines cited are from the text edited by G. H. V. Bunt, *William of Palerne: An Alliterative Romance* (Groningen: Bouma's Boekhuis, 1985).

8. This set consists of samples that have been prepared for computer colla- tion out of the total corpus of 6,100 scanned lines: 700 lines from *Cleanness*, 350 lines from *Sir Gawain and the Green Knight*, 300 lines from *The Parlement of the Thre Ages*, 200 lines from *Morte Arthure*, 200 lines from *William of Palerne*, 200 lines from *The Wars of Alexander*, and 250 lines from *Alisaunder of Macedoine* (*Alex- ander A*).

9. Duggan, "Shape," pp. 566–72.

10. The edition is by E. Kölbing and Mabel Day, eds., *The Siege of Jerusalem*, Early English Text Society, OS No. 188 (London: Oxford UP, 1932). I depend on the textual notes to this edition for the variants discussed.

11. Charles S. Peirce describes the "retroductive" process by which Kepler, in a long series of stages, modified his theory to bring it closer to the facts of the positions of Mars as reported by Tycho Brahe. Peirce called this cycling between theory and observed fact "the greatest piece of Retroductive reasoning ever produced," in his *Collected Papers*, I, ed. Charles Hartshorne and Paul Weiss (Cam- bridge, MA: Harvard UP, 1931), p. 31.

12. Hoyt N. Duggan, "The Evidential Basis of Old English Metrics," *Studies in Philology*, 85 (1988), 153–55.

13. A key part of the tautology, buried at the level of the choice of variants, is the assumption that all authorial lines are metrical. This assumption is used to dis- miss significant numbers of particular lines as not authorial. Elsewhere I have dis- cussed the flaw in Duggan's statistical argument that leads to his assumption that "the aberrant pattern is not and cannot be authorial" (Duggan, "Shape," p. 572). See Thomas Cable, "Middle English Meter and Its Theoretical Implications," *Year- book of Langland Studies*, 2 (1988), 54–58.

14. Langland occasionally has an *-ly* where a single syllable is required by the meter, but the other alliterative poets avoid this structure virtually 100 percent of the time. Chaucer's use of *-ly* in rhyme with single-syllable words ending in [i:],

such as *synfully* and *fy* (*Man of Law*, B 79–80), shows the availability of the modern form at this time. A consistent conclusion to draw is that the two forms existed as alternants in the late fourteenth century (as they had to have done at some point). As with other features, including elision, the phonological conventions of the iambic pentameter and of the backward-looking alliterative poetry are not always the same.

15. T. S. Eliot, *Collected Poems 1909–1962* (New York: Harcourt Brace & World, 1963), p. 56.

16. W. K. Wimsatt, Jr. and Monroe C. Beardsley, "The Concept of Meter: An Exercise in Abstraction," *PMLA*, 74 (1959), 586.

17. Marie Borroff, "Reading the Poem Aloud," in *Approaches to Teaching* Sir Gawain and the Green Knight, ed. Miriam Y. Miller and Jane Chance (New York: MLA, 1986), p. 194.

18. This procedure serves as an additional example of R. B. Braithwaite's "tendency statements" as described in Chapter One—a procedure that sets up the identification of an unknown property.

19. Peirce, *Collected Papers*, II, p. 375.

20. Henning Andersen, "Abductive and Deductive Change," *Language*, 49 (1973), 775.

21. See Richard Feynman, *The Character of Physical Law* (Cambridge, MA: MIT Press, 1965), pp. 156–73.

22. See Noam Chomsky, *Rules and Representations* (New York: Columbia UP, 1980), pp. 136, 139; Noam Chomsky, *Knowledge of Language: Its Nature, Origin, and Use* (New York: Praeger, 1986), p. 55.

23. Lines cited are from the editions by Walter W. Skeat, *The Wars of Alexander*, Early English Text Society, Extra Series No. 47 (London: Trübner, 1886); and *Alisaunder of Macedoine* (or *Alexander A*), Early English Text Society, Extra Series No. 1 (London: Trübner, 1867). Only variants labeled A and D appear in both manuscripts of *Wars* (unlabeled lines appearing in Ashmole but not in Dublin).

24. Fernand Mossé, *A Handbook of Middle English*, trans. James A. Walker (Baltimore: Johns Hopkins UP, 1952), p. 64.

25. Hoyt N. Duggan, "Final *-e* and the Rhythmic Structure of the B-Verse in Middle English Alliterative Poetry," *Modern Philology*, 86 (1988), 119–45.

26. *Blissfull* (5415) occurs in a context in which an *-e* would make the a-verse metrical, but the syntax does not allow *-e*.

27. Hoyt N. Duggan and Thorlac Turville-Petre, eds., *The Wars of Alexander*, Early English Text Society, SS No. 10 (Oxford: Oxford UP, 1989).

28. This is another reason for not conflating several poets when it comes to fine-grained determinations. Enough is conflated in dealing with a single text transmitted by scribes.

29. Duggan, "Final *-e*," p. 136.

30. Turville-Petre, *Alliterative Revival*, p. 58.

31. Lines are from the edition by G. A. Panton and David Donaldson, eds., *The Gest Hystorial of the Destruction of Troy*, 2 vols., Early English Text Society, OS Nos. 39, 56 (London: Trübner, 1869, 1874).

*Chapter Five*

1. W. K. Wimsatt, Jr. and Monroe C. Beardsley, "The Concept of Meter:An Exercise in Abstraction," *PMLA*, 74 (1959), 585–98.

2. See, for example, the use of pulses by Elisabeth O. Selkirk, *Phonology and Syntax: The Relation between Sound and Structure* (Cambridge, MA: MIT Press, 1984).

3. Helen Gardner, *The Art of T. S. Eliot* (London: Cresset, 1949), p. 30.

4. See, for example, J. R. R. Tolkien and E. V. Gordon, eds., *Sir Gawain and the Green Knight*, 2nd ed. rev. Norman Davis (Oxford: Clarendon, 1967), p. 149.

5. Otto Jespersen, "Notes on Metre (1913)," in his *Linguistica: Selected Papers in English, French and German* (Copenhagen: Levin and Munksgaard, 1933), pp. 249–74; and W. K. Wimsatt, "The Rule and the Norm: Halle and Keyser on Chaucer's Meter," *College English*, 31 (1970), 775.

6. Among studies of the early English decasyllabic line, see especially John Thompson's important work on Renaissance meter, *The Founding of English Metre* (1961; introd. John Hollander, New York: Columbia UP, 1989); and Steven R. Guthrie's response to Halle and Keyser's reading of Chaucer, "Prosody and the Study of Chaucer: A Generative Reply to Halle-Keyser," *Chaucer Review*, 23 (1988), 30–49.

7. Susanne Woods, *Natural Emphasis: English Versification from Chaucer to Dryden* (San Marino, CA: Huntington Library, 1984). On this point my own conclusions differ from those in George T. Wright's fine study, *Shakespeare's Metrical Art* (Berkeley: U of California Press, 1988), p. 300n11.

8. Bernhard ten Brink, *The Language and Metre of Chaucer*, trans. M. Bentinct Smith, 2nd ed. rev. Friedrich Kluge (New York: Macmillan, 1901); James G. Southworth, *Verses of Cadence: An Introduction to the Prosody of Chaucer and His Followers* (Oxford: Blackwell, 1954); Ian Robinson, *Chaucer's Prosody* (Cambridge: Cambridge UP, 1971).

9. Wimsatt, "Rule," p. 778.

10. See Morris Halle and Samuel Jay Keyser, "Chaucer and the Study of Prosody," *College English*, 28 (1966), 187–219; and Halle and Keyser, *English Stress: Its Form, Its Growth, and Its Role in Verse* (New York: Harper & Row, 1971). Cf. my "Recent Developments in Metrics," *Style*, 10 (1976), 313–28.

11. The lines from Gascoigne are cited from the edition by Alexander Chalmers of *The Works of the English Poets from Chaucer to Cowper* (London: J. Johnson et al., 1810), p. 510.

12. "Clear instances" are those in which the third and fourth syllables are the stressed syllable of a noun, adjective, or verb, and the first two syllables occur in function words. This pattern occurs occasionally, but infrequently, in Chaucer.

13. Alan Gaylord, "Scanning the Prosodists: An Essay in Metacriticism," *Chaucer Review*, 11 (1976), 22–82. For Guthrie, Southworth, and Robinson, see notes 6 and 8 of this chapter.

14. See Derek Attridge, *The Rhythms of English Poetry* (London: Longman, 1982).

15. Lines from Shakespeare are cited from the edition by David Bevington, *The Complete Works of Shakespeare*, 3rd ed. (Glenview, IL: Scott Foresman, 1980).

16. Halle and Keyser, "Chaucer," p. 190.

17. Wimsatt, "Rule," p. 775.

18. In addition to Jespersen (note 5 of this chapter), see Mark Liberman and Alan Prince, "On Stress and Linguistic Rhythm," *Linguistic Inquiry,* 8 (1977), 249–336; and Bruce Hayes, "The Phonology of Rhythm in English," *Linguistic Inquiry,* 15 (1984), 33–74.

19. See Thomas Cable, "Timers, Stressers, and Linguists: Contention and Compromise," *Modern Language Quarterly,* 33 (1972), 227–39.

20. Morris Halle and Samuel Jay Keyser, "Illustration and Defense of a Theory of the Iambic Pentameter," *College English,* 33 (1971), 162.

21. George R. Stewart, Jr., *The Technique of English Verse* (New York: Holt, 1930).

22. If one's system of stress rules allows for temporal elements, then a pause would separate the clashing stresses on *white* and *breast,* 4-4-2-(x)-1. However, no system of stress for unmetered language would allow heavier stress on *her* than on *white*—except for emphatic or contrastive stress, and this kind of stress is of course different from tilted metrical stress.

23. Jespersen, "Notes," p. 264.

24. Thompson, *Founding,* p. 70.

25. George Gascoigne, from *Certayne Notes of Instruction [1575],* in *Elizabethan Critical Essays,* ed. G. Gregory Smith, 2 vols. (London: Oxford UP, 1904), I, 51.

26. I am assuming with Stewart and other metrists that an inverted first foot, / x | x / . . . , is more adequately represented as a monosyllabic foot followed by a trisyllabic foot: / | x x / . . . . See Cable, "Timers," for further discussion.

27. Mark Liberman, "The Intonational System of English," diss., MIT, 1975, 272.

28. See Edwin W. Duncan, "Stress, Meter, and Alliteration in Old English Poetry," diss., U of Texas at Austin, 1985. David Hoover in "Evidence for Primacy of Alliteration in Old English Metre," *Anglo-Saxon England,* 14 (1985), 75–96, and in *A New Theory of Old English Meter* (New York: Lang, 1985) has valuable observations on the importance of alliteration in Old English meter, but I would judge that he goes too far in trying to establish the priority of alliteration over patterns of stress.

29. Martin Halpern, "On the Two Chief Metrical Modes in English," *PMLA,* 77 (1962), 177–86.

30. See, for example, Frederic G. Cassidy and Richard N. Ringler, *Bright's Old English Grammar and Reader,* 3rd ed. (New York: Holt, Rinehart and Winston, 1971).

31. Thorlac Turville-Petre, *The Alliterative Revival* (Cambridge: Brewer, 1977), p. 54.

*Chapter Six*

1. Angus McIntosh, M. L. Samuels, and Michael Benskin, *A Linguistic Atlas of Late Mediaeval English,* 4 vols. (Aberdeen: Aberdeen UP, 1986).

2. It should be clear that the lack of discussion of alliteration is not meant to

deny its importance. Alliteration has been marked in every one of the thousands of lines that have been scanned. The present study has nothing new to say on the subject.

3. For a discussion of the transmission of language through the construction of individual grammars, see Chapter Four, section 4.7.

4. See, for example, Hans Robert Jauss, *Toward an Aesthetic of Reception,* trans. Timothy Bahti (Minneapolis: U of Minnesota Press, 1982), especially Chapter Three.

5. Jerrold J. Katz, *Language and Other Abstract Objects* (Totowa, NJ: Rowman & Littlefield, 1981), p. 70.

6. See my "Philology: The Analysis of Written Records," in *Guide to Language Change,* ed. Edgar C. Polomé (Berlin: de Gruyter, 1990), pp. 97–106.

7. Seymour Chatman, "Robert Frost's 'Mowing': An Inquiry into Prosodic Structure," *Kenyon Review,* 18 (1956), 421–38.

8. W. K. Wimsatt, Jr. and Monroe C. Beardsley, "The Concept of Meter: An Exercise in Abstraction," *PMLA,* 74 (1959), 585–98.

9. Egerton Smith, *The Principles of English Metre* (London: Oxford UP, 1923); and George R. Stewart, Jr., *The Technique of English Verse* (New York: Holt, 1930).

10. Stewart, *Technique,* p. 31.

11. See Elias Schwartz, *The Forms of Feeling: Toward a Mimetic Theory of Literature* (Port Washington, NY: Kennikat, 1972), pp. 52–54. See also David Abercrombie, "A Phonetician's View of Verse Structure," in his *Studies in Phonetics and Linguistics* (London: Oxford UP, 1965), pp. 16–25.

12. I have offered my interpretation in "Timers, Stressers, and Linguists: Contention and Compromise," *Modern Language Quarterly,* 33 (1972), 227–39.

13. Karl Shapiro, *A Bibliography of Modern Prosody* (Baltimore: Johns Hopkins UP, 1948).

14. John C. Pope, *The Rhythm of* Beowulf, 2nd ed. (New Haven: Yale UP, 1966).

15. Samuel Jay Keyser, "Old English Prosody," *College English,* 30 (1969), 331–56.

16. Much of the present chapter was rewritten while it was in press, after I had the opportunity of seeing R. D. Fulk's important work in progress, "A History of Old English Meter." Fulk presented part of his argument in a paper at the 1989 convention of the Modern Language Association, "Redating *Beowulf:* The Evidence of Kaluza's Law." On tertiary stress, Fulk draws out the significance of observations that had been made by A. J. Bliss, *The Metre of* Beowulf, rev. ed. (Oxford: Blackwell, 1967), pp. 24–26, 113–17.

17. Max Kaluza, *Englische Metrik in historischer Entwicklung dargestellt* (Berlin: Felber, 1909), pp. 84–85; trans. by A. C. Dunstan as *A Short History of English Versification from the Earliest Times to the Present Day* (London: Allen, 1911), pp. 90–91. In Chapter Six of *The Meter and Melody of* Beowulf (Urbana: U of Illinois Press, 1974), p. 78, I proposed reading *eorl Bēowulfes* with a temporal beat marked △:

```
  1    2   3  4
      /\
  ,   Δ   ,   \  x
```
eorl  Bēowulfes

(It now appears that a pause occurs only when the following compound has secondary stress; the stress on -*wulf*- is tertiary.) A new, elegant analysis of clashing stress finds in compounds, between the clashing elements, a "composition" or "bridging" vowel (lost after 600 A.D.). See Chapter Five of F. H. Whitman, *A Comparative Study of Old English Meter* (Toronto: U of Toronto Press, forthcoming).

18. Verses 232a, 911a, 1187a, 1260a, 1426a, 1681a, 1946a, 2583b, 2650a, 2661b, 2780b, 2921a, and 3173a.

19. Bliss, *Metre*, p. 55.

20. Most of these are problematic or exceptional in other theories as well. They include 1111b, 2424a, 2708a, 2758a, 2767b, 2921b, 3056b, and, containing *Higelāces*, 737a, 758b, 813b, 914a, and 2386b (exceptional because resolution requires secondary stress, rather than the tertiary stress of *Higelāces*). See Bliss's discussion of 1111b and 2767b, containing compounds with *eal(l)- (Metre*, p. 55). On *Hylāc* as the form for the original text, see Eduard Sievers, "Zur Rhythmik des germanischen Alliterationsverses," *Beiträge zur Geschichte der deutschen Sprache und Literatur*, 10 (1885), 463–64. On the possibility of giving a stress to the last syllable of *glitinian* (2758a) and *openian* (3056b), see Pope, *Rhythm*, pp. 304, 361.

21. Most other examples of possibly contradictory D\* types are dubious. These include all the half-dozen or so b-verses: 53b, 1724b, 1997b, 2020b, 2032b, 2432b, and 2863b. See Pope, *Rhythm*, p. 365, and Bliss, pp. 57–58. Pope (pp. 309–310) follows Sievers in reading the infinitive rather than the gerund in 473a, 1941a, 2562a, and 2093a.

22. Geoffrey Russom, *Old English Meter and Linguistic Theory* (Cambridge: Cambridge UP, 1987).

23. D. Robert Ladd, "Phonological Features of Intonational Peaks," *Language*, 59 (1983), 723.

24. See Moira Yip, "The Obligatory Contour Principle and Phonological Rules: A Loss of Identity," *Linguistic Inquiry*, 19 (1988), 90–92. See also John A. Goldsmith, *Autosegmental and Metrical Phonology* (Oxford: Blackwell, 1990), pp. 309–318.

25. See Douglas Pulleyblank, *Tone in Lexical Phonology* (Dordrecht, Holland: Reidel, 1986), pp. 27–66.

26. Barbara M. H. Strang, *A History of English* (London: Methuen, 1970), p. 326.

27. See Harry R. Lewis and Christos H. Papadimitriou, *Elements of the Theory of Computation* (Englewood Cliffs, NJ: Prentice-Hall, 1981), pp. 49–167. See also Barbara H. Partee, Alice ter Meulen, and Robert E. Wall, *Mathematical Models in Linguistics* (Dordrecht: Kluwer, 1990), 433–506.

28. Jerome J. McGann, *A Critique of Modern Textual Criticism* (Chicago: U of Chicago Press, 1983), pp. 23–43.

29. John Hollander, *Vision and Resonance: Two Senses of Poetic Form*, 2nd ed. (New Haven: Yale UP, 1985), Chapter 9.

30. Derek Pearsall, "Editing Medieval Texts: Some Developments and Some Problems," in *Textual Criticism and Literary Interpretation*, ed. Jerome J. McGann (Chicago: U of Chicago Press, 1985), pp. 103–104.

# Bibliography

Abercrombie, David. "A Phonetician's View of Verse Structure." In his *Studies in Phonetics and Linguistics*. London: Oxford UP, 1965. 16–25.

Allen, W. S. "On Quantity and Quantitative Verse." *In Honour of Daniel Jones*. Ed. David Abercrombie et al. London: Longmans, 1964. 3–15.

———. *Accent and Rhythm: Prosodic Features of Latin and Greek: A Study in Theory and Reconstruction*. Cambridge: Cambridge UP, 1973.

Andersen, Henning. "Abductive and Deductive Change." *Language*, 49 (1973), 765–93.

Anderson, J. J., ed. *Cleanness*. Manchester: Manchester UP, 1977.

Attridge, Derek. *The Rhythms of English Poetry*. New York: Longman, 1982.

Bennett, J. A. W. *Langland, Piers Plowman: The Prologue and Passus I–VII of the B text as found in Bodleian MS. Laud 581*. Oxford: Clarendon, 1972.

Bennett, J. A. W., and G. V. Smithers, eds. *Early Middle English Verse and Prose*. Oxford: Clarendon, 1966.

Benson, Larry D., et al., eds. *The Riverside Chaucer*. 3rd ed. Boston: Houghton Mifflin, 1987.

Bethurum, Dorothy. "The Connection of the Katherine Group with Old English Prose." *Journal of English and Germanic Philology*, 34 (1935), 553–64.

Bevington, David, ed. *The Complete Works of Shakespeare*. 3rd ed. Glenview, IL: Scott Foresman, 1980.

Blake, N. F. "Rhythmical Alliteration." *Modern Philology*, 67 (1969), 118–24.

Bliss, A. J. *The Metre of Beowulf*. Rev. ed. Oxford: Blackwell, 1967.

Blockley, Mary, and Thomas Cable. "Kuhn's Laws, Old English Poetry, and the New Philology." Forthcoming.

Bolinger, Dwight L. "Binomials and Pitch Accent." *Lingua*, 11 (1962), 34–44.

Borroff, Marie. *Sir Gawain and the Green Knight: A Stylistic and Metrical Study*. New Haven: Yale UP, 1962.

———. "Reading the Poem Aloud." *Approaches to Teaching* Sir Gawain and the Green Knight. Ed. Miriam Y. Miller and Jane Chance. New York: MLA, 1986.

Braithwaite, R. B. *Scientific Explanation: A Study of the Function of Theory, Probability and Law in Science*. Cambridge: Cambridge UP, 1953.

Brook, G. L., and R. F. Leslie, eds. *Laʒamon: Brut*. 2 vols. Early English Text Society, OS Nos. 250, 277. Oxford: Oxford UP, 1963–78.

Bunt, G. H. V., ed. *William of Palerne: An Alliterative Romance*. Groningen: Bouma's Boekhuis, 1985.

Cable, Thomas. "Constraints on Anacrusis in Old English Meter." *Modern Philology*, 69 (1971), 97–104.

————. "Timers, Stressers, and Linguists: Contention and Compromise." *Modern Language Quarterly,* 33 (1972), 227–39.

————. *The Meter and Melody of* Beowulf. Urbana: U of Illinois Press, 1974.

————. "Recent Developments in Metrics." *Style,* 10 (1976), 313–28.

————. "Metrical Style as Evidence for the Date of *Beowulf.*" *The Dating of* Beowulf. Ed. Colin Chase. Toronto: U of Toronto Press, 1981. 77–82.

————. "Middle English Meter and Its Theoretical Implications." *Yearbook of Langland Studies,* 2 (1988), 47–69.

————. "Old English Meter and Its Musical Implications." *The Union of Words and Music in Medieval Poetry.* Ed. Rebecca A. Baltzer, Thomas Cable, and James I. Wimsatt. Austin: U of Texas Press, forthcoming.

————. "Philology: The Analysis of Written Records." *Guide to Language Change.* Ed. Edgar C. Polomé. Berlin: de Gruyter, 1990. 97–106.

Campbell, A. *Old English Grammar.* Rev. ed. Oxford: Clarendon, 1962.

Cassidy, Frederic G., and Richard N. Ringler. *Bright's Old English Grammar and Reader.* 3rd ed. New York: Holt, Rinehart and Winston, 1971.

Chalmers, Alexander, ed. *The Works of the English Poets from Chaucer to Cowper.* London: J. Johnson et al., 1810.

Chatman, Seymour. "Robert Frost's 'Mowing': An Inquiry into Prosodic Structure." *Kenyon Review,* 18 (1956), 421–38.

Chomsky, Noam. *Rules and Representations.* New York: Columbia UP, 1980.

————. *Knowledge of Language: Its Nature, Origin, and Use.* New York: Praeger, 1986.

Chomsky, Noam, and Morris Halle. *The Sound Pattern of English.* New York: Harper & Row, 1968.

Creed, Robert P. *Reconstructing the Rhythm of* Beowulf. Columbia: U of Missouri Press, 1990.

Dahood, Roger. "*Ancrene Wisse,* the Katherine Group, and the *Wohunge.*" *Middle English Prose: A Critical Guide to Major Authors and Genres.* Ed. A. S. G. Edwards. New Brunswick, NJ: Rutgers UP, 1984.

Dauer, R. M. "Stress-timing and Syllable-timing Reanalyzed." *Journal of Phonetics,* 11 (1983), 51–62.

Daunt, Marjorie. "Old English Verse and English Speech Rhythm." *Transactions of the Philological Society* (1946), 56–72.

Deutschbein, Max. *Zur Entwicklung des englischen Alliterationsverses.* Halle: Karras, 1902.

Dobbie, Elliott V. K. *The Anglo-Saxon Minor Poems.* Anglo-Saxon Poetic Records, vol. 6. New York: Columbia UP, 1942.

Donaldson, E. Talbot. "Chaucer's Final *-e.*" *PMLA,* 63 (1948), 1101–24.

Donoghue, Daniel. "On the Classification of B-Verses with Anacrusis in *Beowulf* and *Andreas.*" *Notes and Queries,* 232 (1987), 1–6.

————. *Style in Old English Poetry: The Test of the Auxiliary.* New Haven: Yale UP, 1987.

Duggan, Hoyt N. "The Shape of the B-Verse in Middle English Alliterative Poetry." *Speculum,* 61 (1986), 564–92.

———. "The Evidential Basis of Old English Metrics." *Studies in Philology*, 85 (1988), 145–63.

———. "Final -*e* and the Rhythmic Structure of the B-Verse in Middle English Alliterative Poetry." *Modern Philology*, 86 (1988), 119–45.

Duggan, Hoyt N., and Thorlac Turville-Petre, eds. *The Wars of Alexander*. Early English Text Society, SS No. 10. Oxford: Oxford UP, 1989.

Duncan, Edwin W. "Stress, Meter, and Alliteration in Old English Poetry." Diss., U of Texas at Austin, 1985.

Eliot, T. S. *Collected Poems 1909–1962*. New York: Harcourt Brace & World, 1963.

Feynman, Richard. *The Character of Physical Law*. Cambridge, MA: MIT Press, 1965.

Fulk, R. D. "Redating *Beowulf*: The Evidence of Kaluza's Law." Modern Language Association Convention. Washington, DC. Dec. 1989.

———. "A History of Old English Meter." Book manuscript.

Fussell, Paul. *Poetic Meter and Poetic Form*. Rev. ed. New York: Random House, 1979.

Gardner, Helen. *The Art of T. S. Eliot*. London: Cresset, 1949.

Gascoigne, George. From *Certayne Notes of Instruction [1575]*. In *Elizabethan Critical Essays*. Ed. G. Gregory Smith. 2 vols. London: Oxford UP, 1904. I, 46–57.

Gaylord, Alan. "Scanning the Prosodists: An Essay in Metacriticism." *Chaucer Review*, 11 (1976), 22–82.

Giegerich, Heinz J. *Metrical Phonology and Phonological Structure: German and English*. Cambridge: Cambridge UP, 1985.

Glowka, Arthur Wayne. "Prosodic Decorum in Layamon's *Brut*." *Poetica*, 18 (1984), 40–53.

Godden, Malcolm. *Ælfric's Catholic Homilies, The Second Series: Text*. Early English Text Society, SS No. 5. Oxford: Oxford UP, 1979.

Goldsmith, John A. *Autosegmental and Metrical Phonology*. Oxford: Blackwell, 1990.

Gollancz, Israel, ed. *Cleanness*. Trans. D. S. Brewer. 1921 orig. ed. without trans.; Cambridge: Brewer, 1974.

Guthrie, Steven R. "Prosody and the Study of Chaucer: A Generative Reply to Halle-Keyser." *Chaucer Review*, 23 (1988), 30–49.

Hall, Joseph, ed. *Layamon's Brut: Selections*. Oxford: Clarendon, 1924.

Halle, Morris, and Samuel Jay Keyser. "Chaucer and the Study of Prosody." *College English*, 28 (1966), 187–219.

———. *English Stress: Its Form, Its Growth, and Its Role in Verse*. New York: Harper & Row, 1971.

———. "Illustration and Defense of a Theory of the Iambic Pentameter." *College English*, 33 (1971), 154–76.

Halpern, Martin. "On the Two Chief Metrical Modes in English." *PMLA*, 77 (1962), 177–86.

Hamel, Mary, ed. *Morte Arthure: A Critical Edition*. New York: Garland, 1984.

Hardison, O. B., Jr. *Prosody and Purpose in the English Renaissance*. Baltimore: Johns Hopkins UP, 1989.

Hayes, Bruce. "Extrametricality and English Stress." *Linguistic Inquiry*, 13 (1982), 227–76.

———. "The Phonology of Rhythm in English." *Linguistic Inquiry*, 15 (1984), 33–74.

Heusler, Andreas. *Deutsche Versgeschichte, mit Einschluss des altenglischen und altnordischen Stabreimverses*. Vol. 1. Berlin: de Gruyter, 1925.

Hieatt, Constance B. "A New Theory of Triple Rhythm in the Hypermetric Lines of Old English Verse." *Modern Philology*, 66 (1969), 1–8.

Hogg, Richard, and C. B. McCully. *Metrical Phonology: A Coursebook*. Cambridge: Cambridge UP, 1987.

Hollander, John. *Vision and Resonance: Two Senses of Poetic Form*. 2nd ed. New Haven: Yale UP, 1985.

Hoover, David L. "Evidence for Primacy of Alliteration in Old English Metre." *Anglo-Saxon England*, 14 (1985), 75–96.

———. *A New Theory of Old English Meter*. New York: Lang, 1985.

Jakobson, Roman. "Studies in Comparative Slavic Metrics." *Oxford Slavonic Papers*, 3 (1952), 21–66.

Jauss, Hans Robert. *Toward an Aesthetic of Reception*. Trans. Timothy Bahti. Minneapolis: U of Minnesota Press, 1982.

Jespersen, Otto. "Notes on Metre (1913)." *Linguistica: Selected Papers in English, French and German*. Copenhagen: Levin & Munksgaard, 1933. Pp. 249–74.

Jordan, Richard. *Handbook of Middle English Grammar: Phonology*. Trans. and rev. Eugene J. Crook. The Hague: Mouton, 1974.

Kabell, Aage. *Metrische Studien I: Der Alliterationsvers*. Munich: Fink, 1978.

Kaluza, Max. *Englische Metrik in historischer Entwicklung dargestellt*. Berlin: Felber, 1909.

———. *A Short History of English Versification from the Earliest Times to the Present Day*. Trans. A. C. Dunstan. London: Allen, 1911.

Kane, George, ed. *Piers Plowman: The A Version*. London: Athlone, 1960.

Kane, George, and E. Talbot Donaldson, eds. *Piers Plowman: The B Version*. London: Athlone, 1975.

Katz, Jerrold J. *Language and Other Abstract Objects*. Totowa, NJ: Rowman & Littlefield, 1981.

Keyser, Samuel Jay. "Old English Prosody." *College English*, 30 (1969), 331–56.

Kiparsky, Paul. "Metrics and Morphophonemics in the *Rigveda*." *Contributions to Generative Phonology*. Ed. M. K. Brame. Austin: U of Texas Press, 1972. Pp. 171–200.

———. "The Rhythmic Structure of English Verse." *Linguistic Inquiry*, 8 (1977), 189–247.

Klaeber, F., ed. *Beowulf and the Fight at Finnsburg*. 3rd ed. Boston: Heath, 1950.

Kölbing, E., and Mabel Day, eds. *The Siege of Jerusalem*. Early English Text Society, O.S., No. 188. London: Humphrey Milford, Oxford UP, 1932.

Kuhn, Hans. "Zur Wortstellung und -betonung im Altgermanischen." *Beiträge zur Geschichte der deutschen Sprache und Literatur*, 57 (1933), 1–109.

Kuhn, Sherman M. "Was Ælfric a Poet?" *Philological Quarterly*, 52 (1973), 643–62.

Ladd, D. Robert. "Phonological Features of Intonational Peaks." *Language*, 59 (1983), 721–59.

Lehiste, Ilse. "Isochrony Reconsidered." *Journal of Phonetics*, 5 (1977), 253–63.

Lewis, Harry R., and Christos H. Papadimitriou. *Elements of the Theory of Computation*. Englewood Cliffs, NJ: Prentice-Hall, 1981.

Liberman, Mark. "The Intonational System of English." Diss., MIT, 1975.

Liberman, Mark, and Alan Prince. "On Stress and Linguistic Rhythm." *Linguistic Inquiry*, 8 (1977), 249–336.

Luecke, Jane-Marie. *Measuring Old English Rhythm: An Application of the Principles of Gregorian Chant Rhythm to the Meter of Beowulf*. Madison: U of Wisconsin Press, 1978.

Luick, Karl. "Die englische Stabreimzeile im XIV., XV., und XVI. Jahrhundert." *Anglia*, 11 (1889), 392–443, 553–618.

———. *Historische Grammatik der englischen Sprache, I*. Leipzig: Tauchnitz, 1921.

McCully, C. B. "The Phonology of Resolution in Old English Word-Stress and Metre." *Edinburgh Studies in English Language*, 2 (1990).

McCully, C. B., and R. M. Hogg. "An Account of Old English Stress." *Journal of Linguistics*, 26 (1990), 315–39.

McGann, Jerome J. *A Critique of Modern Textual Criticism*. Chicago: U of Chicago Press, 1983.

McIntosh, Angus. "Wulfstan's Prose." *Proceedings of the British Academy*, 35 (1949), 109– 42.

———. "Early Middle English Alliterative Verse." *Middle English Alliterative Poetry*. Ed. David Lawton. Cambridge: Brewer, 1982. Pp. 20–33.

McIntosh, Angus, M. L. Samuels, and Michael Benskin. *A Linguistic Atlas of Late Mediaeval English*. 4 vols. Aberdeen: Aberdeen UP, 1986.

McJimsey, Ruth B. *Chaucer's Irregular -e*. New York: King's Crown, 1942.

Matonis, A. T. E. "A Reexamination of the Middle English Alliterative Long Line." *Modern Philology*, 81 (1984), 339–60.

Meillet, A. *Les Origines Indo-Européennes des mètres Grecs*. Paris: Presses Universitaires de France, 1923.

Menner, Robert J., ed. *Purity*. New Haven: Yale UP, 1920.

Minkova, Donka. "Early Middle English Metric Elision and Schwa Deletion." *English Historical Linguistics: Studies in Development*. Ed. N. F. Blake and Charles Jones. Sheffield: CECTAL, U of Sheffield, 1984. Pp. 56–66.

———. "On the Hierarchy of Factors Causing Schwa Loss in Middle English." *Neuphilologische Mitteilungen*, 85 (1984), 445–53.

———. "The Prosodic Character of Early Schwa Deletion in English." *Papers from the Seventh International Conference on Historical Linguistics*. Ed. Anna Giacalone Ramat et al. Amsterdam and Philadelphia: Benjamins, 1987. Pp. 445–57.

———. "Adjectival Inflexion Relics and Speech Rhythm in Late Middle and Early Modern English." *Papers from the Fifth International Conference on English Historical Linguistics, Cambridge, England, April 1987*. Ed. V. Law and S. Wright. Amsterdam and Philadelphia: Benjamins, forthcoming.

Mitchell, Bruce. *Old English Syntax*. 2 vols. Oxford: Clarendon, 1985.

Moffat, Douglas, ed. *The Soul's Address to the Body: The Worcester Fragments*. East Lansing, MI: Colleagues Press, 1987.

Mossé, Fernand. *A Handbook of Middle English*. Trans. James A. Walker. Baltimore: Johns Hopkins UP, 1952.

Nespor, Marina, and Irene Vogel. "On Clashes and Lapses." *Phonology*, 6 (1989), 69–116.

Nichols, Stephen G., ed. *The New Philology*. Spec. issue of *Speculum*, 65.1 (1990), 1–108.

Noble, James. "The Four-Stress Hemistich in Layamon's *Brut*." *Neuphilologische Mitteilungen*, 87 (1986), 545–49.

Oakden, J. P. *Alliterative Poetry in Middle English*. 2 vols. Manchester: Manchester UP, 1930, 1935.

Obst, Wolfgang. *Der Rhythmus des* Beowulf: *Eine Akzent- und Takttheorie*. Heidelberg: Winter, 1987.

Panton, G. A., and David Donaldson, eds. *The Gest Hystorial of the Destruction of Troy*. 2 vols. Early English Text Society, OS Nos. 39, 56. London: Trübner, 1869, 1874.

Partee, Barbara H., Alice ter Meulen, and Robert E. Wall. *Mathematical Models in Linguistics*. Dordrecht: Kluwer, 1990.

Patterson, Lee. "The Logic of Textual Criticism and the Way of Genius: The Kane-Donaldson *Piers Plowman* in Historical Perspective." *Textual Criticism and Literary Interpretation*. Ed. Jerome J. McGann. Chicago: U of Chicago Press, 1985. Pp. 55–91.

Pearsall, Derek. "Editing Medieval Texts: Some Developments and Some Problems." *Textual Criticism and Literary Interpretation*. Ed. Jerome J. McGann. Chicago: U of Chicago Press, 1985. Pp. 92–106.

Peirce, Charles S. *Collected Papers*. Vols. 1–6. Ed. Charles Hartshorne and Paul Weiss. Cambridge, MA: Harvard UP, 1931–35. Vols. 7–8. Ed. Arthur Burks. Cambridge, MA: Harvard UP, 1958.

Pilch, Herbert. *Layamons* Brut: *Eine literarische Studie*. Heidelberg: Winter, 1960.

Pope, John Collins. *The Rhythm of* Beowulf. 2nd ed. New Haven: Yale UP, 1966.

———, ed. *Homilies of Ælfric: A Supplementary Collection*. 2 vols. Early English Text Society, OS Nos. 259, 260. London: Oxford UP, 1967–68.

Prince, Alan C. "On Stress and Linguistic Rhythm." *Linguistic Inquiry*, 8 (1977), 249–336.

———. "Relating to the Grid." *Linguistic Inquiry*, 14 (1983), 19–100.

Pulleyblank, Douglas. *Tone in Lexical Phonology*. Dordrecht: Reidel, 1986.

Roach, Peter. "On the Distinction Between 'Stress-timed' and 'Syllable-timed' Languages." *Linguistic Controversies: Essays in Linguistic Theory and Practice in Honour of F. R. Palmer*. Ed. David Crystal. London: Arnold, 1982. Pp. 73–79.

Robinson, Ian. *Chaucer's Prosody*. Cambridge: Cambridge UP, 1971.

Russom, Geoffrey. *Old English Meter and Linguistic Theory*. Cambridge: Cambridge UP, 1987.

Samuels, M. L. "Chaucerian Final '-e.'" *Notes and Queries*, 217 (1972), 445–48.

———. "Langland's Dialect." *Medium Ævum*, 54 (1985), 232–47.

Sapora, Robert William, Jr. *A Theory of Middle English Alliterative Meter with Critical Applications.* Cambridge, MA: Medieval Academy of America, 1977.

Schmidt, A. V. C., ed. *The Vision of Piers Plowman: A Complete Edition of the B-Text.* London: Dent, 1978.

———. *The Clerkly Maker: Langland's Poetic Art.* Cambridge: Brewer, 1987.

Schwartz, Elias. *The Forms of Feeling: Toward a Mimetic Theory of Literature.* Port Washington, NY: Kennikat, 1972.

Selkirk, Elisabeth O. *Phonology and Syntax: The Relation between Sound and Structure.* Cambridge, MA: MIT Press, 1984.

Shapiro, Karl. *A Bibliography of Modern Prosody.* Baltimore: Johns Hopkins UP, 1948.

Sievers, Eduard. "Zur Rhythmik des germanischen Alliterationsverses." *Beiträge zur Geschichte der deutschen Sprache und Literatur,* 10 (1885), 209–314, 451–545.

———. *Altgermanische Metrik.* Halle: Niemeyer, 1893.

Skeat, Walter W., ed. *The Romance of William of Palerne.* Early English Text Society, Extra Series No. 1. London: Trübner, 1867.

———, ed. *Alisaunder of Macedoine* (or *Alexander A* ). Early English Text Society, Extra Series No. 1. London: Trübner, 1867.

———, ed. *The Wars of Alexander.* Early English Text Society, Extra Series No. 47. London: Trübner, 1886.

———, ed. *Ælfric's Lives of Saints.* Early English Text Society, OS No. 114. Oxford: Oxford UP, 1900.

Smith, Egerton. *The Principles of English Metre.* London: Oxford UP, 1923.

Southworth, James G. *Verses of Cadence: An Introduction to the Prosody of Chaucer and His Followers.* Oxford: Blackwell, 1954.

Standop, Ewald. "Der Rhythmus des Layamon-Verses." *Anglia,* 79 (1962), 267–86.

Stewart, George R., Jr. *The Technique of English Verse.* New York: Holt, 1930.

Strang, Barbara M. H. *A History of English.* London: Methuen, 1970.

Ten Brink, Bernhard. *The Language and Metre of Chaucer.* 2nd ed. rev. Friedrich Kluge. Trans. M. Bentinck Smith. New York: Macmillan, 1901.

Thomas, Julius. *Die alliterierende Langzeile des Gawayn-Dichters.* Diss., U Jena, 1908. Coburg: Rossteutscher, 1908.

Thompson, John. *The Founding of English Metre.* 1961. Introd. John Hollander. New York: Columbia UP, 1989.

Tolkien, J. R. R., and E. V. Gordon, eds. *Sir Gawain and the Green Knight.* 2nd ed. rev. Norman Davis. Oxford: Clarendon, 1967.

Turville-Petre, Joan. "The Metre of *Sir Gawain and the Green Knight.*" *English Studies,* 57 (1976), 310–28.

Turville-Petre, Thorlac. *The Alliterative Revival.* Cambridge: Brewer, 1977.

Watkins, Calvert. "Indo-European Metrics and Archaic Irish Verse." *Celtica,* 6 (1963), 194–249.

Whitman, F. H. *A Comparative Study of Old English Meter.* Toronto: U of Toronto Press, forthcoming.

Wimsatt, W. K., Jr. "The Rule and the Norm: Halle and Keyser on Chaucer's Meter." *College English,* 31 (1970), 774–88.

Wimsatt, W. K., Jr., and Monroe C. Beardsley. "The Concept of Meter: An Exercise in Abstraction." *PMLA,* 74 (1959), 585–98.

Woods, Susanne. *Natural Emphasis: English Versification from Chaucer to Dryden.* San Marino, CA: Huntington Library, 1984.

Wright, George T. *Shakespeare's Metrical Art.* Berkeley and Los Angeles: U of California Press, 1988.

Yip, Moira. "The Obligatory Contour Principle and Phonological Rules: A Loss of Identity." *Linguistic Inquiry,* 19 (1988), 90–92.

# Index

University of Pennsylvania Press
MIDDLE AGES SERIES
Edward Peters, General Editor

David Anderson. *Before the Knight's Tale: Imitation of Classical Epic in Boccaccio's* Teseida. 1988

J. M. W. Bean. *From Lord to Patron: Lordship in Late Medieval England.* 1990

Uta-Renate Blumenthal. *The Investiture Controversy: Church and Monarchy from the Ninth to the Twelfth Century.* 1988

Daniel Bornstein, trans. *Dino Compagni's Chronicle of Florence.* 1986

Betsy Bowden. *Chaucer Aloud: The Varieties of Textual Interpretation.* 1987

James William Brodman. *Ransoming Captives in Crusader Spain: The Order of Merced on the Christian-Islamic Frontier.* 1986

Robert I. Burns, S.J., ed. *Emperor of Culture: Alfonso X the Learned of Castile and His Thirteenth-Century Renaissance.* 1990

David Burr. *Olivi and Franciscan Poverty: The Origins of the* Usus Pauper *Controversy.* 1989

Thomas Cable. *The English Alliterative Tradition.* 1991

Leonard Cantor, ed. *The English Medieval Landscape.* 1982

Anthony K. Cassell and Victoria Kirkham, eds. and trans. *Diana's Hunt. Caccia di Diana. Boccaccio's First Fiction.* 1991

Willene B. Clark and Meradith T. McMunn, eds. *Beasts and Birds of the Middle Ages: The Bestiary and Its Legacy.* 1989

G. G. Coulton. *From St. Francis to Dante: Translations from the Chronicle of the Franciscan Salimbene (1221–1288).* 1972

Richard C. Dales. *The Scientific Achievement of the Middle Ages.* 1973

Charles T. Davis. *Dante's Italy and Other Essays.* 1984

George T. Dennis, trans. *Maurice's Strategikon: Handbook of Byzantine Military Strategy.* 1984

Katherine Fischer Drew, trans. *The Burgundian Code: The Book of Constitutions or Law of Gundobad and Additional Enactments.* 1972

Katherine Fischer Drew, trans. *Laws of the Salian Franks.* 1991

Katherine Fischer Drew, trans. *The Lombard Laws.* 1973

Nancy Edwards. *The Archaeology of Early Medieval England.* 1990

Margaret J. Ehrhart. *The Judgment of the Trojan Prince Paris in Medieval Literature.* 1987

Patrick J. Geary. *Aristocracy in Provence: The Rhône Basin at the Dawn of the Carolingian Age.* 1985

Julius Goebel, Jr. *Felony and Misdemeanor: A Study in the History of Criminal Law.* 1976

Avril Henry, ed. *The Mirour of Mans Saluacioune.* 1987

J. N. Hillgarth, ed. *Christianity and Paganism, 350–750: The Conversion of Western Europe.* 1986

Richard C. Hoffmann. *Land, Liberties, and Lordship in a Late Medieval Countryside: Agrarian Structures and Change in the Duchy of Wrocław.* 1990

Robert Hollander. *Boccaccio's Last Fiction: "Il Corbaccio."* 1988

Edward B. Irving, Jr. *Rereading* Beowulf. 1989

Stephen C. Jaeger. *The Origins of Courtliness: Civilizing Trends and the Formation of Courtly Ideals, 939–1210.* 1985

William Chester Jordan. *The French Monarchy and the Jews: From Philip Augustus to the Last Capetians.* 1989

William Chester Jordan. *From Servitude to Freedom: Manumission in the Sénonais in the Thirteenth Century.* 1986

Ellen E. Kittell. *From* Ad Hoc *to Routine: A Case Study in Medieval Bureaucracy.* 1991

Alan C. Kors and Edward Peters, eds. *Witchcraft in Europe, 1100–1700: A Documentary History.* 1972

Jeanne Krochalis and Edward Peters, ed. and trans. *The World of Piers Plowman.* 1975

E. Ann Matter. *The Voice of My Beloved: The Song of Songs in Western Medieval Christianity.* 1990

María Rosa Menocal. *The Arabic Role in Medieval Literary History.* 1987

A. J. Minnis. *Medieval Theory of Authorship.* 1988

Lawrence Nees. *A Tainted Mantle: Hercules and the Classical Tradition at the Carolingian Court.* 1991

Lynn H. Nelson, trans. *The Chronicle of San Juan de la Peña: A Fourteenth-Century Official History of the Crown of Aragon.* 1991

Charlotte A. Newman. *The Anglo-Norman Nobility in the Reign of Henry I: The Second Generation.* 1988

Thomas F. X. Noble. *The Republic of St. Peter: The Birth of the Papal State, 680–825.* 1984

Joseph F. O'Callaghan. *The Cortes of Castile-León, 1188–1350.* 1989

William D. Paden, ed. *The Voice of the Trobairitz: Perspectives on the Women Troubadours.* 1989

Kenneth Pennington. *Pope and Bishops: The Papal Monarchy in the Twelfth and Thirteenth Centuries.* 1984

Edward Peters. *The Magician, the Witch, and the Law.* 1982

Edward Peters, ed. *Christian Society and the Crusades, 1198–1229.* Sources in Translation, including The Capture of Damietta by Oliver of Paderborn. 1971

Edward Peters, ed. *The First Crusade: The Chronicle of Fulcher of Chartres and Other Source Materials.* 1971

Edward Peters, ed. *Heresy and Authority in Medieval Europe.* 1980

Edward Peters, ed. *Monks, Bishops, and Pagans: Christian Culture in Gaul and Italy, 500–700.* 1975

Clifford Peterson. *Saint Erkenwald.* 1977

James M. Powell. *Anatomy of a Crusade, 1213–1221.* 1986

Donald E. Queller. *The Fourth Crusade: The Conquest of Constantinople, 1201–1204.* 1977

Michael Resler, trans. *EREC by Hartmann von Aue.* 1987

Pierre Riché (Jo Ann McNamara, trans.). *Daily Life in the World of Charlemagne.* 1978

Jonathan Riley-Smith. *The First Crusade and the Idea of Crusading.* 1986

Barbara H. Rosenwein. *Rhinoceros Bound: Cluny in the Tenth Century.* 1982

Steven D. Sargent, ed. and trans. *On the Threshold of Exact Science: Selected Writings of Anneliese Maier on Late Medieval Natural Philosophy.* 1982

Robert Somerville and Kenneth Pennington, eds. *Law, Church, and Society: Essays in Honor of Stephan Kuttner.* 1977

Susan Mosher Stuard, ed. *Women in Medieval History and Historiography.* 1987

Susan Mosher Stuard, ed. *Women in Medieval Society.* 1976

Ronald E. Surtz. *The Guitar of God: Gender, Power, and Authority in the Visionary World of Mother Juana de la Cruz (1481–1534).* 1990

Patricia Terry, trans. *Poems of the Elder Edda.* 1990

Frank Tobin. *Meister Eckhart: Thought and Language.* 1986

Ralph Turner. *Men Raised from the Dust: Administrative Service and Upward Mobility in Angevin England.* 1988

Harry Turtledove, trans. *The Chronicle of Theophanes: An English Translation of anni mundi 6095–6305 (A.D. 602–813).* 1982

Mary F. Wack. *Lovesickness in the Middle Ages: The* Viaticum *and Its Commentaries.* 1990

Benedicta Ward. *Miracles and the Medieval Mind: Theory, Record, and Event, 1000–1215.* 1982

Suzanne Fonay Wemple. *Women in Frankish Society: Marriage and the Cloister, 500–900.* 1981

This book has been set in Linotron Galliard. Galliard was designed for Mergenthaler in 1978 by Matthew Carter. Galliard retains many of the features of a sixteenth century typeface cut by Robert Granjon but has some modifications which gives it a more contemporary look.

Printed on acid-free paper.